I0837265

MEMOIR

OF

ELIZABETH NEWPORT.

COMPILED BY

ANN A. TOWNSEND.

"And they that be wise shall shine as the brightness of the firmament; and they that turn many to righteousness as the stars forever and ever."—DAN. xii. 3.

PHILADELPHIA:
JOHN COMLY, 144 N. SEVENTH STREET.
1874.

PHILADELPHIA:
MERRIHEW & SON, PRINTERS.

PREFACE.

A desire having been expressed by many friends that some of the remarkable incidents connected with the ministerial labors of Elizabeth Newport be preserved, a Memoir has been compiled with the hope that it may prove instrumental in encouraging others to a faithful adherence to the "Light within," which was her guide through life.

Although it has already appeared in Friends' Intelligencer, it is now published in book form as a means of more generally disseminating a knowledge of the principles and testimonies promulgated by this devoted handmaiden, upon whom had been bestowed unusual gifts, which were eminently used in Truth's service.

T.

MEMOIR

OF

ELIZABETH NEWPORT.

She "being dead yet speaketh."

Elizabeth Newport was born in the city of Philadelphia, on the 19th of 2d month, 1796. Her parents, James and Margaret Ellison, were members of the Society of Friends. They had four children, John B., Elizabeth, William C., and Martha B. Ellison.

Margaret Ellison, the mother of E. Newport, was the great grand-daughter of John Rodman, an Englishman who lived in Barbadoes, but who with his brother Thomas settled in Rhode Island in 1683. John was a minister of the Society of Friends, having been convinced of its principles through the preaching of George Fox. *

---

* The following account of the courage of John Rodman, recorded by his daughter and copied from

The mind of E. N. in very early life was made sensible of divine visitations, to which, in writing to a Friend many years after, she thus refers: "At the early age of five or six

---

the original manuscript, was found among the papers of E. N.:

"My dear father, John Rodman, lived at Block Island, N. E., of which he owned a large part. At the time of the war in 1690, a French privateer anchored in the harbor. J. R. and several of the inhabitants were at the public landing when the ship sent her boat ashore with a few hands, one being an Englishman.

"They requested a pilot into Rhode Island. Some of the people went on board, of whom the Captain inquired the strength of the Island.

"Soon afterward, the ship's boats were manned, and the men well armed took all that were at the harbor, prisoners. Next morning my father was permitted to go to his house under guard, to see what had become of his family. He found several of the inhabitants, both men and women, gathered there. After some time, a number of the privateers collected together, and one of the crew, a Maltese or Mulatto, with a drawn sword in his hand, ordered all the men up stairs. They complied except my father. He was asked why he did not go. He said one prison was as good as another to him, but, (pointing to us) he added, that is my wife and those are my

years, I was so forcibly impressed with the love of my heavenly Father, that I earnestly desired that He would take me out of the world rather than that I should live to offend Him." According to her mother's testimony,

children, and I will not leave them. With hard threats they made a flourish with their swords as if they would kill him, but after a warm debate among themselves, they granted him his family. Then a neighbor wanted to go with us. My father told the men he believed her to be an honest woman, and her husband was not on the Island, therefore he would not leave her, if they killed him. With a demonstration of rage and disappointment, as if nothing but death would satisfy them, they consented that she should also go. But after this was the greatest trial—how to release those who had been left by their husbands and fathers. At last he told them that he would leave none of the women, and if they would, they might kill him, and he bared his breast with undaunted resolution. One of the gang made a pass at him which another parried. Then one of them ran to the door and shot a fat hog and ordered my father to dress it, (as a stratagem to get rid of him.) He told them he had never done such a thing in his life, but the men up stairs could do it. Finding they had not the power to execute their base designs, the supposed prisoners were called down stairs, and thus it ended."

she "was always an obedient and loving child." Her countenance even in childhood wore the pensive hue for which it was remarkable through life.

She was educated at the boarding school of her uncle Eli Hillis, at Wilmington, Del. Her sedate and quiet manner was an example to her school-mates, by whom she was beloved. Some of these are still living, and hold in grateful remembrance the influence which she exerted over them at that important period of their lives. When about fifteen years of age, she became a teacher in her uncle's school, and won, in no ordinary degree, the love of the pupils.

Subsequently she became a member of her aunt Edmund's family, who resided in Alexandria, Va. Her relatives were Baptists by profession and were desirous that Elizabeth should attend their religious meetings with them. She went a few times, but not finding the spiritual food she required, she preferred attending the meeting of her own Society, although it was comparatively small, and she was obliged to go alone. Here, under the ministry of Edward Stabler, her religious convictions were confirmed.

She sought retirement and obtained the strength she needed in seasons of quiet, when her spirit was brought into close communion with the Divine Mind.

By nature she was reticent and peculiarly sensitive, and shrank from public notice, but she had at times a foreshadowing of a service, which would be required of her if she was faithful to the manifestations of duty. She was surrounded by those who mingled with the fashionable world and conformed to its customs; but she could not be persuaded to use what are termed "compliments," although the refusal to do so sometimes subjected her to ridicule. She was told by her acquaintances that they wished she would cease saying *thee* and *thou* and talk like the rest of them. At one time she accepted an invitation to a public entertainment without knowing the character of it. Upon arriving there she entreated her friends to take her home, feeling herself entirely out of place in a theatre.

After a few months had elapsed, the desire to be near her mother induced her to return to her native city. Soon afterward, she accepted the position of principal in a public school, called the "Model School," which was conducted upon the Lancasterian system.

By her self-control and gentle yet firm discipline, she gave entire satisfaction to the "directors," who acknowledged her influence for good over the children, by whom she was greatly beloved. Her health becoming increasingly delicate, she was obliged to resign her responsible position, much to the regret of both teachers and scholars. The following letters are descriptive of the estimation in which she was held by one connected with the school.

MODEL SCHOOL, May 26th, 1820.

Dear Sir:—It is with extreme concern I acquaint you that Miss Ellison's health is such that she is not able to perform the arduous duties of her station in the school. Her situation is very delicate, if not dangerous; and I think prudence requires that she should not persist *any longer* in making exertions here, beyond her strength, which may be attended with serious affliction to her friends.

Her management of this school, and also of the Adelphi school, fully shows how eminently qualified she is for a teacher; and it is a matter of grief to me that she must necessarily relinquish a place which she has filled with so much credit to herself, and so much to the advantage of the girls under her care. I believe they will all cry when she leaves them, and I feel myself more than half inclined to bear them company. She is certainly one of the most excellent of the earth; and a life so precious should by all means be cherished. You will therefore see the necessity of appointing a person to succeed her as early as convenient. I am most respectfully, your obedient servant, JOHN ELY.

To ROBERTS VAUX, ESQ., *President of the Board of Control of Public Schools.*

MODEL SCHOOL, May 26th, 1820.

Much esteemed Friend:—I received your note of this morning, and painful as the thought is to me of your leaving the school, I have nevertheless complied with your request, which, as you see, is nothing less than to solicit the removal, from near me, of a very dear friend. The enclosed copy will show how I have executed my commission. If I have said more than you authorized me to say, I must beg leave to observe, justice requires that I should thus far bear testimony to your merit, which from long acquaintance I know to be such as cannot fail to be gratifying to your friends; you will therefore, I presume, impute it to the only true motive. However seriously we shall all regret your absence from this school, as I am persuaded it will be for your good, I can say nothing against your determination. With the greatest respect and esteem I must subscribe myself your friend, most sincerely,

JOHN ELY.

TO MISS ELIZA ELLISON.

The health of our Friend, after she gave up teaching, gradually improved, though she never became physically strong. In the year 1820, she and Jesse W. Newport were married at Friends' Meeting-house on Green street. In the 11th month following, a certificate of removal was granted them to Philadelphia Monthly Meeting, of which they were members until 5th month 20th, 1824, when they were again united in membership with Friends of Green street Monthly Meeting.

Of their eight children two died when young. The circumstances attending the removal of one of them, a beautiful child of twenty-two months, were remarkable. In the spring of 1826, the house caught fire one night, and the two little children were taken to a neighbor's for safety, and put in bed with the children. It subsequently proved that these children had measles, though unknown at that time to the parents. Elizabeth's mother, who was very ill at the time, died in a few days after the fire. The night after the funeral, as E. N. was sitting by the cradle of her child, she heard this language as audibly as if spoken by a human voice, and it seemed as if it might have been that of her mother: "Fear not Eliza, another and a greater trial awaits thee: this night two weeks thy little Margaret shall be taken from thee." The child being apparently in perfect health, it made a deep impression upon her mind, and she went to her sister's room and told her what she had heard. The next day her little daughter was taken sick with measles, and died as she had been foretold.

Under the affliction of the double bereavment, she thus wrote to a relative. "I have been supported at times even to my astonishment, but nature will and must feel! The cup that has been given me to drink is bitter! but it is necessary for me to turn from the endearments that press upon my recollection, and seek for strength in looking beyond them to the enjoyments of which the loved ones now fully partake."

E. Newport was a *practical* woman. She attended to the details of her household with discipline and economy. As a wife and mother her ministrations were affectionate and tender; and her example in self-denial, patience and forbearance was worthy of imitation. Amid varied trials she was a true help-meet to her husband. Her considerations for his comfort and for the happiness of those around her, often occasioned her, *apparently*, to lose sight of her own share of trouble, which with her sensitive and sympathetic nature must have been keenly felt. By her faith and trust in the Source whence strength is derived, she was not only sustained herself, but was abilitated to bear others up in seasons of discouragement. Her father-in law, who had been a member of the family since her marriage, was often heard to say, "Eliza is a wonderful woman practically as well as spiritually." About the first of the year 1829, she appeared in public as a minister, a service for which she had long been under the preparing Hand. Of her exercises at this time, she thus wrote to her brother, W. C. Ellison:

PHILADELPHIA, 1 mo. 25th, 1829.

My dear brother:—Hast thou supposed my silence has proceeded from a want of sisterly affection? No, I am assured not! I have wished much to write to thee, but "the way did not seem to open." Dear brother, this day week in a public meeting I was made willing to appear as a fool for His sake who has ransomed my soul, and "plucked my feet out of the miry clay," and "put a new song in my mouth," and in a measure "established my goings." I never before spent such a week as the last. Words fail to give thee an idea of the quiet, peaceful enjoyment I have experienced. Thanks are due alone to the dear Father who has promised that He will never forsake those who trust in Him. He has indeed marvellously sustained me! Mountains of obstacles have been removed, and I have known him to be strength in weakness; blessed be His holy name! Last Fourth-day morning I felt, at times, as if I could not bear the weight of a grasshopper, and through anguish of spirit it was made clear to me beyond a doubt, that I must go to Cherry street Meeting. I went, and was abilitated to do all that I was commanded to do. He is not a hard Master, my precious brother! On Fifth-day, in our Monthly Meeting, my spirit was bowed under the offering of a vocal supplication; and again, this afternoon, I had to give utterance to the exercise which was clearly presented. But what anguish and bitterness of soul did it seem necessary I should pass through ere I was made willing to appear as a fool before the people. The divine promises are yea and amen forever! and I have faith to believe that as I hold fast to the shield which has been anointed, I shall be preserved to the end.

In that near and dear tie that binds us together as children of the same dear parents, I remain thy tenderly attached sister,

E. N.

Her gift was a peculiar one, but it was exercised in simplicity. She was frequently led to address individual states. A Friend in attendance at Green street Meeting, in the Tenth month of 1830, thus wrote: "Our dear Eliza sweetly addressed a state similar to my own. She spoke of the necessity of thankfulness even when the singing of birds was not heard in our borders. She said the life of a Christian is one of fluctuations. That we ought not to expect nor to wish always to abound, but rather be ready to thank Him who sometimes poured into our cup the oil and the wine, and sometimes in His infinite wisdom saw meet to strip us of every comfort."

The same Friend, under date of 3d month, 1831, says: "Again I heard E. N., in their (Green street) Monthly Meeting. She began with the query 'can these dry bones live?' In the first meeting, she had thought the language applied to herself, but it still lived with her. She felt that the Power by which Lazarus was raised, was both able and willing to say 'Loose him and let him go.' How impressive were her words touching even this flinty heart of mine! and I was ready to conclude that to me it belonged. Dear child!

may she be enabled to keep close to that arm that has through much tribulation brought her thus far on her journey heavenward."

From the records of Green street Monthly Meeting, it appears that her ministerial gift was acknowledged by that meeting the 21st of 4th month, 1831. As her gift enlarged she was remarkable for her prophetic vision and discernment of character. This occasioned her seasons of deep humiliation, but as she was faithful to what was required of her, she experienced the fulfilment of the promise, "as thy day so shall thy strength be."

In the Fifth month of 1832, she obtained a minute to attend New York Yearly Meeting. She was accompanied by Sarah Noble, a member of Green street Monthly Meeting.

During this visit, in a letter to her husband, she says: "These are seasons of trial and deep proving. May I stand firm as with my feet in the bottom of Jordan! I have again and again been baptised unto death, and yet have been able to 'wash and anoint.' There are times when the captive spirit is made to rejoice, and there is a liberty felt to enjoy the Society of my Friends; then again, there is a seal placed upon my lips and the way is closed; but my desire is to be able to adopt the language, 'Thy will, not mine be done.' The company of Sarah Noble is grateful to me. Our dear little babe keeps well and is good. My, Friends James Haviland and wife, are truly kind, and I feel at home in their house."

Letters from E. N. to Sarah O. Pierce.

SIXTH MONTH 10th, 1832.

My dear S.—I have just closed a letter to James and Phebe Haviland, and weary as I am, I can scarcely say why I attempt to write to thee this evening. I am alone, and although not bereft of all consolation, the spring is so low and I am so faint, that there seems to be no strength left to draw water from thence, and yet no real satisfaction in anything short of it. In these seasons of extreme strippedness I feel the necessity of being disrobed of all self-adornings—of waiting as at wisdom's gate, endeavoring to know a daily dependence upon the divine Source for knowledge without looking backward or forward—to the right or the left.—Oh! for patience to hold out to the end—for faith to believe in

God, for strength to trust in Him and for submission to yield all unto Him! Why, my Friend, should I write thus to thee? because it is somewhat relieving and nothing forbids it. I should like to answer dear J. Comly's note, received before I left home, but there is no qualification for it at present. I feel him as one toward whom I am no longer bound to manifest reserve, and I wish I was worthy of his love in the same proportion.

Thy letter was received, for which I am grateful. Thou must not rate thyself too low. There is a possibility of being too poor as well as too rich—too much depressed as well as too much exalted. Thou had nothing to do with the depression thou noticed. I felt that morning, in a very powerful and peculiar manner, the necessity of watchfulness, and it all arose from the want of strictly waiting in patience upon the Divine Mind.

It is not worth while to trouble thee with my conflicts of feeling, suffice it to say that mine is a tribulated path, rendered more so for want of a perfect resignation, both as regards outward concerns and my spiritual food; that I be content with a crumb, or to wait in a state of perfect nothingness all the days of my appointment. I have verified in my experience that I am not to "live by bread alone, but by every word that proceeds out of the mouth of God." My increasingly beloved friend, desire for me a firm footing upon that rock, against which the storms and tempests beat in vain.

Thy sincerely attached friend,

E. NEWPORT.

Another.

At the time the tidings of thy illness reached me, my dear S., my mind was wrapt in thought of thee—was busy in retrospective view. There was a sense of endearment and also a feeling of sympathy for which I could not account. It is wonderful what in the infinitude of time and space, the mind, that active yet incomprehensible *something*, can take in! That however the frail tenement may suffer, yet the soul can wing its flight to realms of bliss where distress and pain cannot enter, and there hold communion with the Spirits of the just made perfect and have a foretaste of the full fruition of happiness that shall be known when these earthly tenements shall be consigned to their mother earth, and God the Father of love shall welcome us to "a house not made with hands, eternal in the heavens."

Have just returned from evening meeting, where there was gathered a vast multitude. A. Peaslee was lengthy in testimony, and John Jackson spoke for half an hour. After him, one of our own members followed, and the predominate feeling with me was, what cannot faithfulness do! it surely wonders can perform! by it the simplest gift is made to bud and blossom even as the rose. . . .

From a sense of a lack of qualification to write of latter time, I have entered into an investigation to see if it resulted from supineness; but I am satisfied that, however desolate at seasons the heart may feel, there is cherished therein a pure flow of affectionate feeling toward those esteemed as dear friends. Tell L. S. that I often think of her, and she is of the number toward whom love has not waxed cold. . . E. N.

E. N. visited the families of Abington Monthly Meeting in 1835, with a minute of unity from her own Monthly Meeting. The only record of this visit at command, is an allusion to it, taken from a letter to her family, in which she says, "We have met with great kindness; my faith has been put to the test, but Truth has gained the ascendency, and in some instances in a remarkable manner. We visit eight or ten families in a day, and my physical strength holds out. I have already realized hard things to be made easy, and bitter things sweet. May I ever bear in mind that He who has been strength in weakness will ever be the same if faith fail not."

In 1836 a minute was granted her by Green Street Monthly Meeting, to visit Meetings and Friends within the limits of Ohio and Indiana Yearly Meetings. Sarah O. Peirce (now Plummer) and Ezekiel Tyson accompanied her. In a recent letter from the former to a daughter of E. N., the following condensed account of that journey is given:

RICHMOND, 9th mo. 23d, 1872.

Dear M.—My impressions of thy dear mother's labors throughout that arduous journey are, that they were deeply heart-searching, and calculated to awaken the slumberer, to arouse the lukewarm and to bring conviction to the erring.

The first meeting we attended was the Quarterly Meeting at Salem, Ohio, held on Seventh-day, in which she was engaged in a lengthy living testimony. At the close of the meeting, agreeably to her request, information was given that on the next day a meeting would be held in that house for the people of the town who were not in the habit of attending any place of worship. It was a large gathering, and here was verified a prophetic remark of a minister in allusion to thy mother's prospect, while the subject was claiming the attention of the Quarterly Meeting. It was on this wise: "There will be seasons of public service when thou wilt feel the need of having as it were 'a face of *brass*'"—with more of the same import. Men sat opposite her, who with looks of scorn and derision appeared to be determined, for a time, to face her down; but ere long their heads were bowed under the powerful testimony and affecting appeal made to their higher nature. The subject of intemperance was impressively dwelt upon, and its horrors forcibly portrayed! One individual beyond middle age was solemnly admonished to abandon it at once. At the close of the meeting a man between fifty and sixty years of age left the house, and taking a bottle from his pocket, emptied the contents upon the ground. He then returned and made his way through the crowd, and taking thy mother's hand in both of his, with the tears running down his cheeks, he thanked her warmly for the message delivered to him, adding, "it was all for me, and with the help of God I will never taste another drop."

On another occasion a meeting had been appointed some miles ahead, whither we went without a pilot. On our way, not noticing the fording place over quite a broad stream, we came to a very dilapidated bridge. Ezekiel Tyson stopped the horses, remarking, the bridge looked unsafe. He then walked through it, and upon returning asked what we should do. Thy mother replied, "Be quiet a little while." After a few moments of stillness she said, "If Sarah is willing to risk it I am. I feel as if we can cross in safety." I replied, "I rely on *thy faith*," and we did cross it in safety.

The evening after the close of Ohio Yearly Meeting there was a large company at the house of the friend with whom we had been staying. Sometime after supper the stream of social converse ceased to flow, and the minds of several ministers appeared to be under exercise. At the request of thy mother the young people were looked for, but they were not found. Several communications were offered by other friends, and about 10 o'clock a number of persons took their leave, while others retired; but thy mother kept her seat, feeling no liberty to move. Near 11 o'clock the young people returned, and then the pent up exercise found utterance in a solemn admonition and warning, expressive of a painful foresight of the life of one of the young women, unless there was an immediate and firm resistance of a besetting temptation. It was a remarkable and favored season, but one deeply trying to thy mother's sensitive nature. These young people followed us from meeting to meeting for a number of miles. At one time, a friend joined our little company, and remained with us about three days, piloting us from place to place. His presence was oppressive to us and we made an effort to induce him to go home. At the time of the appointed meeting in his neighborhood we went directly to the meeting-house. Before going into meeting thy mother said to me, with great earnestness, "Do not accept an invitation to that man's house, I do not wish to go there." "Nor I neither," I replied, thinking at the same time that she would see that we would have to go, though I said nothing like it to her. After meeting, the first remark thy mother made to me was, "Oh! Sarah, we must go to that man's house and stay all night without any invitation."

She soon saw that the situation of his family demanded his constant attention, and she was at once introduced into an agonizing exercise.

After tea the family with great difficulty were collected, endeavors being made by all of them to prevent thy mother from speaking; but she was emboldened to raise her voice while this very man was talking. She made an effort to suppress the utterance of hard things, but she found her peace consisted in telling him that which was revealed, and the transgressing nature in him was searchingly and closely addressed.

3

She was informed, after our return home, that circumstances had developed which gave sure evidence that her impressions were *all correct.* Thy dear mother's friend,

SARAH O. PLUMMER.

Letters written by our friend while prosecuting this western journey, as well as at other times when absent from home on religious visits, furnish evidence that notwithstanding the trying nature of the services to which she was frequently called, she was not unmindful of her beloved family from whom it was her lot to be often separated.

The following extracts are expressive of the yearnings of her maternal heart, and also of her faith that those whom she had left for her "Master's sake" would be cared for, though deprived of her immediate care and oversight.

WAYNESVILLE, 9th mo. 24th, 1836.

My Dear J.—I have been sadly disappointed in not hearing from you in this place! How are the dear little ones? Oh! the mother's heart goes out to them with deep yearning love. I try to be as cheerful as possible. I left you *all* in the hands of the dear Father.

We attended an appointed meeting at Elk

on Sixth-day. It was a trying time. How the riches and glory of this world shut out the precious life! Toward the close of the meeting a little life seemed to "bubble up." On Seventh-day I was scarcely able to sit up, but it was a precious meeting.

On First-day at Richmond it was different. Oh! what wading! Surely it was a time never to be forgotten. After meeting a peaceful serenity clothed my mind. A friend who I believe shared my exercise and felt the state of the meeting, said, "What greater evidence can be given than that some of us could put our hands on the heads of those addressed." Ezekiel and Sarah are excellent companions.

RICHMOND, INDIANA, 1836.

Truly the mother's care and anxieties have increased tenfold since the winter commenced, but I have striven hard against them. I think we shall enjoy home when we get together again. It was a bitter cup I had to partake of when I found that we would be separated longer than we had expected. The roads have been very bad. Our pilot, a Friend who was one of the earliest settlers in the country, said, they were worse than he had ever before known them. The extreme point of our journey was sixty miles from Richmond, at Fall Creek, where we had a season of heavenly enjoyment. There is a precious little flock there. From thence we went to another little settlement of Friends, where although there were a number of goodly ones, yet we had a laborious meeting on account of the departure of some from the blessed principle of light and life. Our next meeting was held in a Friend's house, where there was close service. From thence we travelled to another settlement of Friends, had a meeting in a new private house and dined with the friends afterward. Then we returned to Berlin, where live many valuable Friends. Here I found a mixture of the bitter and sweet. The exercises both public and private were beyond expression. Joseph Plummer went with us through all and shared the labor. He is a valuable friend. I have desired at times that this cup might pass from me, but thus it is! 21st—Later. No mistake, we are now on our way home! We left Richmond with peaceful minds.

Letter to M. Hilles from E. Newport.

WAYNESVILLE, 9th mo. 23d, 1836.

I cannot enter into the particular account

of meetings. Our time has been occupied, and peace of mind has been the result. Have had three in Methodist meeting-houses, and one in the Court House at Hillsborough, from which I was favored to return with the answer of peace, though I went forth weeping and with fear and trembling. I have had a dread of those meetings because here the mouth has been opened and the tongue loosened to speak of "faith and doctrine," which are the "chief corner-stone" of some men's belief. I have proven that the Lord remains to be strength in weakness.

An addition by S. O. Pierce.

I have taken the pen to say that dear E. wrote the preceding, when on account of physical infirmities she ought to have sought repose. The maternal interest and solicitude thou expresses for her, induces me to think that some little account of her from another would not be unacceptable, which must be my apology for this freedom; and I know not that I can better convey the ideas I wish to, than by quoting a passage from a letter I received this evening from Samuel Myers (formerly of Washington) now of New Lisbon. He is a minister much esteemed. He was with us at many meetings and was as a father or brother to us. He says: "I have conversed very little on any of the subjects connected with Elizabeth's visit to this country, yet from circumstances that have come to my knowledge, and from my own feelings, I believe I have a further confirmation, if any were needed, which to me were not, of the correctness of her ministry. I see and feel abundant evidence of its being life to the living, and 'as bread cast upon the waters will be found after many days,' strengthening many minds and encouraging them in obedience to every manifestation of duty. My prayer is that those who have been so powerfully revisited through her instrumentality may be found faithful, and that she may be encouraged to bear up under the great weight of depression which she suffers to come upon her, and place her confidence in the protection of her Divine Master, who, I have not a shadow of doubt, will sustain her under all her trials until the work assigned her is finished." To this I may add, that I have been comforted with the clear evidence both external and internal which has been afforded, that there are many who could feelingly subscribe to the above testimony, and I know of none who would dissent therefrom. Had I room I might narrate several incidents that would be confirming. Please think of and remember us as travellers who need the sympathy and prayers of their friends.

S. O. PIERCE.

Letter to M. Hilles from E. N.

WAYNESVILLE, 9th mo. 27th, 1836.

My Dear Aunt.—My last letter was not satisfactory for two reasons. One was that my mind was too much depressed for my own profit, and I have ever found that when this was given way to, it unfits for social commingling of any kind. I came here too much under the influence of fear, yet I trust it has been a profitable season to me, inasmuch as I have been renewedly confirmed that all who desire to be found faithful must stand upon their own footing—must be impressed with the necessity of keeping the eye single and of retiring within and waiting upon their own gift in order that the will or mind of Truth may be manifested, and its dictates be obeyed in child-like simplicity. The meeting for

Ministers and Elders commenced at 11 o'clock on Seventh-day; it was an interesting occasion, much excellent counsel being given. It appeared that there had been a mistake about the time of convening; some came at 10 o'clock and others at 11 o'clock. The discussion about it went far enough, but ended well. Dear H. P. Wilson told G. Hatton, after meeting, that she was glad she was right even if he was wrong. I have been with Hannah considerably and think her an example of humility and resignation. We did not enter upon the state of society on Seventh-day morning, but adjourned until 3 o'clock on First-day afternoon. Some friends objected to this time as being unsuitable, and hoped it might be avoided in future. One gave as a reason that some might be sent to neighboring meetings and they would be straitened. G. H. said that when Friends came to meeting, they came to attend to the business of it without regard to days. The meeting was an exercising but a very instructive one. A committee was appointed to visit the select subordinate meetings, then adjourned to meet on Fourth-day morning. Owing to indisposition I was obliged to leave in half an hour. This has been a good Yearly Meeting; there are many concerned friends, but expression is too much confined to a few. On Fifth-day we had a session five hours long; the meeting was interesting, and I did not experience as much physical exhaustion as on some previous occasions. George Hatton paid a visit to women's meeting and was very powerful in testimony. There were many short communications that were impressive and expressive of a concern that the Light Within might be our guiding star. It was a searching time in which I had my share of exercise. The epistles which have been received were excellent. A committee has been appointed to gather up the fragments for subordinate meetings. I think the Yearly Meeting will close to-morrow. After all other labor was finished I found it my duty cheerfully to submit to the appointment of a meeting at Waynesville. Thou mayest suppose that in the midst of so many valiants it is particularly trying. I would *willingly* attend a meeting appointed by another. Letters from home have not reached us, which has been a great disappointment, but we have had renewed cause to feel that we are in our right places, and as we have labored for resignation it has been mercifully granted. We had a close and exercising sitting in a Friend's family last evening. Ruth Pyle, Hannah P. Wilson and others, dined there, but many left before supper. Heavenly peace was the reward, and that is worth purchasing at any cost! My dear aunt, desire for me, thy unworthy child, a steady course of obedience, with a single eye unto Him whom I desire to serve, so that when permitted to return to my beloved family and home, I may be more faithful in the performance of all duties, social, relative and religious. My love to Cousin C. I have felt much on hearing of her indisposition, and the desire accompanies the feeling of sympathy, that what she is passing through may teach her the instability of all earthly hopes and where to look for wisdom and instruction. It is only as this lesson is perfectly learned and cheerfully applied that peace is known. She, however, is aware of all this. For my Cousin E. I have been also led to desire that she may purchase the precious boon, though at the price of all her beloveds. "Buy the truth and sell it not," and if, my dear, thou art obliged to relinquish all, turn not away sorrowfully; thou wilt be rewarded, for eye hath not seen nor ear heard, neither hath it entered into the heart of man to conceive those glorious things which are in store for those who love the appearing of the blessed son and sent of the Father, and are willing to receive him in the way of his coming. The love and sympathy of our friends is cordial to us. E. N.

In 1837 E. N. attended New York Yearly Meeting and some meetings within its limits, accompanied by Lydia Longstreth, from whose memoranda the following particulars are gathered:

On the 26th of Fifth month, we arrived in New York, and were kindly received by N. S. Merritt and wife. On First-day morning attended the meeting at Greenwich, which, though dull in the beginning, ended with life and power. In the afternoon we were at Rose Street Meeting, and in the evening had an interesting religious opportunity in N. S. M.'s family. Our friends, James and Phebe Haviland, have recently passed through a severe trial in the death of a beloved daughter, aged about thirteen years. They were favored with consoling evidences that she was prepared for the change, and her close was remarkably calm and peaceful.

On Second-day, the first session of the Yearly Meeting, the Epistles from the different Yearly Meetings were read. There was also a discussion relative to Friends uniting with others in Anti-Slavery Societies. After much had been said pro and con, E. Newport observed that although there was a diversity of sentiment, she thought there was no cause for discouragement, while the paramount desire was to be guided by the Light within—that our footsteps should be directed by infinite Wisdom. The minutes for Friends in attendance from other meetings were read, and a committee appointed to unite with men Friends in considering a proposition for a change of discipline in relation to marriage. Third-day morning the state of society was proceeded in as far as the sixth query. My heart was made to rejoice by Elizabeth's faithfulness to what she felt required of her at the house of the friend where we dined. In the afternoon E. visited the men's meeting under a deep exercise. The women's meeting was occupied by a visit from Nicholas Brown; judgment was placed upon the offender and encouragement given to all who were seeking the right way. On Fourth-day attended a meeting for divine worship at Rose Street. Dined at Richard Field's. After a season of solemn silence E. addressed several present in a very beautiful manner. In the afternoon meeting Susanna Jewett bore a testimony to plainness; regretting the departure from simplicity of our young people. Martha Smith was concerned that the axe should be laid to the root of the corrupt tree, that the inconsistencies of those who were older might be destroyed. Elizabeth Newport brought into view the regard for plainness and simplicity held by Elias Hicks, which extended to the furniture of houses and to superfluities in general. In the evening we took tea with the interesting family of George F. White, where we saw gaiety combined with humility. E. had much religious service, with which unity was expressed. On Fifth-day a long communication on the subject of Slavery was read, and a committee appointed to consider what disposition should be made of it. E. N. was not well enough to attend meeting. In the afternoon the women's meeting was visited by George Truman and H. W. Ridgway; both were concerned to hold up our ancient testimony to the importance of taking heed to the Light within, which could alone lead into paths of safety. E. N. was better on Sixth-day and attended meeting, though much exhausted at its close. Dined at Amos Willets', where E. found it her place to speak words of encouragement to those who had gathered into a solemn quiet. In the afternoon extracts from the document on Slavery were produced by the committee and read. The voice of the meeting favored their being sent to the Quarterly Meetings, but two or three Friends thought it was like moving in the dark. After a solemn supplication from our friend R. Hicks, the meeting concluded under a flow of gospel love and sisterly affection.

We spent the evening at J. Brown's. His wife is a member of our religious society, but he is not. She is in delicate health; the language of encouragement flowed freely to both from E., who was followed by Martha Smith with a similar exercise. Margaret Brown appeared in supplication, and J. Foulke being acquainted with the family felt required to confirm the correctness of E. N.'s testimony.

On Seventh-day we bade farewell to Nicholas and Margaret Brown, and prepared for going to Jericho in pursuance of E. Newport's religious concern. James Haviland took us in his carriage, and although the day was mild and genial, and nature was clothed in beautiful verdure, my spirit was depressed by an humbling sense of the nature of the service in which we were engaged, and my desire was to be kept near the heavenly Guide, so that our labor might be attended with the divine blessing. The weather was very pleasant on First-day morning, and at 10 o'clock we assembled with friends of Matinicock Meeting. Information having been given of our prospect of being there, a large number gathered, and it was a favored time with our friend E., upon whom fell the vocal labor. In the afternoon had an appointed meeting at Jericho, which was large and in which Elizabeth had close service. Returned to James

Haviland's to lodge, where we spent the evening sociably, though Elizabeth seemed bowed with the weight of service before her. Went next morning to a Friends to breakfast, which was a trial to E., she feeling that close work was called for. Made several family visits through the course of the day, in which bread was divided with the hungry, and the cup of water shared with those who were athirst. Attended an appointed meeting at Westbury and went home with Rachel Hicks; here Elizabeth had precious service in words of comfort to our dear friend, who had a week previously consigned to the grave the form of her beloved father, Gideon Seaman, he having been an invalid for several years. Third-day visited a friend to whose family E. had much encouragement to offer. She felt the importance of there being much tenderness extended to the children, as she believed there were those among them who, if faithful to the teachings of the blessed spirit, would make much greater advances in the Truth than had been before known among them. We had an appointed meeting at Glen Cove, held in a school-house; we were accompanied by James and Phebe

Haviland; there was a large collection of people and we had an excellent meeting. R. Hicks was in attendance and shared the vocal labor. Called to see a friend who, on account of sickness, was not able to be at the meeting. The language of consolation was offered, and he was recommended by E. to seek for a state of quiet and resignation in times of trial; she believed that He who had promised that the seed of the righteous should not want bread, would care for his wife and little ones. At Oyster Bay we had a meeting in the same house where George Fox and some of his cotemporaries had preached. A considerable number of people came together, for whom E. feelingly expressed her concern for their spiritual welfare, and a feeling of love overspread the meeting. Called at the house of a friend whose mental faculties were impaired by age, but we were kindly received by his children, a daughter and two sons. A number of their friends had been spending the day with them. E. exhorted them to take heed to their footsteps, and follow closely the true spiritual guide, that they might receive the crown of peace.

Lodged at James Haviland's. Next morning after breakfast a number of friends called, among them Sarah Wood, daughter of Samuel Wood, of N. Y. She wished to encourage E. Newport to be faithful to the gift with which she had been entrusted, and to walk in obedience to the light manifested in relation to the little ones among her brethren and sisters; after a season of spiritual refreshment we parted with our friends in love and tenderness.

We attended a meeting at Bethpage, where information had been given that B. Mather expected to attend. After he had spoken to the people, Elizabeth had a close testimony to deliver, under the belief that some were letting go their hold on Truth's testimonies. Dined with a friend, for whom E. had much encouragement; but warning and counsel were extended in an impressive manner, to one whom she felt was on the brink of ruin.

After dinner, E. pointed in a direction to which her mind was drawn, and then in another, towards which there was a similar feeling. In following the course indicated by her, we were brought to a friend's house, who had an afflicted child, where our sympathies were deeply enlisted; and then as before, heeding E's impressions, we visited a family, the father of which had recently become a member of our Society. Elizabeth had much to say to him in regard to the importance of taking heed to the inward Monitor, and encouraged him to read the Scriptures, as they are truly "profitable for doctrine, for reproof and instruction in righteousness."

Called afterward to see Jesse Merritt, where, after a time of silence, words of sweet counsel were imparted, and then parting kindly, we returned to Jericho.

Next day took breakfast with a family, with whom lived an aged father remarkable for his talents. Elizabeth's concern was illustrated by a beautiful garden, in which it is necessary to pull up the weeds; and when we see the weeds growing in our neighbor's garden, we should not hesitate to destroy these also, although the censorious might say that the briers and thorns were not all rooted out of our own. At Cow Neck the meeting began at 11 o'clock. Here the danger of procrastination was forcibly brought into view, and warning given to those who were in the habit of it. Encouragement to those who were not members was extended, and the desire feelingly expressed that what might appear as stumbling-blocks among our members, should not be regarded as defects in the principle of Light which we profess, but rather as a disregard of the illumination of Truth by individual minds. In the Preparative Meeting, the case of a young woman who had married contrary to our order, was introduced. Elizabeth urged Friends to deal gently with her. She was surprised at the dinner-table to find we were at the house of the father of this young friend. She was attractive in appearance, and was reminded of the responsibility which rested upon her, as there were several younger children.

Had a meeting at a Friend's house, the benches being made of boards resting upon logs. There were many present, and after a time of solemn silence Elizabeth spoke to them of the importance of individual faithfulness. B. Mather also had something for the people, and throughout there was a sense of the Divine Presence, uniting us in the feeling of love for all, both black and white. When we were alone with the family, E. had this consoling language in reference to the Friend who had so kindly opened the way for the meeting, "When the billows roll over thee, seek thou refuge in stillness!" Our hearts were drawn closely together, and this text arose in my mind, "Surely the Lord was in this place, and I knew it not." Went to I. Carpenter's, where there was a number of young people, to whom E. felt her mind drawn immediately as we entered the house. We were soon seated in silence, when two of the young women were exhorted not to slight the *third* call, to leave the vanities of the world, and they would be instrumental in strengthening their brethren. If they were faithful they would be called to unite with her in the labor of telling others what had been done for them.

Rode 12 miles to an appointed meeting at Flushing. Elizabeth was led to address one whom she believed held the principles of infidelity. Benjamin Mather, Ruth Spencer, Phebe I. Merritt and Dorothy Golden were all present and had some service. Dined at S. Hicks'; they have a beautiful place fronting Flushing Bay. The garden at the back of the house was filled with a great variety of fruits and flowers, and the green house contained the choicest exotics. All these things will not ensure health or happiness. S. Hicks was confined to his room with illness, which E. told him she felt was not unto death. Attention was directed to the treasures which are not perishable. The children were especially kind, bringing us fruits and flowers, and we parted from them in much love. We visited several families in the course of the afternoon, in all of which E. had appropriate counsel to offer, and for those unduly discouraged there were words of hope and cheer.

As we turned homeward and rode through the beautiful valley with the river winding its course through it, I could but remember the many testimonials of kindness which we had received from the inhabitants of Long Island, and especially from J. and P. Haviland, who had been with us at all the meetings, and had entered into our exercises with deep feeling.

We were now about to part with them, and it caused us more fully to realize the tender sympathy and unity which had existed between us. We crossed the ferry at Williamsburg and lodged at N. S. Merritt's. Elizabeth did not feel at liberty to return home without having a meeting at Brooklyn. Arrangements were made for one that evening. We dined at Richard Fields'. Our hearts were tendered with the retrospection of much we had passed through since we were last under their hospitable roof. Elizabeth was brought into near feeling with our Friends, and encouraged them to a faithful discharge of what they felt required of them in order rightly to perform their day's work. Went over to Brooklyn and called at Robert Haviland's. Elizabeth earnestly appealed to some who were there gathered, to give up that which would prevent them from walking in the path designed for them. The meeting in the evening was quite large, and E. had considerable to communicate. We returned to New York to lodge, and next morning were at Hester street meeting, where E. addressed some who, she felt, had turned from the simplicity of the gospel and were endeavoring in their own wills to please the people ; this she considered even more reprehensible than receiving *money* for preaching. Dined at Abraham Shoemaker's, where E. was led into deep exercise, and feelingly portrayed the states of some who had been unwilling to obey the requisitions which truth had demanded. In the afternoon went to Greenwich Meeting, to which Friends and others had been invited at E's request. The house was filled and all were addressed, but particularly those who were not members, of which there were a large number. We accompanied our Friend Phebe I. Merritt to Richard Cromwell's—his wife is a niece of Phebe's. A number of Friend's came in after tea and we had a solemn and interesting meeting. All were encouraged to a faithful discharge of duty; but some in an especial manner, who it was believed had been called to the work of the ministry were reminded of the responsibility which rested on them, not only as individuals, but on account of others to whom they might be helpful. Lodged at N. S. Merritt's, and in the morning bade them an affectionate adieu, as with thankful hearts we left for our own beloved homes. At the Monthly Meeting in the Sixth month, Elizabeth Newport returned the minute granted her for the above visit with an endorsement expressive of unity with her gospel labors, by those whom she had visited.

In the Tenth month of 1837 E. Newport was again called upon to leave the endearments of home and enter that field of labor to which her natural feelings were greatly averse. She informed her Monthly Meeting of her concern to visit the families of Darby Monthly Meeting, Pa., and those of Wilmington, Del., for which a minute of concurrence was furnished her. Ann W. Longstreth and Thos. B. Longstreth accompanied her in the visit to the families belonging to Darby, and it is to be regretted that T.'s notes concerning it have been mislaid. A letter written to his wife contains a summary account, the substance of which is here given.

Eleventh month 10th, 1837.

. . . We are at our dear friend Rachel Hunt's, and this is the first time that I have had time to write. The committee who plan our visits keep us very busy and the appointments are made several days ahead. We pass through many heights and depths. Our sufferings are at times truly agonizing; we go from house to house, as it were, blindfolded, and Elizabeth, through deep baptisms, has to bring into view "the hidden things of Esau," often to the confounding of the worldly wise, as well as bringing to naught the understanding of the prudent. I feel that our exercises are about as heavy as I can bear, but I hope to be able to hold out to the end. One circumstance may serve to illustrate the nature of E.'s service. A friend was visited who was shown very clearly his spiritual condition, and this was represented as being in striking contrast with that which he knew when he made covenant with his God as he followed the plow in his father's field. He could but accept the message that had been delivered, as one of divine inspiration, as he had never to any one divulged the spiritual exercises through which he had passed in his youth, and which on that occasion had been so truthfully presented by our friend. Thus forewarned he turned from the path which he saw was a dangerous one, and became a remarkably useful member of the community.

Sarah Noble, an Elder of Green Street Monthly Meeting, expressed a concern to accompany Elizabeth in her visit to the families of Wilmington Monthly Meeting, which was fully united with, and a minute was granted her for that service. During the prosecution of this visit, while they were at a Friend's house in Wilmington for the purpose of a religious opportunity, a stranger came into the room. Elizabeth's feelings were arrested and she turned to him with the language, "'Seek ye first the kingdom of heaven and its righteousness and all things necessary shall be added unto you.' This, my brother, is one of the most forcible testimonies of the blessed Jesus, and it is peculiarly adapted to thy condition. It is my desire that thou may comprehend it, may appreciate it, may dwell upon it. I feel irresistibly drawn toward thee in tender sympathy, &c., &c."

In about a week she received from him the following letter :

WILMINGTON, Dec. 15th, 1837.

Madam,—The stranger whom you met in a family of Friends which you visited last week, and whom you personally addressed, cannot forbear to write a few lines to you, to which he is encouraged by your rational and philosophic maxim—"That profession constitutes not religion." I too believe and profess this axiom of true toleration. Ever since I have learned to think philosophically, I have made a distinction between theology and religion, and whoever does not thus distinguish, mistakes the *shell* for the *fruit*. Your admonition, my Christian sister, was one peculiarly adapted, as far as I can judge of myself, to my condition and such as I *greatly needed*. Political struggles and severe trials of six years exile, have hardened and blunted my feelings, and my pride under misfortune, my animal fortitude, have overwhelmed my religious feelings. I have murmured against the Almighty more for my helpless country than for myself. Your admonition was solemn but not terrific. In answer to your apprehension of my enquiry into the principles of Friends, I declare my belief in a God *mentally* revealed to man, by which the unlettered savage, who knows nothing of the decalogue, is shown what is right and what is wrong. This invisible agent, call it what we may, and without which no positive religion can be founded, or even recognized, is the scale by which I measure the perfection of existing religious professions, and the more a religion departs from rationality, the nearer is its approximation to superstition, to fanaticism. Having been often on the verge of death and temporal annihilation by state prisons, I have never been tempted to forsake these self-evident truths which I have acquired in exchange for Roman Catholic absurdities. I shall be glad to hear from you madam.

"Polish Exile."

In E. Newport's last illness she alluded to this person, and said she many times had felt forcibly impressed to write to him, but was not faithful, and when she was informed that about a month after the reception of his letter, he had met with an untimely death, she suffered deeply because of her unfaithfulness.

On another occasion they visited a family

where one of the sons had but a short time previously been discussing, with a friend of his, the subject of revelation. Elizabeth addressed this son very emphatically, repeating *three* times the language, "Tamper not with revelation."

A family consisting of father, mother and a son, an only child, was called upon, and there happened to be present two young giddy girls who were not members of our Society. E. felt no liberty to give expression to her feelings until they should leave the room, which they were invited to do. They complied with manifest displeasure. She then addressed each member of the family, speaking very closely to the son and warning him of the injurious influences of his thoughtless female companions, which if not withstood would lead to ruin. After she had relieved her mind with the family, she proposed that the two girls should be invited in. She told them their presence had closed the way for utterance in relation to the family, but she now felt it right to tell them her feelings in regard to themselves, which she did very pointedly and earnestly. The young man did not profit by the advice given, and had to suffer the penalty of transgression.

Another family which they visited was brought before E. N.'s spiritual vision in a remarkable manner. She addressed their different states so pertinently that one of them remarked aside to a friend who accompanied her, "She has read us all through as if she had known us all our lives. What kind of a woman can she be? She has told me all things that ever I did!" He answered that she was alone guided by an internal sense of feeling.

The religious services within the districts of Darby and Wilmington Monthly Meetings were in keeping with our friend's usual fidelity to and trust in her spiritual guide. The states of the people were often portrayed in so remarkable a manner, that there was no room to doubt but that her knowledge had been received through divine revelation. The acknowledgment was not unfrequently made by the visited that no one save the great Unseen had been cognizant of the facts which had been related.

Her minute was returned to her Monthly Meeting with an accompanying minute from those meetings of unity with her services.

Our friend Ann Jackson, of West Chester, attended the Monthly Meeting of Green Street, held Twelfth month 20th, 1838, with a concern to visit the families belonging thereto, and also those who were in the habit of attending our meetings who were not members. Elizabeth Newport expressed a similar concern which had been resting upon her mind for some time. Both friends were encouraged to pursue their prospects under the direction of divine wisdom. Elizabeth Townsend, an Elder of Green Street Monthly Meeting accompanied them.

The following extract from a letter to E.'s daughter M. alludes to this public offering: "United with the love of a daughter, I recognize a companionship of the nearest and sweetest character. May this bond increase with added years and with the development of truth upon thy understanding ere the cares of life and the love of the world intercept the growth of the pure seed of the kingdom. And may there be a centering to that divine oracle whence issues light and knowledge, that so in the decline of those powers that I sometimes am ready to conclude are even now on the wane, I may have a staff to lean upon, even that of an armor-bearer made strong through the discipline of the cross. This has been our Monthly Meeting day, and in order that the vital spark may be preserved alive, I was induced to present for the consideration of my friends a concern that I have long felt to visit such of our members as duty may require. It obtained the approbation of the Meeting, and although it cost me much to make the avowal, peace has followed, and I am thankful that it is a service that will not call me from home."

A minute of the Monthly Meeting of later date says, that this labor of love was gratefully received, and was accomplished to the peace and satisfaction of those engaged in it.

Extract from a Letter to M. Hilles.

THIRD MONTH, 13TH, 1839.

. . . . Rachel Hicks and Amos Willets and wife made us a very pleasant visit. There seemed to me an unusual degree of sweetness about R. H. She and Harriet J. Moore had an opportunity in our family which was solemn and impressive. R. spoke particularly of the sweetness and solemnity of her feelings; the interview was grateful to me. Since then I have met them at Burlington Quarterly Meeting. I went to our Meeting hesitatingly, as there seemed no way open to proceed. I left the meeting and was followed by my friend, M. A. Hallowell, who encouraged me to attend to my feelings, and she thought that she would accompany me. She would have mentioned it to me the day before, but the roads were so bad that she was discouraged. She and her husband now felt prepared to go, and she believed we would get along. The way thus opening, we got off as soon as possible and lodged at Elisha Hunt's. My mind was laboring under a heavy exercise next morning, insomuch that breakfast was almost untasted. S. Hunt was an invalid at that time, and we were invited into her room, where I hoped to receive a word of comfort. I was longing for a closer re-union of the Divine Spirit, so that doubts and discouragements might be removed and fully overcome. But there seemed nothing for me to take hold of but the language,

"Behold I go bound in spirit to Jerusalem," etc. No consolation from human lips was afforded me. How ardently did I desire that if I were in my place, that quietness and assurance might once more cover my tossed spirit. I saw that I must leave all outward things, and soon my mind attained a state of peaceful poverty. When we arrived at meeting it was gathered, and I felt weak and faint, but said nothing. Soon after we entered, Lydia P. Mott spoke. R. Hicks then appeared in supplication and I was favored with the answer of a fullness of peace and joy and great tranquility. . . . .

E. N.

At a Monthly Meeting held Fourth month, 1839, E. Newport informed the Meeting that she felt a religious obligation to make a visit to the families of Philadelphia Monthly Meeting. Sympathy and unity were expressed, and she was encouraged to a faithful discharge of duty. Our dear friend, Susanna Haydock, an Elder of Philadelphia Monthly Meeting, was her companion and fellow-burden bearer in this arduous concern. Many remarkable visits were made in which the spirit of prophecy enabled E. N. to see many things which since have been verified. After addressing several individuals in a certain family she expressed her interest and sympathy in one of the younger children, and exhorted him to yield to the impressions made upon his mind, and against which he had rebelled until deep suffering was his portion; she felt that continued disobedience would result in his being left in doubt and darkness, but faithfulness would meet with an ample reward, and he would have to become a public Minister of "the Word." The mother, who had not been aware of the dispensations through which her son had passed, and was still enduring, was greatly troubled in the belief that Elizabeth was entirely mistaken, and her faith in her mission was considerably weakened. Before very long, however, she had a clear evidence that the facts were in accordance with E. N.'s feelings, and she could not feel satisfied without making a full acknowledgement to her of her doubts, and the manner in which they had been removed. This son, as was predicted, is now a valuable Minister of the Gospel.

In another instance, where there was a large family of sons and daughters, Elizabeth addressed them with a power that had a tendency to bring conviction with it. She then particularized one son upon whom she felt that the anointing oil had been poured, and that if faithful to his calling he would have to invite others to enter the Lord's vineyard and labor in His cause. To one of the daughters she spoke, tenderly alluding to what she believed she would have to pass through. That it would be her privilege to nurse her beloved father who would ere long be taken ill—that by her devoted care, the pain which he would have to endure would be in a degree assuaged; and after all had been done, and his loved form committed to the dust, in a brief space she would follow him to the mansions of bliss. Trying as this was to some of the family at the time to hear, it proved a true prophecy. Within a few months the father and daughter were taken hence, and in not a very long time, the son alluded to, was acknowledged as a gospel Minister.

Our friends were at another place, the family being strangers to E. N. The committee were surprised to find quite a number of young people—some of them, they learned, were married children of the friend visited, who had come for the purpose of being at the meeting. After a season of quiet, E. addressed the head of the family, but suddenly paused. Then entered into an explanation of the testimonies held by Friends in contradistinction to those adhered to by the "Established Church" and those called "Evangelical" in their belief. This was done in a remarkably clear and concise manner, and the meeting was pre-eminently satisfactory. A day or two after this occurrence, the friend, at whose house they had been, inquired of one of the committee if E. Newport had been told that the young people who were present had been unsettled upon those subjects which she had so clearly explained. He was told, she was an entire stranger to them all, and knew not to whose house she was going. He said *he* was entirely satisfied that that was the case, but the children thought she must have been informed of the doubts which they had felt, or she could not so exactly have alluded to them.

In another case a meeting was held with a family, and as was almost the universal practice of E., its members were individually addressed—but Elizabeth's mind was not relieved; after sitting some time longer, she asked if the family, except the father and mother and one she denoted, would leave the room. They did so, and then E. presented what had been opened to her spiritual vision, and earnestly urged the individual to abandon an intended purpose; if it was persisted in, it would embitter and render unhappy the future. This word of caution was not acted upon, and the result was as was portrayed.

A Friend, who is at this time an active and useful member, can remember the power with which E. N. addressed him during this season of deep baptisms wherein she was led as one whose natural vision had been obscured by the brighter light which shone around her pathway. He was admonished to renounce more fully the strong will of the creature, so that the Master might lead him into the valley of humility and by the still waters; so that the still small voice might be more perfectly heard, and a preparation received to call upon others to serve the Majesty of Heaven, who in condescending goodness was ready to unveil His glory to the waiting and watchful mind.

The families of Spruce Street Monthly Meeting were visited by our friend in the latter part of 1839, she having obtained a minute of concurrence from her Monthly Meeting for that purpose. Among her brethren and sisters of this part of the heritage she went forth as one called of the Lord to distribute bread to the hungry, and consolation to the afflicted, bearing upon his spiritual banner the inscription of "Glory to God in the highest, peace on earth, and good will to men." In a number of instances she foresaw the work designed for certain individuals, who, if *faithful*, would become as bright and shining lights in the camp of our Israel; but if lukewarmness and indifference were suffered to gain the ascendancy, they would appear but as beautiful vessels marred upon the wheel. With yearnings of spirit she looked upon some of these, hoping to see ere the end of her earthly pilgrimage the fulfilment of the bright vision which her faith induced her to believe was no idle chimera. She had often to feel that a want of faithfulness to the inward monitor on the part of individuals, occasioned her to appear as a false prophet, but that gave her much less uneasiness than that these bright immortals should not so use the Master's talents, that at His coming they might receive the answer of "Well done."

Within a year most of the families belonging to our Monthly Meetings in this city, beside many others who were in the habit of attending our meetings, had thus an evidence of divine love and sisterly regard.

From numerous testimonies in relation to this service, it is believed that it had a tendency to unite spirit with spirit, so that the gospel could flow as a stream direct from the Fountain of Life, whereby the weary were refreshed, the weak strengthened, and all were encouraged to take heed to the impressions of the inward monitor, that they might become faithful stewards of the manifold gifts which had been bestowed upon them by a beneficent Creator.

Extract from a Letter to M. Hilles from E. N.

. . . "We were favored to get through the prospect which I mentioned to thee to the peace of our minds. I believe we could all unite in this. I find more and more occasion to feel dear old friend S. Haydock as a true mother in Israel. She told me when we were together on last First-day, when she and David Ellis kindly accompanied me to West Philadelphia Meeting, that she had been nearly united with me though in great suffering most of the week, and that she had lost one whole night's sleep querying why is it so? I informed her that in some severe baptisms through which I had passed, I had desired to know if she was separated from me; her answer was, "my dear, never more nearly united." One of my communications lately at Cherry Street gave rise to many conclusions, and much talk; but S. H. expressed much satisfaction, and as soon as she was near enough to me, sealed it with a kiss. Many and deep have been my plungings of latter time, but if they only have the blessed effect to deepen in the root of life, they will be numbered among the blessings in disguise of a kind and overruling Providence."

In the First month, 1840, a minute was granted E. Newport by Green Street Monthly Meeting to visit Byberry Monthly Meeting, but the way not opening for her to perform the visit she returned the minute in the Third month with this information—she felt the reward of peace for having thus far been faithful to what had been required.

FLUSHING, WESTBURY, AND JERICHO.

She obtained a minute in the Fourth mo., 1840, to visit the families of Flushing, Westbury, and Jericho Monthly Meetings. It appears from the diary she kept at the time, and from which the following account of the visit is taken, that she felt a restriction in regard to having a female companion.

James Haviland, who at that time resided near Jericho, L. I., had for years been resting under a similar concern, and his friends united with his joining with Elizabeth in the service. She commenced her religious labor by attending Westbury Monthly Meeting, of which she says: "My mind was introduced into a sense of the state of things among the people, and after a season of deep, silent travail, in which I was reminded of the language, 'except ye eat the flesh and drink the blood of the Son of man, ye have no part in Him,' I was enabled to give utterance to my concern greatly to the relief of my mind." Dined with a friend who appeared to have every earthly comfort around him, but I seemed required to remind him of the perishable nature of all the cunning devices and contrivances of men.

Arose next morning under a depressed state of feeling, and it was long before the cause of it was made known; but at length the waters were divided; a firmament was placed in the midst dividing the waters that were above from the waters that were below.

Had a close time at meeting and a *very* close testimony in men's Monthly Meeting. Commenced on Sixth-day to visit families in company with James Haviland. I felt it right to go without a female companion, and Friends not objecting to it, we thus proceeded. Amid some dry, tough labor, we found one hopeful young plant toward whom the full tide of testimony flowed, and also some precious spirited old friends. During

Seventh-day's services there were occasions to give forth strong unwavering testimonies in boldness and fearlessness. The language at the close of one address was on this wise: "Sell what thou hast, give back the price, giving usury for usury if it be required." The cause for this I feel no anxiety to know —sufficient for me is the answer of peace.

First-day attended meeting at Bethpage—a close service—the mind much bowed through the day, it being hard work to the flesh to be found in a constant state of application of mind; and thoughts too were interwoven of some beloveds left behind, so as almost to exclude enjoyment.

On Second-day felt a state of greater resignation, so that the work was not so trying to the creature, though closely proving, it being necessary to speak plain things, and even to invite the children sometimes, after my mind was relieved in regard to them, to leave the room. Visited 10 families to-day —silent in two. Excused from mental labor, there being no entrance nor capacity to receive.

Third-day. The distances between the families this morning gave us much riding, and in the afternoon after I had laid down, I received a message that an individual wished to see me. I found it to be one to whom some plain things had been spoken, and he was not willing to receive them, and wished me to recall what I had said. I replied, that I believed what had been delivered had been under the influence of the same feeling that had visited my mind for years. Upon a re-examination I felt that I had nothing to do with it, having received my reward—a peaceful covering of spirit—and this being not jostled in the least by a *close* investigation, with a renewed flow of love toward him, I could leave the result with Him to whom all secret things are known.

In the afternoon visited the school, and then went to V. H.'s, where we had a comfortable religious opportunity—some deep travail of spirit, and some close counsel which was well received, and I believe occasioned a fellow-feeling of gospel unity under which we parted after tea.

By previous arrangement met with a young man at James Haviland's whose history was unknown to me, but toward whom, after a time of silence, the gospel stream flowed freely.

On Fourth-day rode 16 or 18 miles to visit an invalid. He was confined to his room, and seemed weak, but to my feelings it appeared as if spiritual strength was equally needed; a hard plodding exercise in which there was an endeavor to bring into view the necessity of experiencing a state of emptiness and want ere food could be relished. His responsibility also, as a possessor of spiritual gifts was alluded to. In another part of the house we had a meeting with several who were not members. Counsel and encouragement were freely given, which was acknowledged as truth by an elderly man, who said that "he had been told very much how it had been with him all his life." Called at the house of a Minister who was too much engaged with his outward concerns to come in and sit with us a little while.

Visited two families before meeting, in one of which the labor might be compared to pulling at the oar. In the other, no mental labor, so was excused, of course, from vocal service.

I had no liberty to proceed in the family visits at Jerusalem until after First day, when I expect to attend their meeting. In the neighborhood of Bethpage made several visits. On Sixth-day, visited 10 families and rode 14 or 15 miles; retired for the night in a peaceful state of feeling but extremely fatigued. Yesterday, at R. Powell's, we were instructed in silence with the exception of some expression to an Indian girl, who, being very curious to see us, had been invited into the room. On Seventh-day made seven or eight visits, in one of which we were again instructed in silence, at which there was some disappointment, it not being what was desired; but I dare not offer anything of my own, and not having anything given me I had nothing to hand forth.

In several visits close labor was called for, but in each case the individual was open and received the message kindly.

Attended meeting at Jericho on First-day. My mind was calm and tolerably free from exercise, nevertheless it was a low time, in which the language was uttered, "strangers shall stand and feed your flocks, and the sons of the alien shall be your ploughmen and your vine dressers." There were some panting after the water of life, and to these the language of encouragement flowed freely. Were at Jerusalem in the afternoon at a meeting appointed by a Friend from Brooklyn. On Second-day visited 13 families, and met with much cordiality among some who were not members, many of whom appeared to be in a state of readiness to receive a blessing.

After visiting 9 or 10 families and riding about 20 miles, we returned to J. Haviland's with grateful and peaceful hearts. The calm and serenity through the evening seemed almost unalloyed; but the next day was a season mostly of suffering—spent it in writing and resting with an occasional attempt to read, but the prospect of going to Flushing was a painful one. Kept mostly in my chamber, which was a great treat. It is difficult sometimes to lie as low and abased as certain requisitions call for, when we feel that the testimony which has cost much is laid waste or become a matter of public criticism. The change from the evening previous, when there seemed not one cloud to be seen in my horison, I believe, was needful to prepare my mind to enter again into suffering.

Seventh mo. 5th.—Visited twenty-five families since we came to Flushing—a different kind of service required from that mostly experienced on this Island.

Seventh mo. 8th.—The last of our labor in this district. We have altogether visited about thirty-four families, which has required much riding; and this, with considerable physical weakness, has caused us to make slow progress.

Fifth-day attended meeting, which was silent, but there was hard rowing "against wind and tide," and no possibility of even getting into the stream which leads into the ocean. Visited four families under great trial and mortification of self. The state of some young friends, unbelieving in the pure principle, which alone was my dependence, was sensibly felt; however, truth soon arose into dominion, though not very high, but sufficiently to know that it was above all, and it proved a favored season. In the afternoon we met with some precious spirits, who were counselled to sell all and take up the Cross, while to some, further advanced, encouragement was offered in love and sympathy. On Sixth-day we visited several others, whose various conditions were pointed out, but not in much freedom, there being an impossibility for the stream to raise higher than the fountain. Were at meeting at Flushing on First-day, which was a time of deep suffering, but some relief was obtained through expression.

Visited five families in the afternoon—all seasons of mental suffering and close labor, producing a state of exhaustion, in which the physical powers were fully overcome for a considerable time.

Left Flushing on Third-day afternoon for Cow Neck. A valuable Friend of this meeting accompanied us through all the visits, to mutual satisfaction. Were at the select preparative meeting at Westbury, and on the day previous were at Cow Neck—both of these meetings were favored; utterance was furnished, and there appeared to be a preparation to receive what was handed forth.

From thence went to S. H.'s, from an unexpected impression that it was the right time to call there, although I had the information that his wife was from home. This did not deter us, and we had an evidence that "wisdom is profitable to direct" not only as to the right time, but to divide at right times. Returned after this opportunity to Jericho, and next day paid the remaining visits in that meeting.

On Seventh-day Silas Carl came for us, and we went with him to Westbury. His house was our home, and his wife was exceedingly kind.

On Fifth-day were at Westbury meeting. It was a trying season and a silent one, in that I could rejoice.

In looking over my experience, I have great cause for thankfulness, in that the promise has been so often verified: "I will be to thee mouth, tongue and utterance."

Attended Westbury Monthly Meeting on Fourth-day, which to me was a painful time, as I had to utter plain things; and although in much weakness of body and mind, I believed it was in the authority of Truth—the force of the Truth was not, however, received, nor understood by many. Had a solemn opportunity in S. Carl's family before leaving, and then returned to Jericho to attend the Monthly Meeting there. This was a time of favor to be remembered by me. Truth in its authority arose above all opposition. May the praise be ascribed to Him to whom it is forever due. Parted with S. C. and wife with regret; S. having been with us through most of the visits in Westbury.

On Sixth and Seventh-day visited about ten families each day. A close application, in which both the mental and bodily powers were much exhausted.

Attended meeting on First-day. This was one of the occasions in which the measure of suffering required to be filled up for the body's sake, was hard for the natural part to endure. The pangs and throes of those who are baptized for the dead are inexpressible. Forever be magnified the name of Israel's God, in that as there is a willingness to follow Him closely, He endows with sufficient faith to keep the feet on the "stepping-stones," though far separated sometimes. But as the eye is kept single, the evidence of the

King's signet will be seen upon the testimony, and this must be acknowledged even by the wisdom of men. In the afternoon visited three families, who were not members. As a whole, I consider this the most trying day since I left home.

Several families were visited on Second-day, and I had renewedly to feel that we have indeed a gracious Father, who condescends to our weaknesses, and enables to fulfil the allotted work. Returned to our friend, James Haviland's, late in the evening, and in the morning we had a solemn opportunity, in which vocal supplication was called for, and we parted in unity and sweet feeling."

A communication was subsequently received by Green Street Monthly Meeting from Flushing Monthly Meeting, acknowledging the labors of Elizabeth Newport among them to have been acceptable.

In the Seventh month of the same year, she was furnished with a minute from her Monthly Meeting to visit the families of Chesterfield Monthly Meeting, and also those of persons who were in the habitual attendance of that meeting who were not members.

This minute was duly returned, with the acknowledgement that the service had been satisfactorily performed.

RICHLAND, HORSHAM AND CONCORD.

In the Tenth month of 1840, E. N. again left home with a minute of unity from her Monthly Meeting to visit the families of Friends constituting Richland, Horsham and Concord Monthly Meetings. Ann W. Longstreth of Green street, Philadelphia, and John H. Andrews of Darby, Pa., were her companions.

From a diary kept by J. H. A., and letters to his family, the following details are gathered:

Elizabeth Newport and Ann W. Longstreth attended the Preparative Meeting of Stroudsburg, which is composed of about fifteen families and is a branch of Richland Monthly Meeting. They then came to Quakertown, where John met them with his own conveyance. Darby Monthly Meeting not occurring till the 24th of the month, he was not able sooner to obtain a minute to accompany them. On the 26th they attended the Preparative

Meeting at Quakertown, when the prospect of visiting families was fully united with by both men's and women's meetings. J. H. A. says "there appears to be a great openness to receive us and E. seems in good spirits. I was never more sensible of my many weaknesses, and often marvel that my mind should have been impressed with a sense of this duty which I believe is required at my hands. Perhaps it is for my own good, not that I expect to be able to render much assistance to E." In thirteen days they visited sixty-seven families and attended the meetings which came in course. On Second-day, the 7th of Twelfth month, they returned home. It would seem by the following note written to the wife of J. H. Andrews, that E. Newport had not been certain of the favor of having a companion who was abilitated to enter into near feeling with her exercised and sometimes deeply tried mind. The "good spirits" which J. H. A. alluded to can be therefore readily understood.

M. Andrews. My Dear Friend:—I feel that I want to tell thee that the company of thy dear husband is truly grateful, though an unexpected favor. I really feel as if there was cause rather "to thank God and take fresh courage," than to allow discouragments to enter, although the trial of leaving home is one that I think no one can understand who has not been similarly tried. I hope thy mind will be sustained in patience and faith under the separation this winter, and thou wilt have a share of the spoil! In much sisterly feeling, thine affectionately,

E. NEWPORT.

Horsham Monthly Meeting occured on the 30th of Twelfth month, and our friends were in attendance. In the evening they visited the family of Demas Worrell, (a minister). E. had much excellent service, to the satisfaction of all. On Fifth-day morning they visited an elderly friend who dressed exceedingly plain. E. was so close and searching in her remarks, that John says, "I was alarmed, yet did not doubt the authority. As soon as we entered the carriage, Isaac Parry turned to Elizabeth and said, I love thee and have good unity with thy service. The remark was as the 'oil of gladness' to our drooping spirits. We visited seven families that day and seven yesterday, although it stormed hard. To-day E. has been very poorly, indeed the exercise of her mind is so great that her physical powers seem scarcely able at times to support her. Those sitting quietly at home can form no idea of the travail of spirit it requires for this family visiting. Isaac Parry staid with us till this morning, and I can say he has been as a near and dear father to us all. He told us he was *very* unexpectedly united in this work. He watches over E. as a parent over a child, encouraging her 'to reveal the whole counsel of God without the fear of man.' And I have no doubt he would often have marvelled if he had not been a firm believer in the all-sufficiency of the Power which unfolds and reveals the states of the people to Elizabeth's mind.

I think there is a good degree of openness to receive the gospel-word, though in some places the hearts of the people seem closed. Last evening we had a great meeting at a friend's house; it commenced at 8 o'clock and continued till after 10 o'clock; after a remarkable address to the young people they were all requested to withdraw; then the parents were impressively addressed. It was a very precious time to us all. Isaac said E. was rightly led. I can say with all sincerity that no one can travel with E. Newport without admiring the power which clothes her mind and enables her to declare without fear that which is adapted to the states and conditions of the people. We visited to-day a family which was large, several sons and a number of daughters. E. was led to address a state present in a remarkable manner, and portrayed the exercises of mind through which he was passing. He appeared deeply impressed; sat still a few moments after the meeting broke up, and then arose and went out without speaking to any one, but when we got into the carriage he came and took each of us by the hand. I think he will not soon forget the testimony."

. . . . . "This is one of the coldest days I ever felt. We rode four miles to Horsham Meeting. A. Garrigues made a few remarks, then J. Foulke, and after him Elizabeth delivered a lengthy and impressive discourse, which I think will long be remembered by many present.

We dined at Isaac Parry's, and had an interesting opportunity with his family. He requested the children to dwell under what they had heard, and not to talk about it. In the afternoon visited several families. I. P. told me that 'E. had a right view of all these people—that he had full unity with her and her mission.' I narrate these things to show how a mind like I P.'s is drawn in close feeling with E., although some may doubt and find fault. And Oh! saith my spirit, may the labor of our dear friend sink deep into the minds of those who have had the opportunity of sitting under her ministry! It has, I think, been a favored visitation to many in the neighborhood, and I firmly believe it is in the ordering of Divine wisdom that she is sent on these missions of Gospel love!

We are getting along comfortably with visiting families. Have not laid by, though there have been five or six stormy days. E. and myself have both been poorly, but have kept going—she is so anxious to get through! She is wonderfully strengthened, far beyond anything I expected, both in body and mind. Her exercises continue as close and searching as ever. I. P.'s daughter told him she wanted him to go with us, and to continue to help Elizabeth all he could.

. . . . "Since I last wrote we have experienced some of the most exercising times I have ever witnessed. I think they will never be forgotten by the visited. I have seen the parent so overcome as to weep aloud, even as we read that Joseph wept when he was made known to his brethren; and the same effect produced when the spirit of supplication was poured forth for the children, with a power which touched hearts that were comparable to the flinty stone; and for those that were wounded the oil and the wine were dispensed for their healing.

On First-day, the 24th, attended Horsham Meeting, then returned home, having visited 155 families within the verge of Horsham Monthly Meeting."

During this journey Elizabeth wrote to her husband, saying: "If I had known exactly what would have befallen me when I left home in the weak state I was then in, I do not see that I could have undertaken it, though I fully believe I would have declined in strength, mentally and physically, if I had refused; and this at last brought me to submit. But the mind has been borne up beyond what I could have expected. Still it has been hard for flesh and blood to bear, as poor John can testify! I believe if I am resigned to do all required of me, when I am at liberty to return, I shall bring home the sheaves of peace. My dear friend, T. B. L., has frequently been the companion of my mind, though not often very anxiously, believing that all will work together for his good. His sickness is not unto death, but unto the glory of God.

My companions and myself have been much united in travail and exercise, and I believe this mission will not close our service, for by the eye of faith I have been given to behold a large field of labor opened. Love to the precious children toward whom the solicitude of a mother's heart flows with ardent concern. May thy mind, dear M., [then 12 years old] early learn subjection to that Power which I am sensible is even now operating upon the little leaven. . . . .

Friends are still very kind and attentive, but none of these things relieve the mind of the weight of the work, or render the task a desirable one."

"1st mo. 28, 1841.—We attended Concord Monthly Meeting. The next morning commenced visiting the families of Chichester Preparative Meeting, a branch of Concord Monthly Meeting. When I take a view of what we have passed through within a few days, I hardly know whether it *can* be compared to former services. Joseph and Hannah Dodgson will remember that Elizabeth remarked, the morning they left, that "there was some hard work to be done that day," and they will also remember that I told them that I knew where we were going, but that she did not. Well, I never heard closer or more searching exercises—words can but faintly describe them. . . .

At one place we visited Elizabeth was concerned for some frivolous and light young people who were present. She clearly shewed them the danger they were in. The exercise was pointed and close, and was very impressive. I hope the counsel to them may be treasured up.

On Fifth-day we attended Chichester Meeting. Elizabeth was so poorly that she kept her seat while speaking. She addressed a young man in so plain a manner, that the case could not be misunderstood by any; his poor father shed many tears. She then spoke to another, and told him he had not come there with his own accord. Poor fellow! he did not raise his head. It was a day of visitation to them all. Elizabeth has a heavy cold, and her throat and breast sore and painful, but strength is mercifully given to our admiration!

Notice having been spread of our being at meeting, it was the means of gathering a large concourse of people of all classes. The meeting was a long one, but so wrapt were the assembly during the whole time of E.'s speaking, which was an hour and a-half, that I never sat a more quiet meeting. Truth reigned triumphant over all, to the humbling of many minds. There are many whose faces are turned Zionward, and whose cry is, "Who shall show us any good." E.'s mission to these was to direct them to a Teacher that cannot be removed into a corner, but who, if they attend to His voice, will lead and guide them into all truth. She is impressed with the belief that there are many in this neighborhood, not of our Society, who, if faithful, will come forth as able advocates of the cause of righteousness.

No description of the meeting alluded to could convey an idea of it. The efficacy and power of her appeals to those present must have been *felt* to be fully appreciated. E. was led to supplicate on behalf of different states, and among them one who had given way to intemperance, and who had been powerfully addressed in her communication. After the prayer, the meeting settled into a state of profound stillness, and remained under that covering to its close. Several who were not Friends came to me, and desired a visit. Although E.'s mission is a close, searching one, it has been kindly received. At one place a man, not a member, dressed himself in plain clothes to deceive Elizabeth, but she brought him out in his true colors, and he was spoken to very closely. His family desired another visit, but I think E. feels released. Visited a friend, into whose state Elizabeth entered very closely, telling him of his faults and the necessity of obedience to the Light within, in order to know an overcoming. A few days afterward he met me, and said, I am much obliged to thee for giving E. Newport a full portraiture of my character. I replied that I had never mentioned his name to her; she knew nothing about him; all that she said to him was from a sense of spiritual discernment; that she is guided by the Light within, and is never willing to listen to any external information, and we never tell her anything."

When our friends called upon another family they were up stairs. The wife remarked to her husband and children, "Now let us all go down and see what the old witch has to say to us." They sat a little while in silence, when E. turned to the mother and said, "I must tell thee I am not an old witch." A solemn quiet followed, and the meeting broke. The lesson was a painful one, but must have been fraught with deep instruction.

At another place, one of the sons did not wish to come into the room, and said to his mother, "The Friend only comes to get something good to eat and drink." After they were gathered, E. turned to the boy, and said, "I came here neither to eat nor to drink;" She then delivered her gospel message.

At another house, where the family were apparently all assembled, Elizabeth said to the wife, Is thy husband at home? she answered, No. When will he return? Cannot tell exactly when. They sat a little while in silence, when E. in a low voice requested her companion to open a certain door, and to the surprise of the company, a man stood in the door-way. Elizabeth invited him to take a seat and addressed him in a remarkable manner. She told him that she was impressed that he was standing outside the door to listen, but was not willing to sit with them.

After having had a very interesting opportunity with a family, she returned in a day or two and asked to see a relative who lived in another part of the house. She told this individual that she knew nothing about him save from her sense of feeling; but she had returned to warn him that his days were numbered, and that his mind and thoughts were too much absorbed with earthly things. That it was time he sought to lay up spiritual treasures—he could not take his gold and silver, which had become idols, with him. This person was rich, but E. did not know it. He seemed impressed by the earnestness which accompanied the communication; he lived but a few months after this interview. He had lost his wife and children sometime previously and had since devoted himself to making and *saving* money.

In a letter to his wife, J. H. Andrews says: "I feel like giving a sketch of a visit we had to a family who were not members, that you may see how the mind can be directed when its sole dependence is upon its divine Teacher. E. N. was led to address the head of a family, who it was said was looking toward uniting himself with Friends. His state was delineated in a remarkable manner, and no doubt to his satisfaction.

We were seated in a small room with the man and his wife; in an adjoining room through which we had passed sat a young woman—the door into this room had been left open about six inches. As soon as E. had finished speaking to the person above alluded to, she said 'I am bound as in prison in sympathy with a state in the next room, and I cannot pass away without saying to thee my brother,'—she then went on in a most powerful manner to describe his condition as deplorable, and made a fervent appeal to him to lead a better life. We were amazed, not knowing that any one was in that room except the girl whom we saw. Soon, however, a *foot* appeared before the crack of the door and was immediately withdrawn; this was after E. had been addressing an unseen person for some time. I was impressed with the feeling that the man was sitting against the partition, and as soon as the meeting broke, I arose and found a rough-looking man against the wall, and three men and a boy were also in the room. The men soon slipped away, and when we were seated in the carriage the boy was the only one to be seen. Here was another trial for E.'s faith. The reasoner stepped in to persuade her that she had been mistaken; but instantly she had a secret impression to look at his foot. She saw that it was not the same she had seen through the door.

There were four men standing near a wheelwright shop close by, and as we passed, E. remarked, that the man who was standing with his back toward us was the person she addressed. She had before seen no part of him except his foot, but I recognized him as the individual who sat by the partition. I relate this one instance, but there are many remarkable ones which prove that while our friend keeps close to her Guide, the Spirit of Truth, there is no danger of her being deceived.

On First-day the 21st, attended Stanton meeting in the morning and Wilmington in the afternoon, at both of which Elizabeth had deep searching labor, but was favored to relieve her mind. On Third-day were at Darby Monthly Meeting. After a solid opportunity in our family to the comfort and satisfaction of all, E. Newport returned to her home in the evening. In conclusion, I may say, that although we had to pass through many deep trying baptisms, I have had to admire the wonderful manner in which E. was led from house to house, opening the states of individuals in the power and authority of Truth and with a clearness that left not a doubt of her being directed by the pointings of Him who had called her to the work."

Extract of a letter from E. Newport, written at Concord.

SECOND MONTH 6th, 1841.

. . . . Not more acceptable to the parched mouth is the cooling and refreshing draught that issues from the juttings of the rock, than to my feelings was the little packet received from home this evening after a hard day's service. The roads were rough, and the six families we visited were widely separated. I am much oppressed with a cough and cold, but this did not excuse me from close service, which was relieved only by utterance. It was given in simplicity, void of slavish fear. Indeed I have felt there never was a time when I have experienced less of a disposition to falter or to rely upon externals, or to look to man, than through this visit, and if I mistake not, the necessity for this will continue to the end of the service. Close as have been the exercises, still I have been supported through all, and have generally been able to wash and anoint under an evidence, that my Guide will not allow me to err, so long as there is a concern to watch the "stepping stones" and sway neither to the right hand nor the left. After Monthly Meeting we went to Chichester and were at meeting there on First-day. It was a free time in which the mind was relieved. On Second-day we returned to attend the Select Meeting, which was a season of deep exercise to me; but as I waded through the deep and waited till my measure of suffering was filled, the command was given and an alarm was sounded in the camp. At the conclusion of the meeting, Hannah Oakford turned to me and said, "I can say amen to that testimony." We returned to T. Marshall's, where many friends were gathered. After some conversation, silence ensued and a solemn covering overspread our little company. My concern was first expressed. This was followed by a testimony from Mary Hunt, after which Alice Chandler appeared in fervent supplication. The next day was one to be remembered, but I believe Truth reigned over all. The spirit of supplication was poured forth under a sense of nothingness of the creature, unto Him whose power was magnified. The business meeting was an exercising one, but it was a favored season.

Rode to T. D's, six miles over a rough country ; J. and H. Dodgson accompanied us. Had a religious opportunity in Thomas' family. J. Dodgson testified to its being a time of spiritual refreshment.

Went on our mission next morning and paid such a visit as hitherto I had never performed. My mind was supported on the ground not of external evidence, for I needed something more sure to build upon. My voice was raised with no fear save the fear of God. I deeply sympathised with the individual, but I felt that I must reveal to him the whole counsel as given to me." . . . . . .

In the 12th month E. N. informed her Monthly Meeting that her mind was turned toward a class within the three Monthly Meetings in which she was then engaged, that was not embraced in her minute. After due deliberation she was encouraged to follow the pointings of Truth in regard to the additional service.

Horsham Monthly Meeting forwarded a minute to the Monthly Meeting of Green street, by which it appeared that the labors of our friend E. N. had been satisfactory.

A similar communication was received from Richland, in which it was stated "The labors of Elizabeth Newport have been promotive of love among us."

REMOVED TO ABINGTON, PA.

In the Fifth month of 1841, a certificate of removal was furnished Jesse Newport and family to Abington Monthly Meeting, Pa.

Letter to J. H. A.

ABINGTON, 7th Month 4th, 1841.

I hope no unfavorable construction has been placed upon my silence as relates to my interest and esteem for thee, whose kindness and sympathy have so often been cordial to my feelings. Thou hast been often, my brother, as a prop and a staff when I have been faint and weary. Thy unwearied attention and watchfulness, have called forth deep and heartfelt gratitude to the Author of all our sure mercies. I considered it an unspeakable favor to be provided with a companion in all respects so suitable, and so entirely congenial with those peculiar feelings from which I suffer in going from door to door. I say *peculiar*, because I believe there are but few so weak as I; and thou, my friend, understood these weaknesses and could and *would* bear with them. Since our removal to A. I have had repeated evidences of our being in the right place, and generally there has been witnessed a quietness of spirit which has preserved from anxiety; and yet I feel the necessity of watchfulness and introversion of mind that there may be daily experienced "a conscience void of offense toward God and man. It was said formerly by one of experience that "a christian's life is a continual warfare," but I have been ready to conclude that the obedient mind may witness a time of rest from this warfare. Be that as it may, I believe in the language of the Psalmist that "Light is sown, for the righteous and *joy* for the upright in heart." This text has been of late the companion of my thoughts, with an increasing desire that the eye may be kept so singly directed to the light that there may be a more perfect understanding of those mysteries of the kingdom which are reserved for the "upright in heart" —that there may be experienced a perfect and divine harmony which inspires the acclamation of "Glory to God in the highest, on earth peace and good will to men." Surely here the mind may experience a rest from its labors, and be brought to participate in a foretaste of that bliss, of which those enjoy the full fruition who hold out to the end. We had to-day a very large meeting. Edward Hicks was favored. His doctrine in relation to "Salvation by Christ," to the spiritually minded was clear and comprehensive and perhaps sufficiently so to all. The subjects upon which he spoke were well adapted to the meeting and were feelingly delineated. His beloved friend Isaac Parry was with him.

E. N.

A Visit to the Families of Baltimore and other Monthly Meetings.

In the Tenth month, 1841, Elizabeth Newport informed her Monthly Meeting that she felt it required of her to visit the families of Baltimore Monthly Meeting, and other meetings as the way might open. This was united with. T. B. Longstreth and wife were her fellow-laborers in this service.

From desultory notes, made by L. L., the following particulars are gathered:

10th mo. 24th, 1841.—"Left home in a private carriage with my husband, to accompany E. Newport in a visit to Baltimore. In order to lessen the fatigue, our friend Elizabeth left us at Wilmington, and proceeded with good company in the cars, and consequently reached Baltimore before us. We arrived in time to attend a part of the Second-day morning meeting, in which the concern prevailed for the promotion of truth and righteousness. Through the sittings of the Yearly Meeting we were edified, and under a covering of sweet solemnity it closed on Fifth-day at noon."

A letter from E. Newport, dated Baltimore, 11th mo. 6th, 1841, informs her family of her safe arrival. She says: "I was glad to be able to participate in the instructive exercises which claimed the attention of Friends relative to the subjects introduced by the reading of the 3d Query—subjects which involve great responsibility; and under the deep and heartfelt convictions of my own insufficiency, I was brought renewedly and fervently to seek Divine aid in the fulfilment of them. I was led to examine and endeavor to ascertain in what I had been delinquent. How was I overwhelmed with grateful emotions when the language was sounded in my mental ear, 'She has done what she could.' May I never give occasion for this evidence to be revoked! I did not accept it as an assurance that I had always maintained the watch, and exhibited a consistency of deportment which would illustrate a perfect conformity to the spirit of love, but rather that the motive having been sincere it was accepted, and the sins of omission and commission were passed by, as the mind sought counsel and strength from Him who remembers we are dust and compassionates our infirmities.

"The meeting closed on Fifth-day morning, and we went to Elk Ridge in the afternoon. The Elders of Baltimore Monthly Meeting did not think it necessary for us to wait till after their Monthly Meeting before we proceeded in the concern to which I have felt particularly called, and from which I believe I never shrank with greater dread. I do not know that I have ever been more sensible of support and aid in the *moment* of need. The promise has been fully realized that 'I will go before and prepare the way.' The way has been made in the hearts of the people to our astonishment." . .

T. B. Longstreth adds: "At E.'s request I write, and can inform you that we have been greatly favored with a home in this city. M. Gillingham is a truly sympathetic friend, and has sometimes accompanied us. We have visited nine or ten families per day. Sometimes the work was hard and very trying to the poor instrument, who has been nevertheless faithful and fearlessly disposed to reveal the whole counsel, so that she may be clear, as she says, 'of the blood of all men' in the day of reckoning. We shall probably get through our work in this city about the 14th, and proceed to Indian Spring and to Sandy Spring. I am inclined to think even then we shall not be at the end of our labor. The prospect of further service has already dawned. At the Monthly Meeting yesterday, there was a decided expression of approbation with our visit so far as we had gone."

Extracts from Letters.

BALTIMORE, 11th mo. 14th, 1841.

Thy letter, my dear J., was most welcome after a fatiguing day, in which 15 families had been visited. Although the nature of the exercises was less trying than sometimes, the poor weak body was very weary.

We are still at the house of our kind friends J. and M. Gillingham. Have visited 138 families. We spend no idle time. The visits so far have been signally owned. There has been often much manifestation of tenderness on the part of some who are in the strength of manhood. Still it is a work to which the natural feelings are so averse, that it is hard for me to be submissive. My social and conversational powers seem narrowed into a very small compass, so thou seest there is much to mortify self; but I know that this needs reducing again and again; and if in this reduction there is no loss, but rather an increased evidence of Divine life and love, I can even rejoice that I am made worthy thus to fill up my measure of suffering. L. is very pleasant and agreeable, and I hope will continue with me to the close of the visit. T. keeps his post faithfully. Love to the dear children. Oh! these separations, how hard they are to bear! . . .

11th mo. 30th, 1841.

"I feel it to be a great favor to have the opportunity of converse through this channel with the dear ones left behind. I have found it a hard struggle to divest my mind of home; but fervent are my aspirations after resignation. The work is one in which 'no flesh can glory.' My experience has brought to mind the condition of the blessed Master, when He trod the wine-press alone. My prayer has been earnest that this baptism may be continued until it performs its renovating office, and the spirit is weaned from all external dependencies. I can truly say, thus far the Lord has been a helper in the needful time. Neither matter nor the power of utterance has been withheld, but has been given at the required moment. Through the Yearly Meeting I had not much vocal labor. It was a time of great interest and instruction, many of the testimonies being of a nature to 'clinch the nail' that had been driven." . . .

L. L.'s Diary.

On First-day were at Elk Ridge Meeting. Returned to Baltimore in the afternoon and visited two families on the way. Made some visits in the evening. On Second-day were similarly engaged. There was an openness to receive the message of love, which produced great tenderness of feeling; but upon the whole the day was a trying one. Being among strangers, we felt the need of walking circumspectly, and therefore of washing and anointing, and not appearing unto men to fast. Made a number of interesting visits within the past two days.

Attended Monthly Meeting; it was a low time. On First-day were at Old Town meeting, and made several visits in the afternoon in the suburbs. Third-day was spent in visiting Friends living in the city.

Eleventh month 11th.—Went to the Eastern district. Made a visit in the evening, in which the labor was attended with the power and demonstration of the Spirit in a remarkable manner.

On First-day morning we were at Lombard street meeting. I felt a concern that I might neither sit nor stand in another's way, and also deeply felt the importance of rendering obedience to our heavenly Leader. How true, that when He commissions, ability is afforded and knowledge given what to say and when to say it! May I never again distrust His power! Verily He fills the heart and satisfies the thirst and thus strengthens for renewed exercises! The evident manifestations of truth caused me to rejoice, and I could adopt the language, "One hour in Thy presence is worth a thousand elsewhere." Our labor in Old Town seems nearly completed; we may mention the call upon Esther Townsend as being signally favored. In some other visits there was a loud call to awaken to the responsibilities connected with a social and religious life. At Jacob Lafetra's, after a time of silent waiting, words of comfort and encouragement were administered to us by J. L. which had a strengthening effect. The afternoon was spent in preparing to leave

Baltimore. A number of Friends were collected at J. Gillingham's. We had a solemn opportunity with the family and recommended them still to adhere to that divine principle in the soul which is able to give us a knowledge of the Lord and the power of His grace."

T. B. L., in a note to a friend says, "We have accomplished the visit to the families except the small branch of Indian Spring, for which we start early in the morning. We have visited about 175 families. Some very trying seasons have been passed through. The mind on each occasion having to become as a blank sheet of paper, ready for that impression which alone can enable the feeble instrument to hand forth that which will minister to the wants and the conditions of the people. I believe our visit in this city has resulted as satisfactorily as is often the case with this kind of close work, which often reminded me of what Nathan said to King David—"Thou art the man." From Indian Spring we expect to go to Sandy Spring and perhaps to Pipe Creek. If I were seated for an hour or two in your domicil I could relate very interesting interviews and occurrences, with which we have met in going from door to door, like blind-folded beggars. Light and wisdom have often been furnished to see how the accounts stood, and suitable counsel has been offered which has generally been kindly received."

Diary Continued.

Proceeded to Indian Spring. Made several calls and were favored to enter into feeling with the visited. Words of consolation were uttered. Were hospitably entertained at G. Bailey's, and it proved a season wherein was known an out-pouring of the holy Spirit for which gratitude was sincerely felt. Lodged at Betsy Snowdon's, a free-hearted woman, who had a short time previously liberated her slaves. Her mind appeared turned in an earnest search for Truth.

On Sixth-day it rained, but we were favored with an excellent guide, who, being on horseback, opened the *gates* for us, which are numerous even on the public roads; we passed through 13 in the distance of 4 miles. Our friend was not merely helpful by removing the obstacles in our outward path, but his spirit was strengthening and encouraging to

10

us in our trials and deep provings. We visited the families which came in our way and lodged at R. Hopkins'. In the evening we had a meeting with the family, which was truly a favored season and a time of individual visitation. On Seventh-day made a religious visit in the morning and spent the remainder of the day in pleasant social converse. On First-day all of the family went to meeting, some on horseback and others in a carriage. The meeting was small, but was owned by the divine Presence. Rode 6 miles to dinner. In the afternoon made a family visit which was particularly trying to Elizabeth.

In the evening had another meeting which appeared very satisfactory to all and was edifying to me.

On Second-day it was very stormy; R. P. accompanied us to Caleb Stabler's. C. took charge of us and we made one family visit, but felt that we should be better satisfied to obtain the concurrence of the elders of Sandy Spring, before proceeding further. We were taken to the house of Deborah Stabler, who gave us a hearty welcome, and we were refreshed both in body and in mind under her hospitable roof. Next day it was decided we should enter again upon our mission. Although encouragement was offered whereby our weak hands should be strengthened, yet it was a low time and earnest were our desires to be directed only by that Power which can alone qualify to visit "the seed."

We have finished our visits to the families of S. S. meeting; may the labors of love prove as bread cast upon the waters that will be found after many days.

Letter from E. N.

ELEVENTH MONTH 24th, 1841.

My dear J.—Left Baltimore on Fifth-day for Indian Spring, taking the families of friends as they came in the way. A young man, quite fashionable in his appearance, offered to pilot us. No doubt it is in divine appointment. After a testimony of some length had been delivered in his own family, we sat a full hour in perfect silence, when it was broken by the torrent of feeling in his breast finding vent in tears. I am now writing in haste at the house of T. Stabler, about six miles from Sandy Spring. The meeting at that place was one not soon to be forgotten or erased from the catalogue of favors. If help had not been granted at the right time, the poor instrument would have fainted, but thanks be to Him who giveth the victory! To Him belongs the glory! that my soul knows right well. The communication was short and of individual import. After its delivery I could have placed my hand upon the head of the person to whom it applied. A dear old friend, an elder in the church, sealed the testimony, as did Deborah Stabler also. She is a minister, and upwards of 77 years of age. E. Stabler, whom I knew in my early life when I spent a winter in Alexandria, accompanied us through S. S. neighborhood. Many baptisms of various kinds had to be endured, but I feel clear of that place. Oh how disappointed I feel! Instead of attending meeting and then pursuing our journey, I find I am bound in spirit and must visit a branch of Pipe Creek Monthly Meeting, and partake again of bitter waters in going from house to house. May resignation be arrived at so that a state of tolerable cheerfulness can be maintained.

Diary Continued.

"Our course was directed toward New Market—called Bush Creek Monthly Meeting. Our kind friend E. Stabler did not leave us until he placed us under the care of his hospitable friend John Talbot. Were at Bush Creek meeting in the morning; at its close the proposal to visit the families was united with generally, and John Talbot was appointed to bear us company. We made some visits in the afternoon, when it commenced snowing. Visited three families in the evening. In the morning started in our carriage, but had not gone far before we were overtaken by a friend in his sleigh, who came to help us through the snow, and who rendered us important service. An opportunity with the family of J. Russell, with whom we dined, closed the service of visiting families in this district, and we returned to New Market.

The 30th of the 11th month started for Pipe Creek, having Caleb Ogburn for pilot. We reached Wm. Shepherd's at 4 o'clock in the afternoon, weary and worn with our ride. Next morning the thermometer had fallen to

7°. On Fourth-day attended meeting. Friends were willing to receive a visit and we commenced at once.

We found a gloom cast over the neighborhood of Pipe Creek on account of the illness of J. Moore, one of the older members of that meeting. A few days terminated his sufferings. On the occasion of the funeral, Friends, according to custom, met at the Meeting-house, and it proved a very solemn and interesting opportunity. The rain prevented our doing more that day.

First-day attended Monallen Meeting, which though rather a low time, was not an unprofitable one to many. The concern to visit the families expressed by Elizabeth, was united with ; Wm. Ellis felt a wish to accompany us, which being also approved, we set out with J. Wright as pilot. The very rough roads retarded our progress, the families in some instances being miles apart; but the visits were satisfactory. Made a number of visits and returned to J. Wright's and had an opportunity in the evening with his family, which had a tendency to gather us near the fountain of blessings, where we were remembered by Him who opens His hand and dispenses thereof to the humbled and contrited spirit.

We made one visit before meeting. It was their usual week-day meeting, and was a large gathering. Elizabeth was greatly favored in opening and explaining subjects calculated to interest and instruct; afterwards visited a family in which there was deep exercise; it was very evident that it had a good effect.

From thence we proceeded to Opossum Creek, which to us was noted for the stony road and the hard spiritual labor which had to be performed. We could but notice in various instances how beautifully the little children and infants behaved at meeting, although at home they were as restless and noisy as could be well imagined.

12th month 29th.—To-day finished the remaining visits, a few of which were to persons not members, but professors. Some states were easy of access, but not all.

Next day, on our homeward track, we made several interesting calls. Lodged at I. Tudor's. Left next morning for Petersburg. Made visits to several families, in which it could be sensibly felt that it was necessary that Truth should be laid to the line, and judgment should be tested by the plumb-line. The evening was spent in reading such parts of the Scriptures as the mind was drawn toward, and we felt that it had been profitable and edifying.

First-day went to meeting. It was a time of deep exercise. Made a pleasant visit to J. Townsend and family, who had removed from Chester County. Sweet and appropriate counsel was tendered to the young people, and much encouragement given to attend to the Divine principle within them.

Second-day morning.—Called on a family who were not members of our Society, but they very cheerfully laid aside their washing to receive our visit. The father was a man about 90 years of age, possessing all his faculties except his eyesight. They seemed very thankful for the visit.

On Third-day made some very pleasant visits, which revived the drooping spirits and gave room for hope that there will be a revival in this place if there is a continued attention to the Light whence knowledge is derived.

12th mo. 15th.—It seems now as if we might continue with our faces "Eastward." Language fails to convey the feelings of pleasure that arise with the prospect of again mingling with our families at home. A number of persons called to see us, and E. had a few words of encouragement for them. On the way to Warrington our carriage was taken through a mill-dam, the water coming up to the carriage body. Elizabeth and I preferred crossing over the foot bridge. Made several visits. Next day was a very stormy one; we made a few calls and attended the Preparative meeting at Warrington. In the morn- had interesting interviews with different families.

17th.—A snow-storm rendered it unpleasant travelling. Made two visits, but found the storm too severe to proceed.

On Seventh-day, with a good deal of perseverance, we started, the snow being very much drifted. S. Griest, at whose house we had lodged, went with us to help break the roads; in some places it seemed doubtful whether we should be able to get through the drifts. Lanes were filled half-way to the fence tops, and it was necessary in some instances to take down the fences, which was done without regard to their kind. Several friends volunteered their services, and with their assistance we were enabled to proceed. On First-day were again at Warrington meeting, which was small. In the afternoon rode several miles in the sleigh. Went to see David Cadwallader and wife, both too infirm to get out; they were aged 81 years. Next morning we set out with two strong horses, leaving ours to rest, of which they stood in need. Made only two visits, and returned by moonlight to J. Walker's.

After another day's similar experience, we started for Newberry. Called at a Friend's house, where E.'s communication was eminently calculated to arrest the feelings and turn the attention to the monitor within. The roads were unbroken, and we had great difficulties to encounter, in one place going down an embankment three feet high, and were very near upsetting. The kindness and sympathy of our friends were very grateful.

Reached I. Garretson's before dark, where we were entertained most hospitably. Next morning they furnished us with a sleigh and horses, which gave ours another opportunity to rest. We set off for Monthly Meeting, a number of Friends going with us. Visited several families in Lewisburg.

Twelfth month 23d.—The weather was drizzling, but this did not deter us from persevering in what we felt we had to do. Next morning was a bright, clear morning; the rain had melted the snow considerably, but in some places it was too deep for the carriage. We accepted the proffered assistance of T. Garretson, and made a number of visits. Were at Newberry meeting on First-day, which held more than two hours; and although several mothers had their infants with them, varying in age from seven weeks to ten months, there was no disturbance.

There has been a faithful endeavor throughout this journey to awaken a fresh zeal in the cause of Truth and righteousness, whereby our profession may be held "in deed and in Truth."

Twelfth month 27th.—Some difficulty was experienced on account of the snow, and again we were indebted to our friends for their kind assistance. Were entertained in York by our friends Jonathan Jessup and family. Made several visits.

Twelfth month 28th.—Breakfasted by lamp light, and made a number of calls through the day.

Twelfth month 29th.—Elizabeth felt her mind would not be clear of this place without attending the public meeting. There were three families visited to-day.

Twelfth month 30th.—A rainy day. Made a family visit, and went to meeting. It was a season of deep thought and inward retirement. May it not be unproductive of good. After dinner bade adieu to our kind friends, to whom during the short season of our acquaintance we had become attached, and a deep interest was felt for them.

Genessee Yearly Meeting.

In 1842 E. Newport was furnished by Abington Monthly Meeting with a minute to visit some meetings and families within Farmington Quarterly Meeting, and to attend Genessee Yearly Meeting. In this religious service she was accompanied by John H. Andrews and Ann W. Longstreth. On Sixth month 1st, J. H. A. writes: We commenced our journey, and for several days travelled over a rough and mountainous country, reaching Friendsville on First-day morning just as Friends' meeting had gathered. Found them few in number. Elizabeth bore a living testimony to the efficacy of practical righteousness. After meeting went home with our kind friends Caleb Carmalt and wife.

6th.—In the afternoon visited two families, in one of which E. addressed an individual, who made an open acknowledgement of the truth of what had been told him. Resumed our travel next day over a very rough and stony road. Next morning started at 5 o'clock, and soon found ourselves in a more fertile country.

The 10th was a rainy morning, notwithstanding which we pursued our way to D. Herendeen's at Macedon. John Comly and A. P. Jackson were among those who found a comfortable resting-place under our friend D. H.'s roof.

At the Meeting for Ministers and Elders on Seventh-day, there were seventeen minutes read for Friends from other Yearly Meetings. It was a favored time; some excellent counsel was imparted, calculated to encourage Friends to a more faithful discharge of the duties required of them. It was truly cheering to meet with so many familiar faces at such a distance from our homes.

First-day morning, attended Macedon Meeting. J. Comly and E. Newport had no opportunity to relieve their minds. In the afternoon we went to Farmington and had a good meeting. J. C. and Elizabeth both spoke in an impressive manner.

Arrangements are being made for us to commence after Yearly Meeting our arduous work; and oh! the strippedness and the littleness the mind is introduced into as the time approaches! My prayer is that E.'s eye may continue to be kept single to the light; and I have faith that it will be.

On Second-day some individuals were present who felt a wish to attend the meeting, but they having been disowned it was objected to, although much sympathy was felt for them. There being but one session in the day, the meeting adjourned till 10 o'clock next morning.

During the consideration of the state of Society on Third-day, the meeting was brought under an heavenly influence, and gratitude for the favor flowed freely.

On Fourth-day morning attended a meeting for worship at Farmington, where G. F. White was largely engaged in testimony.

Seventh-day.—Finished the business of the Yearly Meeting. When about to close, E. Newport requested the shutters opened. I trust her living testimony will not soon be forgotten. G. F. White appeared in supplication, and the meeting closed under a solemn covering.

On First-day morning we were at Macedon Meeting which was large. E. N. and J. C. both bore living testimonies to the ever blessed truth, and the people separated under a precious feeling. Returned to our lodgings where a number of friends were gathered. E. Newport and S. Underwood (Hunt) were both engaged in admonition and encouragement in the solemn opportunity which followed.

On Second-day we commenced visiting families within Macedon Preparative Meeting. Our first visit was to a family where the husband was not a member of our Society. The gospel stream flowed freely and he appeared gratified with the meeting. He was a stranger to the views of Friends and manifested much interest when allusion was made to the necessity of coming under the operations of the Spirit of Truth. At the next place, an individual was shown how entirely inadequate he was of himself to advance any good work. E. was led to speak in a very searching manner. I think she will find a wide field of labor in this part of the vineyard. She feels the necessity of holding up the view that it is only as we are influenced by the divine Mind that we can promote the cause of truth and righteousness. A friend called upon E. and offered to unite with her in these visits. This brought her under close trial. To have the help of such a valiant was very pleasing to the natural mind, but she had to feel that the dependence must not be upon man.

We made two visits after the friend joined us, and E.'s way was completely blocked up. She told me that we must either go alone or return home, and said, while she felt that a service was required of her, yet she had no liberty to go with this dear friend, and added, that I had come to take care of her and must act in the case. My mind was brought into deep suffering; I could but contrast my weaknesses with the high position which—held. I mentioned thesubject to J.C. Hesaid, I esteem the Friend and think she has a pure gift in the ministry, but in olden time, one said, "I go a fishing," another said, "I go also," and they went together, but "caught nothing." Our experience was somewhat similar, and we separated. Made three visits afterwards on that day, all of which were satisfactory. On Third-day visited 8 families and rode 22 miles. Elizabeth had great difficulty in making persons believe she had no outward knowledge of them. One man, where we dined, would not be convinced until D. H. had assured him that he had not told her one word concerning any one. The people are not familiar with family visiting, and it seems incredible that such plain truths should be told them. I have faith to believe the labor will be blest.

Have finished our work in this district. We have had seasons of rejoicing together, but the mind was often brought into deep exercise and travail with the suffering seed which in many places was pressed down as "a cart under sheaves."

Our next movement was to South Farmington Preparative Meeting. In the afternoon, in company with Wm. Gatchel, we made a number of visits. On Third-day rode 40 miles in the prosecution of our labor.

On Fourth-day attended their meeting in the morning and visited a number of families. A friend on whom we had called and who was not at home, rode 16 miles for the purpose of seeing us. E. had a most satisfactory interview with her. Many interesting visits were made, and a comfortable meeting with W. G's family closed our labors in that way in South Farmington. Since last Second-day we have attended their meeting, visited 23 families and rode 104 miles. We visited one family where the husband had been disowned. Poor fellow! he had his state opened to him in a marvellous manner. I was told by the friend who was with us, that E. was as true to his case as if she had always known him. She followed him across the Atlantic Ocean in quest of gain, and told him that his whole mind had been absorbed in this one pursuit, but all had ended in disappointment and vexation. This was in accordance with facts. There are many deep baptisms to pass through before the mind can be brought into that state in which it is able to suffer with the suffering seed. The spiritual need of the rich and the poor, the high and the low, have been ministered unto without the fear of man.

On Seventh-day we started for Hamburg, 12 miles beyond Buffalo and 100 from Macedon. Farmington Quarterly Meeting is held there once in the year, and Elizabeth had a concern to attend it and some meetings in the vicinity. It was a stormy day, but we went as far as Rochester. On First-day morning attended the meeting of Friends in that city. No notice had been given of our being there, but the house was full. Elizabeth soon arose and said her mind had been singularly impressed with what might be considered a *novel text* viz :—" These Quakers are a strange kind of people to come here and sit in silence. What good can be accomplished in that way ?" Very soon two meetings of other denominations, which were opposite, closed, and a large number of people crowded into our house. E. illustrated the doctrines of the Christian religion in a more forcible and impressive manner than I had ever before heard her. The people were very still and attentive, especially those belonging to other religious organizations. They looked upon her with astonishment. The meeting separated under a very solemn covering. The friend who was with us was asked by a man the name of the preacher; he said he had become dissatisfied with "church doctrine" and to-day he had heard the true Christian doctrine, and he thought he would go to Quaker meeting; he would at least have to go again. He had heard a bad account of the Quakers, but he had liked this sermon very much. His wife was with him and seemed also deeply impressed. In the afternoon we resumed our journey, accompanied by several friends.

4th. Second-day rode through a portion of the best country I ever saw. Passed through Buffalo and lodged at an Inn about a half mile beyond. A great many Indians who had been in the city to see the celebration of "the Fourth," in going to the Buffalo Reservation, about five miles distant, passed the house where we were staying. They were generally sober. I saw many more white persons than Indians intoxicated. Rode this day 57 miles. On our way to Hamburg next morning, we passed through the Indian Reservation. Their improvements greatly exceeded my expectations. The soil is very fertile, and their crops were equal to their white neighbors. Attended the Quarterly Meeting for Ministers and Elders in the afternoon. It was a comfortable meeting. E. had much service that appeared adapted to the states of those gathered. Next day attended Quarterly Meeting. It was an humbling time—some, who were filled with the world's policy, were melted into tears. Elizabeth went into the men's meeting and had good service therein. The meeting was large and ended satisfactorily. The people here look upon E. as a highly favored instrument, and are astonished that her ministry is so wonderfully adapted to the different states among them. The "Youth's meeting" held to-day was considered the largest ever known in this part of the country. The house was crowded; many stood, and all the windows and doors were full. H. Sexton arose as soon as the people were gathered and spoke for an hour. E. followed her and impressively addressed a state present. I have no words to describe the power of the ministry of both H. and E. Some who were not members came 20 miles to attend this meeting. It was a time to be long remembered by many.

8th of the month. H. Sexton having the approbation of Farmington Monthly Meeting to attend some meetings in this district, joined us, and we attended an appointed meeting at Boston, held in a Free-will Baptist House. When we arrived many people were gathered on account of the funeral of a Presbyterian. The doctrine held forth was very adverse to our views in relation to the resurrection of the material body, etc. After this service was over our meeting commenced, and while it was a close and searching time, I felt it was a season of favor. Next day had a large meeting in the Methodist meeting-house at Eden. Both H. and E. had much to communicate; some minds were reached, but upon others not much impression was made.

On First-day we were at Collin's; a great concourse of people assembled. After the house was filled, benches made of plank the length of the meeting-house were put outside of all the windows and doors; carriages were drawn up as close as they could stand, and were filled. E. had some of the closest labor I ever remember in a Friends' meeting, but it was admitted to have been in place. H. also had appropriate service. In the afternoon rode nine miles to another meeting appointed in a Free-will Baptist-house, Friends' meeting-house being too small. Elizabeth addressed the people for an hour and a half; she was clear and powerful on the subject of a free gospel ministry, for the want of a true perception of which many had been turned from the true Guide. Individual states were impressively addressed, especially the lukewarm; these were shown the influence they exerted over others. G. M. Cooper had a meeting appointed for us at the Cataraugus Reservation. We went in heavy wagons over the worst roads I ever saw, a distance of four miles. We met in their council house. Our friends E. and H. addressed them through an interpreter. It was an interesting occasion. After the women had finished speaking, Samuel Gordon, a chief, came forward with an interpreter. He was 92 years old, and was taken a prisoner by the Indians when he was 17 years of age and had lived with them ever since. Samuel made a feeling address, expressive of his gratitude for the good counsel which had been imparted, and hoped it would be treasured up. Then a young chief addressed his brethren in their own language, and J. Cook also encouraged them to attend to what they had heard. The natural grace and elegance with which they spoke was remarkable. E. wished to visit Oliver Silverheels, a chief who was ill with consumption." E. Newport, in a letter to her family, gives some additional particulars of their visit to Cataraugus. She says, "We had a refreshing visit to the chief, Oliver Silverheels, at his own hut; he understood our language, but wished an interpreter, so that his wife and children should also know what was said. He is very weak and feeble with consumption, but appears in a blessed state of mind. He thanked us warmly for coming.

His knee was my prop while a blessing was vocally poured forth, and our tears and prayers were mingled with those of the red-man. It was a precious season not soon to be forgotten.

We saw there a babe eight days old who was fastened to a board just its length and shaped a little like a cradle at the head, but had neither sides nor rockers; the head only of the little creature was to be seen, the rest of the body being tightly laced or bound to the board with strips of fine cloth nicely embroidered. I did not see how it could move either toe or finger. The most genteel dress for the women is, a square of fine broadcloth.

This people are deliberate in all their actions, and are never known to whip their children; but they take them in the woods and seat them on a log and talk to them a long time. They are divided into two classes in religious Faith, and style themselves Christians and Pagans. The latter class are those who profess to believe in Quaker worship, and in the guidance of the Good Spirit. The *Christians* seek information of the missionaries and profess a belief in the doctrines taught by them. One of the missionaries being present at our meeting, took offence at my advice to the Indians to attend to the counsel of their chief, and said "I should have directed them to the minister." I knew nothing of the two parties. The chiefs who were at the meeting were of the Pagan party. The women are inferior to the men in point of mental culture. Those in Buffalo are in a much higher state of cultivation, their opportunities having been greater. Our meeting with them was deeply interesting. The interpreter was a handsome young man and was engaged to be married to "a nice white woman."

At the close of the meeting several of the older people came up, shook hands with us, and expressed their gratitude as well as they could. The women carry their pappooses on their backs. Some of the children are pretty and look very cunning. We were well satisfied with our visit.

We have to feel sometimes as if the standard of Truth has fallen in the streets, and as if the call to Friends was to rally to the

"Strong Tower." I feel comforted in having left you all in the hand of our heavenly Father. Every tried feeling finds a solace in the thought that hitherto His arm has graciously supported me. It has been my defence and my deliverance from storms and tempests, which have at times whirled their cruel blasts around me. As a cool and refreshing shower on a sultry day, or as water from a clear brook, were the tidings contained in the sheet filled so nicely by those whose names are indelibly written upon the tablet of the heart. It came seasonably, for I was in need of that kind of refreshment. The physical powers were worn and weary, though the spirit had been sustained in so much as to enable me to adopt the language of one formerly—"Thou hast been strength in weakness—riches in poverty—a present help in the needful time." . . . .

E. N.

J. H. A.'s Diary Continued.

On Third-day morning we had a meeting at Abbott's Corners in a Presbyterian meeting-house. The minister belonging thereto was the same who officiated at the funeral to which I have previously alluded. He said he did not think that the language at that time, in relation to those who preached for *money,* was too severe, it was not harder than such deserved. He offered the meeting-house again for our use, which we felt it right to accept. Elizabeth and H. Sexton had both much to say and it was an excellent meeting. I never saw so much openness in the minds of all classes to receive Friends. The Orthodox Friends at Hamburg offered their benches to accommodate us, and many of the "*strictest*" attended some of our meetings and said "Elizabeth preached true doctrine!" After the last meeting, we had not gone more than a quarter of a mile, before E. said to me, "we must go back to Boston."

The next day we had another appointed meeting there; the notice was short but the house was filled and the meeting was a favored one. The labor was close on account of a lukewarm spirit. We rode 7 miles to attend this meeting, the same distance to dine, and then 8 miles to attend another meeting at the Buffalo reservation at 3 o'clock. The Council

House is a large building, finished very much after the manner of modern "Churches." The house was full. The Indians were well dressed and it was a deeply interesting occasion, far surpassing that at Cataraugus. We had the Chiefs from all the reservations assembled in council. The interpreter was a young man who expected to marry a white girl, the teacher among them. His native grace was striking. H. first spoke to them, then G. M. Cooper, after which E. had considerable to communicate, and at the conclusion of her impressive discourse she addressed the young interpreter. I cannot portray the scene; every tender sympathy was enlisted for the poor Indians under a view of their past and present trials. E. appeared in supplication without an interpreter, and under its baptizing power many of the Indians shed tears. I can only give the outline of our labors. I am entirely convinced my peace consists in being here.

14th.—Fifth-day spent in Buffalo and had a meeting in the evening in a Unitarian Church, which was satisfactory. At this meeting a circumstance occurred of an unusual character. Elizabeth found that, contrary to the usual practice among Friends, she must read a portion of Scripture. Turning to J. H. A., she asked him to turn to the 14th chapter of John. He replied, thou must do it thyself. Finding there was no other way for her, she arose, opened the bible before her at the very place she desired, and read the first 12 verses of that chapter, and then proceeded with her discourse. When asked why she did so, she said, " I found I could not reach the minds of the people in any other way. The discourse which followed was said to be remarkable for power and perspicuity.

On Sixth-day morning rode 23 miles to the Falls of Niagara, where we spent several hours in wonder and amazement.

16th.—On Seventh-day travelled 25 miles to Elba and had an appointed meeting at 3 o'clock. Some very close doctrine was delivered to a man who was intemperate. He was seriously warned to retrace his steps.

17th.—Rode 13 miles to breakfast and then 4 to meeting. In the afternoon had an appointed meeting at Rochester, which was a very favored time.

On Second-day morning attended the funeral of Allan Frost's daughter, aged about 17 years. In the afternoon were at an appointed meeting at 4 o'clock, after which we rode 16 miles. Travelled this day 30 miles. We can but believe that the "back is fitted for the burden," when we take into consideration the frail physique of E. N.

The mind of our friend was drawn southward. We found the place to be a settlement of Friends who have an indulged meeting about 51 miles up the Gunpowder River; it is a branch of Rochester Monthly Meeting. We had an evening meeting there on the 19th, composed mostly of those not in membership with us. E.'s testimony was a powerful one to the all-sufficiency of the light within for the guidance of man.

Her effort was to call away from men, from books, or any outward help; of which I have no doubt there was great need, for though the people are zealous, they do not appear to be spiritually minded.

Had an appointed meeting at Woodsville on Fifth-day evening in a school-house. There are a very few Friends in the neighborhood, and usually they hold their meetings in a private house. The school-house was crowded, a number came from Danville, 2 miles distant. Several men who were not members, were spoken to so clearly that they acknowledged that "their states were opened in so remarkable a manner, that it caused them to marvel like the woman at 'Jacob's well,' for they had found one who told them all things that ever they did."

On Sixth-day we rode about 44 miles to Scottsville. The next afternoon had a meeting at Wheatland. Next morning, after a religious opportunity in W. Cornell's family, with whom we had lodged, went to meeting at Henrietta. E. had close work with individual states. Elizabeth's mind not being clear of Rochester, we returned to that city, and Friends meeting-house being small, the Baptists offered theirs for an evening meeting. The house was crowded, also the aisles, windows and doors, and the street, as far as the voice could be heard, was filled with an attentive audience. It was computed that 500 people went away who could not get near enough to hear what was said. Hundreds were there who knew nothing of the principles and testimonies of Friends and had never heard a woman preach. E. illustrated the views held by our Society and clearly demonstrated the testimonies of Truth as we understand them, and also what constitutes a pure gospel ministry. Said she had no controversy with any *true minister*, but had no sympathy with one who "would preach for hire, or divine for money" which seemed too much like making merchandize of the gospel. She directed all to the "light within," which ever preserves from sin, if man is obedient to its teachings in the soul. For more than an hour the people sat in remarkable silence, listening to the words as they fell from her lips. A solemn quiet reigned even in the street; it was such a time, the people say, as was never before known in that city. There was a convention being held, and many strangers from miles around were in the town, and most of them were at the meeting. A number who have attended E. N.'s meetings, have said that her testimonies upon the subject of a hireling ministry "are searching, but are clear and convincing." I have been told by many persons of different denominations, that the truth was spoken with such authority they could not but unite with her. There is abundant evidence, that He who sent her is able to open the way in the hearts of the people ; it has indeed been marvellously manifested ! Many zealous professors of religion have been shaken to the centre. The sketch that I have given falls short of the reality, but no praise belongs to E., except as a *faithful* servant of the Lord.

28th. — Fifth-day attended Farmington Monthly Meeting, held at Macedon. E. N. had close labor on account of several different states present. In the afternoon a number of friends called to see us and we enjoyed their company. On Sixth-day went to Palmyra to visit the families of that Preparative Meeting. Were met by Pliny Sexton, he having been appointed to accompany us in the service. There were 14 families, and the visits all proved very satisfactory.

On First-day we were at Farmington Meeting, where E. had much service. On Second-day we commenced visiting the families of Farmington meeting, and after some very refreshing seasons, with a great deal of hard labor, we completed our work on Sixth-day, the 5th of the month. H. Pound was with us throughout these visits, and he told me that "he was well acquainted with all their members, and in no instance could he have described them more truthfully than E. had done, although she was a stranger to them all." He had often found it necessary at the close of a visit to tell the people that nothing had been said about them to E., and to encourage them to receive her testimony as a visitation from their heavenly Father.

7th.—On First-day attended Macedon meeting, which was large and satisfactory. We had expected to proceed at once to Williamson, but E. felt it required of her to attend the funeral of George Smith, an elder of South Farmington meeting. The succeeding four days were occupied in visiting families.

On First-day had a large meeting composed of all classes. E's discourse was lengthy and impressive. Then returned to D. H.'s, having ridden to-day about 18 miles. Soon after we arrived, Hugh Pound came, saying he had forgotten *one* family. It was then evening, bu it had been such a burden upon his mind, he had ridden 6 miles to inform us. The next day he took us to see the Friends. We then proceeded to Waterloo. Spent next day there and had a meeting in the evening in a Baptist Meeting-house. On Fourth-day were at Julien meeting, and on Fifth-day were at Galen.

19th.—Sixth-day started for home. Our daily rides varied from 40 to 45 miles. Proceeded in a direct course and landed Elizabeth safe at her own home on the 25th of the 8th month, 1842.

A Letter from E. Newport to M. Hilles.

ABINGTON, ELEVENTH MONTH 2d, 1843.

My Dear Aunt:—After having been absent from meeting on account of indisposition for six or seven weeks, I went on Second-day and obtained liberty to attend Bucks Quarterly Meeting, to visit the meetings constituting it and appoint some meetings among those who are not members of our Society; but I feel as yet very unlike it in every necessary requisition or qualification; and it is to me a great matter to set out again upon so important an engagement after a longer season of domestic quiet and enjoyment than has been allotted me for several years. This respite has not lessened the weight and responsibility of such a concern. My mind during the year and almost a half that I have been at home, has not been free from exercise, and many times it seemed as if the period was at hand in which to make the offering, but the will has been accepted and releasement given. I trust these seasons have not been unprofitable for me, for indeed I have a great dread of a condition that would step forth in the will of the creature without waiting for the divine command.

It is with heart-felt gratitude that I acknowledge the favor of having a dear aunt who feels such an interest in one who regards herself as unworthy of it, although all my life-long I have received the strengthening influences which have flowed from thy pen, and which have had a tendency often to cheer amid gloom. I have lately been looking over some letters long since written, in which is manifested the same maternal solicitude, mingled with admonition and counsel suited to my condition. The encouragement then given, I feel, could only have proceeded from a mind that had been deeply impressed with the solemn responsibility of one upon whom such a gift as had been given me had been conferred.

While tears of thankfulness dimmed the eye, my prayers were earnest that I might witness preservation from false presentations or imaginations; that there might be such a growth experienced under the sanctifying influences of heavenly love, as to preserve from breaking in upon the silence of an assembly without the constraining power of the gospel. I have sat at times under a sense of suffering during the communications of those I have preferred to myself, and whom I have much esteemed; and have desired by repeated baptisms, (if need be,) to be preserved from kindling a fire of my own to enliven or warm the people, yet I feel assured that I am in as much danger as any one, and that it is only as the eye is preserved in singleness of purpose that I shall witness preservation. . . . .

Soleberry and Kingwood.

In the Twelfth month, 1843, with the approbation of Abington Monthly Meeting, our friend E. N. visited the families of Friends of

Soleberry, Pa., and of Kingwood, N. J. Charles Kirk and Mary H. Schofield (Childs), were her companions in this journey.

Extracts from C. K.'s Narrative.

E. was not drawn to visit all the families, and there seemed some difficulty in the minds of Friends how to proceed. She told them if they would furnish her with the names of their members, she thought, although a stranger to all, she would be enabled to designate such as she was called upon to visit, and this was done. In a few instances those who acted as pilots deviated from the list, but it was of no avail, for she found nothing to do in such families, not even to attempt to centre into the quiet.

On First-day attended meeting, in which the gospel was preached with power. In the afternoon visited several families. There were many deeply proving seasons through this visit, for it seemed as if the "sword of the spirit" had to be turned every way in order to "guard the tree of life."

In one house there lived a mother and married son, making two families. The mother came into the son's apartment, so that there need be but the one meeting, but E. had such close service for the young man that she felt she must ask the mother to withdraw, which was exceedingly trying to her; but by dwelling near the Fountain the streams of which make strong the spirit, she was enabled to accomplish her work satisfactorily. After visiting the families we attended Soleberry meeting, which was a season of great labor, for the people were so eager to hear, that it made hard work for the poor instrument; but E. was favored to keep near her guide and "a holy quiet reigned supreme."

After this meeting we proceeded to Kingwood, N. J. This meeting was composed of but few families. Seasons of heavenly consolation were known among them. We had to feel the importance of having such Friends as pilots as are impressed with the weight and responsibility resting upon those who visit families under a religious obligation, and who can appreciate their inability to enter into conversation especially upon trivial matters. If such as are called upon to perform the needful work of guides from place to place would endeavor to enter into sympathy with those who have gone forth without "purse or scrip" in obedience to their Master's call, there would be a realization of the concern, and these kind friends might become true yoke fellows in the blessed cause of Truth.

To J. H. A. from E. N.

ABINGTON, TENTH MONTH 20th, 1845.

My Dear Friend:—"There are many who willingly cry hosanna to him who cometh in the name of the Lord, but who are not bound enough in heart, to the pure seed of divine light to watch and to suffer with it, when there is no form nor comeliness in it, and when it seems not otherwise to operate in the soul than by making the creature abhor itself." This language of that deeply experienced Friend, Sarah Grubb, so entirely portrays a state which thou my dear friend J., hast been brought into sympathy with in seasons of deep trial and close baptism, that they revive as "life answering to life." So far from any wish to be mounted on the King's horse, the desire is that the Lord's hand may not spare, nor His eye pity until the work of sanctification is completed. When the selfish spirit is humbled and prostrated, how comforting is this language: "Thy light shall break forth as the morning and thine health shall spring forth speedily, thy righteousness shall go before thee, and the glory of the Lord shall be thy reward." . . . . . .

Wrightstown Monthly Meeting.

In the Tenth month, 1846, E. Newport visited the families of Wrightstown Monthly Meeting, accompanied by Elizabeth Paxson and Charles Kirk, both of Bucks County, Pennsylvania.

From memoranda kept by Charles Kirk, the following account is taken.

"We attended Wrightstown Monthly Meeting in which E. had close service. We proposed, and it was united with by Friends, that we should be permitted to make our visits unattended by any of their own members. This arrangement proved satisfactory, and the visit was a remarkable one. It was a time of deep proving, our friend being favored to enter into the states of the visited. They were indeed solemn and interesting occasions.

Among our first visits was one to the house of a Friend who had said several unkind things in reference to E.'s visit, of which of course she was entirely ignorant, not knowing even his name. As we were gathered in silence, and E. was brought under the influence which was sensibly felt as we went from house to house, she addressed this Friend, and repeated the words he had used in relation to her. One evening we rode a few miles out of our direct route to see a family whom E. had a particular wish to visit. We intended to lodge there, but stopped on our way and took supper at another Friend's house. Soon after we left the latter place, E. N. said to me, "I do not think it is the right time for us to go to —— ———'s." We halted a few minutes, and then turned and made a visit to another family. We were afterwards told by the persons whom we designed visiting, that about the time we turned back, one of their children was very badly hurt, and they were obliged to sit up with her all night; so that had we gone there, we could not have had their company.

Arrangements for our visits being always

made the day previously, we were unwilling to fail in their accomplishment, and on one occasion turned out in a severe storm. We had not proceeded far before we had to pass through a piece of timber-land. By this time the storm had greatly increased—the wind blew furiously. E. Newport laid her hand upon my shoulder and said, "I fear the trees will blow over on us." I replied I did not think so, the ground had been very dry, and it had not rained long enough to soften it; but the words had scarcely escaped my lips when I felt there *was* danger. E. remarked, do not let us be too daring. Then we should have turned around, but we were so nearly through the woods, I drove on. As we neared the edge we heard a tremendous crash, but could see nothing, it being immediately over the carriage. In an instant, however, a large limb 8 or 10 inches in diameter fell across the road just ahead of us, which, if it had fallen on us, must have crushed us.

Wrightstown was at this time composed of 157 families and parts of families, who were all visited in the course of sixteen days. The language of encouragement to persevere in well doing was at times extended, while at others, caution and warning appropriate for the occasion were forcibly given. This service was completed on the morning of their "weekday" meeting. While sitting in meeting my mind was impressed that there was one more family to visit. I said nothing until we had nearly reached the house where the Friends lived, when I asked E. if she felt peaceful and happy. She said yes, fully so, with all that is left *behind.* There was no more said, but much felt. When we came to the place I went in to see if the Friends were willing to receive a visit. I found them in the midst of house-cleaning, but the wife said "yes, come in," and arrangements were very soon made for us. A season of solemn quiet ensued, when E. was greatly favored in testimony. She sometimes seemed to know as well what was passing in the minds of her companions as they did themselves, as was the case on this occasion."

Fishing Creek Half-year Meeting.

In the Fifth month, 1849, E. Newport accompanied by Mary A. Hallowell, an Elder from Abington, and James Andrews, from Darby, Pa., attended Fishing Creek Half-year's Meeting and some of the families belonging thereto, E. having obtained a minute for the service from Abington Monthly Meeting. A brief allusion to this journey is contained in a recent letter from Mary A. Hallowell to E. N's children.

. . . . "Although so many years have passed, the events of that visit are fresh before me, particularly the gift of "spiritual intuition." On one occasion we were dining at a Friend's house, when some one began telling of the circumstances concerning a Friend whom we expected to visit. Elizabeth remarked, "I would rather not hear anything relative to those we may visit." The next day we went to the Friend's house, and she addressed him with much power; it was a searching and close testimony. After we left the house E. said to me, "Dost thou know, Mary, that thou worried me this morning?" I was surprised, and asked what I had done? she pleasantly replied "when we first sat down in silence, the thought passed through thy mind, 'what will E. do with what she has heard relative to this man?'" I was amazed, and said "those were my thoughts; after this I shall be afraid of thee"—but I loved her too sincerely to fear her. This was only a positive proof in my own case of what I had often witnessed with others. At one time, after we had attended a meeting wherein she had addressed several states very impressively, she said to me, "It is hard work to speak to those who are not willing to receive—I could feel a rebounding of the word from some." In many instances after sitting quietly with the family for awhile, E. would inquire if some one was not absent, and would await their coming, or if circumstances prevented this, she would defer the opportunity and go again. In one case the absentee was a lad, and when he came, it proved that her mission was particularly to him. Her labor was close, but the reward was *peace.*

She was a member of Abington Monthly Meeting nearly ten years and I knew her well, and can bear my testimony that she fully carried out the injunction of "doing good to all;" her practical life gave evidence of forgiveness and forbearance, of love and charity to a remarkable extent, under circumstaces of a peculiarly trying character.

She was a wonderful woman, possessing the gifts of prophecy and spiritual discernment in a degree that I never witnessed in any other. MARY A. HALLOWELL.

A Letter to M. Hilles from E. N.

ABINGTON, 8th mo. 22d, 1849.

My Beloved Aunt:—Upon my return from Fishing Creek it was my desire to write to thee immediately. This visit, through Divine favor, was performed to the peace and entire relief of my own mind. . . .

We returned home in less than three weeks, after attending all the meetings and visiting most of the families. Some were passed by without the least feeling that would draw us toward them, while we went ten miles out of our way to see others.

In one family we visited I felt that there was labor to be performed, but after sitting some time I mentioned that there was an obstacle in the way. The man Friend said they were all there. So we sat still for some time; I then spoke again to the same import, and he replied there *was* a young man who was at school, who would be home toward noon. We left and returned, and the visit was crowned with peace, and I may add it was as instructive and interesting to my own mind as any that we made." . . . .

On the 21st of Second month, 1850, a certificate was received at Green Street for Jesse W. Newport and family, from Abington, Monthly Meeting, Pa.

Western and Southern Quarterly Meetings.

In the Seventh month, 1850, E. Newport obtained a minute to visit Friends in their families or meetings, as Truth might require, within the Western and Southern Quarterly Meetings. Mary H. Schofield (Childs) was her companion throughout this journey, and from her memoranda the following particulars are extracted. Charles Kirk accompanied them through the Western Quarterly Meeting. M. writes, "On our way to Centre Monthly Meeting called to see our dear friend A. Chandler, who was too feeble in health to get out to meeting. At the Monthly Meeting E. was led to speak prophetically to individuals of both sexes. The next day Kennett Monthly Meeting was large. E. was extensively engaged in testimony. She felt that the work of the Lord might be marred by overzeal, yet it would prosper. He could work by many or by few. She had an interview with the Friend and his wife where we dined, and spoke encouragingly to the former, who she believed was not far from the kingdom. His sympathies had gone forth for suffering humanity, but she felt that there were other baptisms through which he would have to pass ere he could be made a pillar in the Lord's house that should go no more out. At London Grove Monthly Meeting the gospel was sounded and our spirits travelled in unison for the precious children, many of whom were present.

After dinner E. went up stairs to take some rest, but soon came down and said she felt there was no rest for her. She pointed in a certain direction and asked what could be over there that made her feel so heavy-hearted. After a little while she remarked that she would have to go and see, and if the Friend was willing to take her she thought she could point out the way. When they drove out of the lane the Friend said, 'now, Elizabeth, which road shall we take?' She replied, 'turn to the left and follow this road about half a mile.' So she continued to point out the way for several miles, although the road was very winding, and most difficult for a stranger to find. When they came to a certain house she said, 'this is the place.' The wife was an invalid, and it was supposed the visit was for *her*, but the exercise of our friend proved to be for the husband, to whom she was an entire stranger. His state of doubt and unbelief was portrayed, and his condition represented as a fearful one. Though the language was close and searching it was attended with great power, and its authority could be felt. We left him under a feeling of great solemnity, and when we bade him farewell, he remarked, 'I am glad you came.' Since the demise of E. Newport this individual told a friend, with his eyes filled with tears, that all E. N.'s predictions in regard to him had been fulfilled. We visited another family, our friend being wholly ignorant of any trouble therein; but we had not been in the house five minutes before E.'s mind was brought into great distress and suffering on account of the state of things which were opened before her. Her message for the wife was comforting and consoling, but for the husband there was a warning and caution of the most serious nature. We learned afterward that E. had not been mistaken in feeling.

New Garden Monthly Meeting was held at Mill Creek. E. admonished an individual who was resting in the 'tradition of the fathers,' that had turned from the Spirit to the letter; and the language was 'Come away, come away from all these outward dependencies.' At the place where we dined there was a large company, and we had a solemn meeting. E. addressed one who was powerful in intellect; she told him he would have to pass through many deep baptisms, and have to tread 'the wine press alone;' but if he were faithful to the end he would be made a mighty instrument in the hands of the Lord in emancipating those who were in bonds.

At Penn's Grove Monthly Meeting the language to a young woman was 'put away thine ornaments, that I may know what to do with thee.' The person to whom it was applicable felt and acknowledged the power which attended the exhortation.

Next day were at Fallowfield Monthly Meeting, where the testimonies of truth as professed by Friends were brought into view, and also the importance of bearing them faithfully before the world; each one working in that part of the vineyard allotted him. We met with Mary Thorne, a Friend 83 years old, who had walked three miles to attend the meeting.

First-day.—Attended meeting, in which Elizabeth found close service. She felt that there was one present who was on the brink of ruin, and addressed him most feelingly, believing that unless repentance was sought he would be landed in continual sorrow. After meeting a woman with grief depicted in her countenance, came to us and earnestly requested a visit. There were many Friends at the house where we dined, and our dear E. distributed crumbs of heavenly bread among them. In the evening called to see the friend from whom we had received the pressing invitation in the morning. Her husband was the son of a worthy minister who had been gathered to her eternal rest. E. spoke to him in a powerful manner, and our united prayers were poured forth on his behalf. He was tendered and broken into tears, and at one time exclaimed, 'Oh, this is too close!' After the meeting he insisted upon our staying all night. We accepted the invitation, not feeling at liberty to refuse. Next day had a meeting a few miles distant. Elizabeth's service was pointed and touching. After meeting her mind was drawn to visit a family. The husband being absent was sent for, but declined coming; he said the Friend had been told all about him, and he felt that what she had said in meeting belonged to him. A second message was sent, and he still refused. E. then spoke to the wife and children in a most touching manner. She was entirely unacquainted with the circumstances of their family relations, or with anything connected with their history, but she felt that she could not leave the house without seeing the husband. She asked if she could not be admitted into the room where he was sitting for a few moments. He then consented, and at once remarked that she had been made acquainted with the situation of the family. She assured him she had *not*—that she knew nothing from outward information. Her advice to him was pertinent.

At Kennett Square, Charles Kirk felt his mission ended, and John H. Andrews accompanied us through the Southern Quarterly Meeting. Had an appointed meeting in the afternoon at K. S., which was very large. The gospel was preached, and all were encouraged to enter into the work of reformation and to follow the Light within. A caution was extended not to wound the babe-like condition, nor to improperly discourage the tenderly-visited mind. The voice of supplication was heard in our midst, and the feeling of gratitude flowed freely for the favors bestowed.

Took tea at Samuel Martin's, who kept a boarding-school for girls. Before we left the table E. spoke to them very sweetly and appropriately. Before leaving W. Bailey's in the morning, for the purpose of entering upon our labors in the Southern Quarter, E. spoke encouragingly to the family. She then supplicated for them and also for the poor instruments who had endeavored to fulfil their mission in that part of the vineyard. She earnestly besought Him who had put forth to go before, and enable His servants when they had finished His work to return in peace to their homes. This day we rode thirty miles. We were kindly entertained by J. Alston. Another thirty miles ride brought us to Cecil, Md., and to the home of our kind friend M. A. Bowers (Needles).

On Seventh-day attended Cecil Monthly Meeting. The subjects of Slavery and of a free Gospel ministry were profitably dwelt upon, and our sympathies were enlisted for the little band who were present, separated as they were from the body of the Society. We remembered, however, the omnipresence of God, and that He could bless the small company as well as the large assembly. We were much pleased with the manner of their conducting their business, the men and women acting together in perfect freedom and harmony. J. H. A. says of this meeting, "that it held from 11 o'clock till 4 o'clock, including the Select Meeting. I never knew E. more favored or to preach more powerfully, although the meeting was small. Five or six men and a half-grown interesting boy were present, but the women were more numerous. They hold their Monthly Meeting all together, and equally participated in the business. They appeared truly glad to see us, and expressed their unity with the visit. After meeting, a Friend came to E. and asked, with much feeling, if she thought him worthy a visit? She replied, we will dine with thee to-morrow. This engagement was fulfilled. The Friend acknowledged he had widely departed from the instructions of his beloved parents, and had now to suffer. This disobedience to concerned parents brings sorrow to the heart long after they have passed from earth, therefore the wisdom of heeding their advice, remembering the time may come when even "the grasshopper may be a burden."

First-day were at Cecil meeting. There were present several slaveholders. E. had a testimony to bear to an individual who had known better days. A meeting was appointed at Chestertown, in the Court House, where a large company assembled, composed of ministers, lawyers, slaveholders, &c.; enough, I thought to make a feeble woman tremble at the idea of speaking in their presence; but the power of the Father is sufficient for His own work, and He can enable His feeblest instrument to rise superior to the fear of man and preach freely the glad tidings of the gospel even to those highest in human authority. The testimonies of Truth as professed by Friends were held up to view to an attentive audience, showing that we could not unite with an hireling ministry, with holding our fellow men in bondage, with war, nor with calling the Bible the '*word* of God.' E. said that although she had not joined the Abolition Societies of the day, she felt she belonged to one to which every Christian must belong, as she believed that all *Christians* must be Abolitionists. On our way to Chester Neck, dined with a young man who was the only white person about his house. His colored housekeeper had lived with him for 14 years and had her husband and children with her. She was very kind. I felt that she and her family were better off than many of their color. In the afternoon we visited another similarly situated. He owned great possessions and lived in a spacious mansion. Elizabeth had close service. Next day we were at a meeting where Quakerism seemed at a low ebb. One member having often to sit alone. Dined with a young couple to whom E. had words of counsel and sympathy. We knew not till after we left, that the husband, in whom we were much interested, had ever been an "overseer" on a plantation. We think that he would not again accept such a position. As we rode through Chestertown Elizabeth was brought under much exercise of mind with the belief that it would be right for her to have another meeting there.

One was appointed at 11 o'clock next morning. We assembled in the Court House, and after sitting a considerable time in silence, dear E. remarked that she believed her mission, in part, was to those in the next room, and queried if they could be invited in, with the understanding that while she could not feel satisfied without making the request, she wished to leave them entirely at liberty to accede to it or not. A friend carried to them her message, and was told that the Court had met on special business. After a few minutes consideration, however, they adjourned to the meeting-room. Elizabeth arose immediately and spoke in a powerful manner. She then returned thanks unto Him who had not only put forth, but had gone before His frail little ones during their seasons of labor in that part of His vineyard. The audience was respectful and attentive, and the meeting closed in good order.

Attended Centre meeting; it was a rainy morning and there were but five persons beside our company present, but I believe we could have all acknowledged that it was good for us to be there. We entered into sympathy with the few and reflected upon the responsibilites that rested upon *us* because of our many privileges. E. had much to communicate.

At Tuckahoe there was no longer a meeting of Friends regularly held, but there was one appointed for us. The people listened attentively, and one person, not a member, expressed his gratification with our having been there, and invited us kindly to his house. He said truth lost nothing by investigation. E.

N. had explained the views of our Society very fully.

We had an appointed meeting in the Court House at Easton, which was a very large gathering. Many were slave-holders, and not a few were of the rougher class of the community. For some time after E. began to speak the people were quiet; but when the subject of slavery was touched upon, and the view given that every Christian must be an Abolitionist, there was quite a stir, and some left the house, muttering as they went, evidently trying to create a disturbance. They went into a store near by and said if E. had been a man instead of a woman, he would have been carried out of the house. We passed out in safety, but felt that we did not want ever to have another meeting at Easton. As we rode through the town there were some stones thrown at the carriage, which was a mortification to the more respectable inhabitants. Next day attended a Quarterly Meeting in the house where the first Yearly Meeting of Friends on this continent was held. There was much communicated; sympathy was expressed for the living members of the

Church, and caution extended to the lukewarm and indifferent, who were encouraged to arouse from this offensive and unhealthy condition. But few participated in the business of the meeting, which occasioned some remarks relative to the importance of being "faithful in the little." The next day a meeting, called the "youth's meeting," was held in which the gospel was preached by our dear E. N. and supplication was offered on behalf of various classes present. It was a solemn time, and I trust we were all profited thereby. In alluding to this opportunity, J. H. A. says it was a *very* memorable occasion. He also relates the following incident: "To-day we are going to visit one of the largest slaveholders in the neighborhood. As E. N. sat in the meeting at the Court House on Second-day, she saw with her spiritual eye a man who held a great many slaves, but who was a humane man. He was advanced in life, and he lived in a certain direction. Next day she told us of her mental vision. Upon J. D. mentioning a name she said 'Yes, that is the man.' J. Needles went to inquire if he would receive a visit; he replied, 'he would be glad to see us the next day at 9 o'clock.'"

As we pass through the country we are treated with great respect by all classes.

After breakfast, we proceeded to the "Bay Side," 17 miles distant, accompanied by a number of Friends. It is said that there is not in the whole distance, 18 inches of ascent or descent in the road.

Had a meeting in the Methodist meeting-house, composed of an intelligent assembly, many of whom were slave-holders. E. was favored to speak in the demonstration of the Spirit and with power.

After meeting, a colored woman, whose hair was white with age, and who had handed a cup of cold water while E. was speaking, came to us and clasped our hands, while the tears ran down her furrowed cheeks, and she exclaimed, "Bless you! bless you! the Quakers set me free!" How it touched our hearts! we felt glad we had a testimony to bear against this great evil, while we regretted we were not more faithful in its maintenance.

We dined at J. Kemp's, whose wife was a methodist; he was not a member of any religious Society, but with warm Christian feeling he welcomed us to his home. Returned in the evening to our friend J. Dixon's.

On Seventh-day made a visit to an old man whose mother had been a member of our Society. He was a slaveholder but was said to be a humane and kind master. E. had much to say to him which he appeared to feel considerably. He thanked her for her counsel and said he hoped he might profit by it.

Passed through the "Hole in the wall" to a miserable looking place called the "Trap." We had a meeting in the Methodist house, but felt a lack of a religious element among the people. The next day attended our last meeting at Third Haven. A large number of people were gathered. Some from Easton were present. E. quoted the text "Righteousness exalteth a nation, while sin is a reproach to any people;" this was largely commented upon. Then another voice was raised in behalf of Truth's testimonies, showing the importance of bearing them faithfully before the world, particularly that in regard to slavery, that thereby we might become instruments in the divine hand in opening the eyes of those who seem not to see nor understand the nature of that fast which the Lord hath chosen, of opening the "prison doors and letting the oppressed go free. A solemn prayer closed the services of the meeting, when we could have adopted the language, "Return unto thy rest, oh my soul, for the Lord hath dealt bountifully with thee."

We dined with E. Dawson, an "orthodox" friend, and a sister-in-law of our friend John Needles, who had been with us since the Quarterly Meeting; we were very kindly entertained. This family was the only Friend's family in Easton. She holds meetings in her own house, her children sitting with her.

Our friend E. N. felt her mind drawn towards two individuals in different directions of the town. They were unknown to her except as they had been brought before her spiritual vision. She spoke to J. Needles of her concern, and so nearly described the persons and the direction in which they lived, that he had no trouble in recognizing them, and volunteered to inquire if they were willing to receive a visit. They cheerfully assented. The first one upon whom we called was a venerable looking person dressed in a priestly garb. He met us at his door and ushered us into a room richly furnished. He retired into an adjoining room and washed and crossed himself, preparatory, we supposed, to the religious interview. Elizabeth's seat was near him, and she addressed him with much power. She then knelt resting her hand on his knee. It was an impressive scene to behold a frail Quaker woman kneeling before a grey headed Roman Catholic Priest who was a slaveholder, interceding with "the Father" that he might be permitted to obey the injunction to do justly and love mercy, that the blessings of the poor and needy might rest upon him and his name go down from generation to generation, this being told as a memorial of him. His feelings were tendered and he appeared to appreciate the visit. The other visit was also satisfactory.

That evening at J. Dixon's we had a solemn opportunity. Gratitude for the renewed evidence that we should be permitted to return bearing the olive branch of peace was freely poured forth, and also for the favor that the fount of feeling had not only been opened in the hearts of those whom we felt were as 'bone of our bone and flesh of our flesh,' but that the divine image had been recognized in those not of our fold, and that with these also we had been permitted to hold sweet communion. Individual states were spoken to and salutary counsel was given. On the 3d of Ninth month, we bade farewell to our kind friends and turned our faces homeward. On the 5th attended meeting at Appoquinemink, dined at Cantwell's bridge and reached Wilmington that night. On the 8th, arrived at home after an absence of more than five weeks."

At the Monthly Meeting held at Green street in Eleventh month, 1850, a minute was granted E. Newport to visit the meetings belonging to Abington Quarter, and appoint some meetings within its limits. "Much sympathy and unity were expressed with her prospect." Rebecca W. Ellis felt a concern to accompany E. N. in the proposed visit, which was fully united with.

The friends returned their minutes at the next Monthly Meeting with the information that "the visit had been performed to the peace of their own minds."

In the Fourth month, 1851, E. N. informed the Monthly Meeting of her prospect of attending N. Y. Yearly Meeting and of appointing some meetings among Friends and others not of our Society. She was encouraged to attend thereto as Truth might open the way.

In the Sixth month, she informed her friends that the service had been performed and her mind was relieved.

While at Flushing, L. I., during this visit, she thus wrote to her husband and children.

. . . . . . We left New York on Seventh-day to attend the funeral of Abigail Thurston. The Friends met at the meeting-house and it was a satisfactory meeting. From Flushing, T. Leggett took us to Westbury; we are to have an appointed meeting there this afternoon, and then go up the North River on the west side, where I saw my way before leaving home, yet do not know what the location is. I have been mercifully preserved, as I believe, in the line of my duty. The path though hidden sufficiently to continually occasion me to realize my own short sightedness, has always been opened and light unfolded seasonably. Some portion of the Yearly Meeting week, I was like a bird out of its cage, or a child released from school. I felt joyous and light-hearted, and I think I never felt more grateful for such refreshing seasons.

I feel anxious about my dear family, but feel constrained to go on, as ability is furnished, to bind up the broken hearted and aid in restoring the waste places. At no period of my life has the truth been more exalted in my view than on some occasions during this visit.

I must now close in the aboundings of that love which emanates from the inexhaustible fountain. The very outpourings of my soul go out in fervent aspirations for you. I do not wish you to follow me only so far as you perceive that I follow the course which leads to peace; but I ask you all to seek for a more intimate acquaintance with the principle of life in the soul. I was never more sensible that matters, which may be small in themselves, involve great and important results.

Baltimore Yearly Meeting.

In the Tenth month, 1851, our friend again felt herself called to visit Friends and others within the compass of Baltimore Yearly Meeting, and applied to her Monthly Meeting for a minute. Mary M. Evans informed the meeting that she had a concern to accompany E. N. as far as the way might open. Minutes of sympathy and unity were furnished them and they were encouraged to attend to the openings of Truth. James Andrews of Darby, Pa., accompanied them. The following extracts from letters, give some particulars of this visit.

BALTIMORE, ELEVENTH MONTH 12th, 1851.

My Dear J.— . . . . We were kindly greeted by our friend J. Needles, who was waiting with his carriage to receive us. The next day we attended the Monthly Meeting, where a clear sight was given me of the nature of the mission called for at my hands, and although great and arduous, I was enabled to bow in submission. It resulted in our going to Little Falls and visiting some families in that vicinity. We visited a slaveholder and had a free conversation with him upon the subjects of slavery and a free gospel ministry. He was affable and wished further information. As we contrasted the inconsistency of slavery with the principles of Christianity he admitted it to be a curse. I told him that I did not know that he was a slaveholder, but my mind was drawn to some who were not members of our Society, and I felt it right to inquire if he would receive a visit. He said, "how did you know where I lived?" I replied, by impression I pointed out the road and the house. He treated us kindly and expressed gratitude for our coming. Later.—We have just returned from a visit to the slave prison. Oh! how excruciatingly suffering it is to behold these poor objects! My spirit was turned toward them in the night. We were told by one poor creature, who whispered to us and begged us to buy her, that a "parcel" of them were sent there in *the night* handcuffed, to be sold to the far South.

We told them we could do nothing more than pray for them; and they were exhorted to put their trust in that Power which they would find within them, and although they might be treated cruelly, to endeavor to imitate the example of the blessed Jesus; for all the imprecations that they might breathe upon their persecutors would only increase their own sufferings. But if they cultivated the feeling which could enable them to say,

"Father, forgive them, they know not what they do," they might be instrumental in softening the hearts and convincing the judgment of their masters of the wickedness of holding their fellow beings in slavery. A very interesting looking youth of about 20, said he could not read, but his dependence was upon God; he had endeavored to do his best in serving his master, and he was determined to continue to do so. Poor creatures! they thanked us for coming, and their looks and tears were eloquent. Oh it was a hard sight, such as I never wish to behold again! We visited several slaveholders, and were richly rewarded for going. The word flowed freely and the anointing was poured forth on the poor instrument.

Farewell dear ones,

E. N.

CAMERON MIELS, 12th MONTH 20th, 1873.

. . . . . Time will not admit of my saying more than that we expect to go back to Baltimore on Second-day. It has been colder here than for many years past, the thermometer being at 10° this morning. I think about two weeks more will close our labors about Washington, Baltimore and Little Falls. I have not yet been able *continually* to adopt the language "Thy will be done" in relation to the other part of the concern, yet have no doubt as to its being a positive requiring. I do not see why one so unqualified as I feel myself to be, should be sent when there are so many stronger and more acceptable to many people. We have visited several noted slaveholders, and in every opportunity the fear of man has been overcome so that the truth has been spoken fearlessly and no offense given, but often many thanks offered with the acknowledgment that what had been said was the truth.

This morning we propose going to the awful prison. Oh! I have a dread of it, a *great dread* on several accounts! Yet if we can be instrumental in handing one drop of cold water or anything that can comfort the poor creatures shall we shrink from going?" . . .

It was during this religious visit that Elizabeth Newport and her companions, Mary M. Evans, James Andrews and Richard Plummer, made a visit to Henry Clay, who was at that time in very feeble health. Her address to him was appropriate and sympathetic, to which he made the following reply :—

"I am obliged to you madam for this visit, and for the kind interest you have taken in my behalf, and I also appreciate the feeling that impelled you to come. Your advice I acknowledge to be of the highest magnitude, and I shall endeavor to give it that consideration which it so justly merits and demands at my hands. I am aware, madam, that when one like myself has arrived at the age of three score years and ten, and who is as feeble in health as I am, he cannot expect to remain here much longer; yet, madam, when it pleases God to take me hence, I am willing to go; and if Dr. Jackson of Philadelphia, who is expected here this evening, should not be able to afford me that relief for my cough that is sought for, I care not how soon that period may arrive. Though I do not pretend to say that I have a full assurance that all will be well, yet, madam, I have faith in the love and mercy of God, and am not afraid to die."

Soon after our friends entered his room, H. Clay inquired of J. Andrews, whether they belonged to that part of our Society called Orthodox or Hicksites; when told to the latter, a name given in derision, H. C. replied, 'I always regretted the separation in your Society, but if I understand the difference in the two parts, the Orthodox believe in the divinity of the body of Jesus Christ, and the Hicksites in the divinity of His mission."

E. Newport's health becoming increasingly feeble she returned home, and remained till the Second month following, when, accompanied by Tacy Pancoast and Charles Kirk, she again entered upon the service, feeling, as she said, that "until the work was finished there could be no true rest of mind nor body."

Her concern, it may be remembered, was not confined to the members of the Society of Friends, but included a class that rendered the prospect especially painful. For years, her mind had been impress:d with the belief that she would have to visit the Southern portion of our country and plead the cause of the poor and oppressed, and endeavor, in the peaceable spirit of the gospel, to convince those who held their fellow-men in bondage of the wrong they were committing.

From the memoranda of C. Kirk, the following account of this journey is comprised:

"Second Month 18th.—Arrived at B. Moore's, in Fallston, Md. Our first application to visit a slaveholder was not acceded to, owing, I believe, to his not being approached in the right manner. It was necessary for messengers who were sent, to prepare the way, by informing the individual that a Friend was travelling through the country on a mission of *love* and had a wish to visit them. When this course was pursued, none refused. On the 19th, E. was indisposed and in bed all day. The next day we visited a slaveholder, and the day following two of the same class were called upon; toward them the gospel flowed freely, and it was kindly received. They expressed gratitude for the visits. In the afternoon went to Baltimore, and the next morning, attended Old Town meeting, which was a season of deep exercise to dear E. In the afternoon we were at Lombard street meeting, in which was borne a short living testimony. On the 24th, had a meeting in the Old house at Gunpowder, at which several slaveholders were present. The subject of slavery was treated in a clear and powerful manner, and the people listened with great attention. Had a religious opportunity with the family of John Matthews. Two of the neighbors coming in, E. was led to address them with great plainness.

25th.—One of the horses being lame we were obliged to leave him, but we were among kind friends and were furnished with a substitute. In the morning attended Gunpowder meeting, which was large, and it was a time of Divine favor. In the afternoon visited two slaveholders, both satisfactory interviews. One of them, not long after, manumitted his slaves.

26th.—Had a meeting in a Baptist house at Haverford, and in the afternoon one in a school house at Cockeysville. After the morning meeting, Elizabeth had a severe attack of indisposition which kept her in bed until after the hour appointed for the meeting, but she felt so strong an obligation to attend it, that a messenger was sent to explain the reason of our not being punctual and to invite the people to remain until we came. We had four miles to ride, and when we got to the house there was no fire and no way to make one. E. feeling no liberty to leave, we placed her where the sun would shine through the window and wrapped a buffalo robe around her as well as we could; this with the exercise of mind through which she had to pass, prevented her, no doubt, from taking cold. She was led to address an individual in a powerful manner, believing him to be treading a path which would lead to ruin.

27th.—Visited the family of the person who was killed in Lancaster county, while attempting to capture some runaway slaves. The family of a relative was also there, and it was a solemn and interesting occasion. We then returned to Baltimore. 29th, were at Sandy Spring meeting and made one family visit. Dined with a friend who had a poor opinion of Abolitionists.

Letter from E N.

SANDY SPRING, SECOND MONTH 29th.

My Dear J.:—Here we arrived yesterday toward evening, after a wearisome journey, the roads being wet, stony and hilly and occasionally diversified by clay and deep ruts. We have met with extremely kind friends, and have needed such, for beside the attack I had at B. Moore's, I was ill at Gunpowder. We were at the home of Eli Matthews, a dear aged Friend, in his 86th year. Had several appointed meetings from among Friends in that neighborhood, all ending satisfactorily, and also paid several visits; a few of them were opportunities worthy of grateful remembrance. I came away fully relieved and peacefully centered under a renewed conviction that He who promised to go before and prepare the way, had graciously afforded strength and ability in the needful time, for the performance of all that was required. Although the effort was never greater to keep my mind in a state of resignation to endure the trial necessary in going from place to place under attendant circumstances, with the increasing disposition to shrink from public gaze, the evidence of being in my right allotment was clearly manifested; so that every inch of ground we have travelled over thus far has seemed under divine appointment.

When at Little Falls, my mind was so weightily impressed with the service to which

I had often alluded to thee, that, after many hours of suffering, I at last yielded so far that B. H. was written to, and upon our return to Baltimore we were told that there was a prospect of obtaining the Capitol on First-day morning without requiring a vote from the Representatives, and therefore there need be no publicity about it. But after our visit to Gunpowder, we learned that no meeting could be held without a full and clear understanding with all parties, and it was very doubtful even then that consent would be obtained; so that Friends about the Capitol and others who were consulted, thought it not best to make further effort, yet expressed a willingness to do so in case I requested it. Upon consideration I felt entirely released, and great was the relief, particularly as with it I seemed to be excused from all further service in and about Washington. I could say much upon this subject, for it has been one fraught with intense interest and suffering to my spirit, under which there has been at times, as I have apprehended, clear and enlarged views of our standing as a Society in connection with our Government, its constitution and its laws; but

I forbear because I feel that they are among the King's secrets and are not to be divulged except by word of command. . . .

E. N.

Diary Continued.

3d Mo. 1st.—Made arrangements for holding a meeting in the Court House at Rockville, the county town of Montgomery Co. Some friends were discouraged from making the attempt, with the belief that as the Court was then in session it would not adjourn. Elizabeth was obliged to pass through many deep baptisms, but faith triumphed.

2d.—Went to Rockville accompanied by W. H. Stabler, an Elder, and attended the meeting which had been appointed. It was supposed that about two-thirds of the audience were slaveholders. The people were quiet and appeared to listen attentively to the Truth which was proclaimed with life and power. There had not been a Friend's meeting held in that place for 20 years. After the meeting, called at Mahlon Kirk's and had a religious opportunity with the family.

3d.—Attended the Monthly Meeting at

Sandy Spring. E. was favored to preach the gospel with power, especially in the men's meeting. In the afternoon visited three families. One of these persons subsequently manumitted his slaves.

4th.—Visited Fair Hill Boarding School; in the afternoon made a family visit. 5th.—visited several families, some of whom held slaves. The Truth was declared to them in its purity.

On the 6th returned to Baltimore, a distance of 26 miles. 7th were at Lombard street meeting in the morning, which was a favored season. The next day attended their Quarterly Meeting. Elizabeth was silent during the first meeting, but made a visit to the men's meeting, in which Truth reigned over all. 9th.—Visited the families of two friends. 10th.—Had a remarkable visit to a person who was a Methodist and a slaveholder. He acknowledged the Truth of E's testimony. 11th.—Made visits to five families. In the afternoon were at the residence of two slaveholders, one of whom was the owner of 3,000 acres.

Returned to Baltimore, and next day proceeded to Washington. Had a meeting in the Temperance Hall, which was a favored time.

13th.—Rode to Waterford, a distance of 44 miles. The road for about three miles after leaving "the Pike" was extremely bad, and we did not reach Isaac Steer's till after dark. First-day we attended the meeting at Waterford and dined at Miriam Gover's; had religious service in her family, and with several others in the course of the afternoon. We returned to I. Steer's to lodge, where the gospel spring was opened and the pure water flowed freely. 15th.—Dined with a widow who was a member, but her son held slaves. Had a meeting in the family. Then went to Leesburg, the county town of Loudon county, Va. A meeting in the Court House had been appointed for us, which we attended. This was a time of deep suffering for the poor instrument, but she was favored to accomplish her work to general satisfaction. Again returned to Waterford. It was E. Newport's practice, when she visited a neighborhood of Friends, to invite the Elders to an interview and acquaint them with the prospect which she had before her. When the subject of visiting the slaveholders was mentioned, although it was not opposed, yet it was evident that friends felt very cautious in regard to it. This made the burden still greater, if possible, for E. to bear.

16th.—Visited a slaveholder, to whom the gospel was preached in humility and love. Had a meeting in the town of Hillsboro' which was tolerably satisfactory.

17th.—Visited an individual whom E. N. warned of the evil which would befal him unless he repented. The poor man heeded not her counsel, and reaped bitter fruit. He was so exasperated with the Emancipation Proclamation that he sold his farm for Confederate money, and, although advanced in life, joined the rebel army. He lived to return, but his means were exhausted and he died soon afterward. Attended meeting at Waterford. In the afternoon were at a house where the slaves were very poorly clad, and our sympathies were deeply enlisted for them, and also had a religious opportunity with a Friend's family.

18th.—Reached Goose Creek in time for their week-day meeting, which was large. Visited a slaveholder in the afternoon.

19th.—Had interviews with three persons at their separate homes, who had once been members of our Society, but who at that time held slaves. E. N. delivered searching testimonies which we had reason to suppose were well received, as all of them were at Friends meeting on the following First-day.

20th.—Visited an Englishman who owned 900 acres of land and many slaves. Although our friend E. had very close service and the system of slavery was strongly testified against, this person would not allow us to leave without dinner. We submitted, though somewhat in the cross. The wife was sitting upon the floor darning stockings when we first entered the house, and took no notice of us, but after the meeting she was very kind, and obtaining some money from her husband, took E. aside and offered to pay her for the sermon. Visited two sons of a worthy Elder who had become slaveholders, greatly to the grief of their mother and friends. E. was entirely ignorant of any of the circumstances connected with them, but her testimony was powerful and searching.

Lodged at J. Smith's and had an interesting religious opportunity with the family, individual states being feelingly addressed. Next morning were at Goose Creek meeting, in which E. was greatly favored. Dined at S. M. Janney's, after which the family was gathered, and we had a solemn meeting. There was a person present whom we had previously visited, who was a Baptist and a slaveholder. He had also attended Friends' meeting, the first day after we had been to see him. A friendly influence certainly overspread his mind. On First-day afternoon we visited a slave-holder, at whose house we found about twenty of his neighbors gathered. E. proclaimed the truth plainly and fearlessly. Lodged at N. Shoemaker's, and had a religious opportunity in his family.

22d.—Rode thirty miles to Hopewell and found a resting place at our friend Joseph Branson's. This had been a day of intense suffering for our friend E. Her spirit was impressed with a sense of a wrong which had been committed in that part of the country.

A short time previously, a poor slave had been whipped so severely that he died, and his master had attempted to conceal the crime by throwing the body into the river. It was discovered, and the offender brought to trial, and although the evidence against him was clear, the victim being a man of color and a slave, he was not convicted ; but E. knew nothing of this. When we came to the house where this person lived, I asked her if she would like to call there. She replied, after a few moments consideration, "No—*it is too late.*" I heard afterward that he had become so paralyzed, both physically and mentally, that he was incapable of understanding what was said to him. As we journeyed on, Elizabeth asked me to stop the carriage. She then called to the friend who was piloting us and said that there was a man living in that house, pointing to one some distance from the road, that she would like to see. The friend went to the house, but did not find the person at home, but subsequent events proved that our calling was a great advantage to us. This individual was mainly instrumental in opening the way for us to have a meeting in the neighborhood. The meeting was a very trying one, but our dear friend was favored to warn the people, in the spirit of love.

On our way to Winchester, we had been riding, as was frequently the case, for a long time in silence, and just as we entered the town, E. said to me, "There are *five* slave-holders in and about this place, whom we will have to visit. There is one living on the road which we are now traveling, a little way out of the town on rather an elevated situation. We must go there first in the morning. Then when we come out of that house and stand with our backs to it and our faces to the north, there is another place to the right hand; we must go there next." We inquired of the friends with whom we lodged, and they proposed several individuals before the right ones were named, but E. had no difficulty in deciding, when she heard them. Next morning the friend and I called to inquire if a visit would be agreeable to them, and found them all quite willing. He told me afterward that if E. had always known them, she could not have more correctly described them.

23d. Endeavored to make arrangements for a meeting at Berryville, County town of Clark County, Va., but were not successful. 24th. Attended a funeral of an Orthodox Friend. I felt that E. was favored to "divide the word aright." After the interment, the people were invited to the meeting-house. They accepted the invitation regardless of sectarian differences. Thus our friend E. N. had an opportunity to relieve her mind. We then went to Winchester. 25th. Visited two slaveholders--one of them the son of a Friend. In the afternoon had an appointed meeting in Friends' meeting house, wherein a strong testimony against slavery was borne. The meeting was remarkably quiet. 26th. Went to see two individuals who held slaves--one of them a widow; both visits were satisfactory, but particularly the latter. In the evening had a meeting in the Lyceum room at Winchester, where truth reigned over all. 27th. Visited a woman who held slaves. Our friend's testimony was remarkably clear, and the evils of slavery were forcibly brought into view. The uncertainty of life was feelingly alluded to. Dined at a Friend's house and had a religious opportunity with the family. Next morning had a similar one with the family with whom we had lodged. A meeting was held in the Academy at Berryville to a degree of satisfaction. From this place we proceeded to Goose Creek.

30th. Went to Waterford. Visited an individual who had once been a member, but who had become a slaveholder; it was a remarkable time. His tears flowed freely for a long time, and when we bade farewell there was no ability for utterance, but the affectionate grasp of the hand, was expressive of the deep feelings of his heart. We left him with the earnest desire that he might take heed to the counsel which had so evidently reached the witness for Truth in his mind.

Our next visit was to the owner of 60 or 70 slaves. E.'s testimony against the practice of holding our fellow-men in bondage was *very* close, but it appeared to be kindly received.

In this opportunity as well as in others, the slaves were spoken to in a feeling manner, but they were always requested to withdraw before the masters were addressed.

31st Were at Friends' meeting at Waterford, which was a time of favor. Not feeling released from Hillsboro', we went there in the afternoon, and had another meeting in a Methodist house. This proved much more satisfactory than the one held on a former occasion.

Fourth mo. 1st. On our way to Alexandria made visits to two Friends, who were located 18 or 20 miles from meeting. Our home in the city was at the house of Benjamin Hallowell. 2d. Commenced visiting the families of this Monthly Meeting, and made eleven visits between three and nine o'clock, P. M. On 4th day attended the meeting at Washington, which was small, and afterward visited several families. 5th day. After making three family visits, we started for Baltimore. At Bladensburg, we found the bridge was unsafe, and the stream too high to ford. There appeared to be no suitable place to stay all night, and Elizabeth not feeling her mind clear of Washington, we returned. In the morning visited a Congressman on our way to Baltimore, and it proved a most satisfactory opportunity, but still we left Washington with heavy hearts. I never felt more the solemnity of the language used in reference to Jerusalem—"O Jerusalem, Jerusalem, etc." Reached Baltimore, and had a satisfactory meeting in Friends' meeting-house in Old Town.

On the 7th, went to Deer Creek. 8th. Attended Deer Creek meeting, after which, we rode to Nottingham, where he had an appointed meeting next day. Visited a family, in which E. represented things in as true a light, I was told, as if she had been well acquainted with the individual.

On the 10th arrived at our homes with feelings of deep gratitude to Him who had been with us and had so mercifully preserved us through a long and wearisome journey."

The following, incidents which occurred near Baltimore, have been furnished by a Friend who was in company with Elizabeth Newport at that time. "While at the house of a Friend in a neighborhood where she had been attending a Quarterly Meeting, her mind was impressed with an obligation to visit a person who was entirely unknown to her. She described him to her host as one accustomed to the use of the pen, and who exercised a wide influence through that medium. She pointed in the direction in which he lived; after some reflection, the Friend remarked, there was a person answering that description (a non-slaveholder) living several miles distant. A messenger was sent to ask an interview, which was kindly acceded to, and E. N. was led to address him on the subject of slavery, and to exhort him to dedicate his gifts to the service of his Divine Master, and labor for the extermination of an evil, which she felt confident had deeply exercised his mind. It was believed from what subsequently appeared, that the message was felt to be an encouragement to him to do what he could for the abolition of slavery."

When this service was accomplished, she was impressed with a conviction that there was a slaveholder in the same neighborhood who occupied a prominent place in public affairs; and on ascertaining there was such an one, the way was opened, and an opportunity freely granted. She portrayed to him her feelings in regard to himself and his family, and the duty which she believed had been clearly opened to his mind in relation to the slaves which he then held as property. The visit was kindly received and appreciated."

The following letter is from a Friend who was applied to for information respecting E. N.'s religious labors in the neighborhood in which she resided:

"—— ———:—Thy dear mother, whom we remember with affectionate interest, was our guest at three different times. The first time, accompanied by T. B. and L. Longstreth, she remained a week. Her health was feeble in the extreme as it appeared to us, and yet I thought it not improbable that the exercises of her mind, the deep baptisms through which she passed, were wearing upon a body that was not very strong. She appeared to feel much upon starting every morning, and returned every evening exhausted in mind and body, and upon one occasion was just able to reach the sofa and sank into unconsciousness. During that visit her exercises seemed particularly trying to her truly feminine nature. On one occasion, when I thought she had withdrawn because of physical indisposition and followed her to her room, she wept very much, and said she shrank from the work of the day that was before her. Though she assured me to the contrary, I felt my presence an intrusion, and soon left her that she might gather the strength she needed.

And that she found it I know, for she came forth bright and cheerful, and I doubt not with a renewed feeling of dedication to her Master's work. My husband, at her request, accompanied them to the families of our neighborhood, and some visits were felt by him to be very close and searching. We thought her visit to our family a peculiarly favored one. I was absent at the time of her second visit, but heard of some favored seasons on that occasion."

The subjoined extracts from letters written by E. Newport during her late visit, will, no doubt, be read with interest by those who sympathized with her in the probation of going from door to door, imparting in humility and love that with which she had been entrusted as a spiritual ambassador.

Third Month, 1852.

"*My Dear J.*—We arrived in B. from Sandy Spring, whither I went as one blind, save as regarded the direction in which to go, but I was favored to experience the promise verified again and again—'I will go before thee and in the right time will cause light to shine out of darkness.' When I mentioned to R. B. the prospect of a meeting at Rockville, he remarked, it was court time, and he thought it would not adjourn: but we had a large meeting. Wm. H. Stabler, an Elder, went with us. It was a dreaded meeting to me, but it proved satisfactory, and was said to be a favored opportunity. Had several interesting visits to slaveholders." . . .

"GUNPOWDER.

. . . "I have been sick but am better now. Paid visits to two brothers, slaveholders. More true kindness and hospitality I never witnessed. One of them, an old man, told us we 'need not say one word, for go we should not, until we had dined.' "

We parted under a manifestation of great kindness, even down to the youngest son, an open-hearted creature, full of life and fun, but who paid us every attention in his power." . . . .

"HOPEWELL, Third mo. 28, 1852.

My Dear D. and S. Newport:

This morning I had hoped to have opened my eyes in Philadelphia, but instead thereof we are 200 miles distant. We have been as far south as Winchester. Expect to leave here to-morrow for Waterford, of which I had hoped we were clear. The present prospect is to have another appointed meeting at Willisborough, a town about nine miles distant, where we held one in a Methodist meeting-house. This was the only place in this section where individuals left the house when the subject of slavery was touched upon, and now we must go there again. I do not know whether they will stand the *fire* any better or not; but I desire to leave the consequences to Him who has to our humbling admiration so often prepared the way for us. Had an appointed meeting in the meeting-house at Winchester, where the abominations of slavery and the practice of making merchandize of our fellow-beings were strongly depicted. My mind was so absorbed and so entirely free from the fear of man, that I was not conscious such *close* things were said. There was a crowd at the doors and windows, but all were very still; some boys, sons of slaveholders, I was told had clubs, but they sat quietly. We have paid a number of visits to slaveholders, and I have unhesitatingly advanced such views as were required of me. Yesterday we visited a widow who had many slaves. I knew nothing of her, but had to give her to understand how, by impression, I was directed whom to visit, and to explain the consistency of this, with our profession of being guided by the Spirit. I dreaded the interview, but it was crowned with peace. The effects and the evils of slavery with the sufferings it costs, were boldly set forth, and yet we were invited to dine, and even to spend the day. At one place the woman took me out privately and offered me money. I told her "we had sufficient to take us home." But said she, "I want my black people to come up." I replied, "do bring them all." Her husband was a hard master, and the neighbors told us afterwards, that she was a dreadful woman. I addressed the colored people, inciting their attention to the Spirit of Truth to guide and direct them; and entreated them to cultivate love, kindness, forgiveness and forbearance. At parting, the hostess acknowledged that all I had said was true, and she gave us a cordial invitation, if we ever came that way again, to make them a visit. I do not want you to think the way is *easy*. A remark made by Charles, yesterday, will explain our feelings. "We have visited a number, but I think it is no easier to go into this house, than the first one we entered." I deeply feel for Friends here, surrounded as they are by slaveholders. I think the testimony has not been fully sustained by *some*. I *often* feel a sense of the *future suffering in store for our country* on account of this great curse. The land is good, though the roads are intolerable. Charles sometimes pretends to scold about them, and says the people do not deserve to be visited. The slaveholders appear to live more comfortably here than in Maryland.

Your affectionate mother,

E. N.

To Miriam Grover.

PHILADELPHIA, 5th mo. 16th, 1852

My dear friend:—I had not supposed so long a time would have elapsed before the pen would have been resorted to, in order to convey to my friends at Waterford the assurance that a continued sense of their kindness to the poor pilgrims who sojourned with them, and who partook not only of the hospitalities the frail body so much required, but who were also strengthened by the healing balm of sympathy so freely offered. Who that has known its influence when it flows from the fount of pure feeling, can but acknowledge its power to soothe and to heal. I know not that I should be thus employed now if I had not been prompted by T., for I have again been let down as into the deep. Although the garb worn may not be sack-cloth and ashes, yet it is a season when surely neither the singing of birds nor the voice of melody is heard, but one in which no flesh can glory! one in which the continual feeling seems to be to watch, watch!

I feel that I should do injustice to the affectionate sympathy of my nature, not to say that I have had in living remembrance thee and thine, and many precious Friends and others in your vicinity, to all of whom I desire to be affectionately remembered. Although upon my return peace was the answer, yet the feeling of nothingness and insufficiency covered me as a mantle. In attempting to look back, there appears to be nothing in which to sorrow or rejoice. How it humiliates to feel the little that we are capable of doing for each other; but the hope has been, that if there was no good there was at least no harm done.

In that love which emanates from the pure fountain, my beloved friend, farewell. When thou art favored with near access to the altar, forget not one who feels to subscribe herself,

Thy attached friend,

E. Newport.

In the Seventh month, 1853, Elizabeth Newport informed her friends of a prospect which had weighed upon her mind of "visiting such parts of some of the Southern States, as the way might open for, to attend the Quarterly Meetings of Centre and Warrington, and to appoint meetings within their limits, and also to attend Baltimore Yearly Meeting." Much sympathy was expressed by the meeting, and she was encouraged to a faithful discharge of the requisitions of Truth. During the prosecution of this concern, she made a visit to President Pierce, for the account of which the compiler is indebted to one of the Friends who accompanied her:

A Visit to President Pierce.

On the morning of Eleventh month 5th, 1853, in company with William Tyson, of Washington City, I called upon Franklin Pierce, President of the United States, and informed him that Elizabeth Newport, of Philadelphia, a minister of the Society of Friends, was visiting the meetings of her brethren and sisters of the same religious communion in that section, and had felt it right to offer him a visit in the love of the Gospel. The President replied that he would receive the visit with pleasure, at half past 2 o'clock in the afternoon, at which time he directed the messenger in attendance to introduce us into his private parlor, and to inform him of our arrival.

Near the time specified, Elizabeth Newport, Hannah Lukens, her companion, Harriet J. Moore, Rebecca Turner, and myself, reached the Presidential Mansion; soon after which the President entered, and was introduced to the Friends.

He remarked that he had hoped to have the company of his wife, but that she was not well enough to be present. He alluded to the severe bereavement they had sustained in the removal of an only son, and that it had disqualified both of them for the responsible position they had been called to assume. He also alluded to the satisfactory interview he had recently with some Friends from England, who had presented their views on the subject of slavery. E. Newport commenced by reminding him of the feeling of obligation which impelled her to offer this visit, and of the different positions they occupied in life, and yet they were children of one common Father—"One is your Master, even Christ, and all ye are brethren." Under this feeling she could address him as a brother. She then repeated the testimony of the Apostle Paul, "that the grace of God which bringeth salvation, hath appeared unto all men, teaching them that denying ungodliness and worldly lusts, they should live soberly, righteously, and godly in this present world;" expressing the conviction that her brother whom she was addressing had known from a child the stirrings of the grace of God, and that he had not always attended to its blessed teachings, which would have preserved him from evil. She then referred to several incidents in the life of the blessed Son and sent of the Father, and to several of his testimonies recorded in the New Testament; urging upon her listener the obligation resting upon all Christians to follow His holy example.

She repeated his declaration in the synagogue of Nazareth: "The Spirit of the Lord God is upon me, because he hath anointed me to preach the Gospel to the poor, he hath sent me to heal the broken-hearted, to preach deliverance to the captive and recovery of sight to the blind, and to set at liberty them that are bruised." The conviction was expressed, that the responsible position in which he was placed, enabled him to carry out these gospel principles to as great an extent as any one now on the field of action, and she entreated him, in the most earnest and affectionate manner, to give heed to this blessed Spirit, a manifestation of which had been given him to profit withal. As he was obedient to this, he would experience a growth in the Truth, and a qualification to carry out the discoveries which this Divine principle would reveal to the mind, reminding him of the testimony, "If thine eye be single thy whole body shall be filled with light." She adverted briefly to the evils of war and slavery, and the desolating effects they produced upon the human family. In conclusion, she alluded, in the most feeling manner, to the bereavement he and his wife had sustained in the removal of the beloved object of their affection, expressing the sympathy she felt with them, and the hope that they would be reunited in heaven. The object of these afflictions was often to wean us from our attachments to the perishing things of this world, and to gently lead us to seek after that inheritance which fadeth not away. That this might be his happy experience was her fervent prayer, and then when the solemn period arrived, he would realize the state so beautifully described by the poet:—

Sweet is the scene where virtue dies,
  When sinks a righteous soul to rest,
How mildly beam the closing eyes,
  How gently heaves the expiring breast.

A holy quiet reigns around,
  A calm which nothing can destroy—
Nought can disturb that peace profound,
  Which their unfettered souls enjoy.

During the early part of this interesting testimony the President looked steadfastly on the speaker, but soon fixed his eyes on the floor, and at times manifested his emotion by tears. After a moment's pause, he replied nearly as follows: "Madam, I am not a professor of religion, but I can acknowledge the truth of much that you have expressed. It is true, as you suggest, that from a child I have been impressed with the sacred truths of religion, and though I may not have regarded them, I can assure you it is my firm belief, that there can be no permanent reformation, either in an individual or a people, that is not founded upon the obligations of civilization and Christianity. You refer to the difference of our positions in life. I feel there is none; and as you have kindly addressed me as your brother, I can in return call you my sister.

"The responsible position I now occupy is not one of my seeking, or my choice. I feel that it is a path surrounded by thorns, and can assure you I would gladly escape from it. Nothing, nothing, that surrounds me here can soothe the agonies of my crushed heart. You have adverted to the subject of war, and let me assure you that I regard it as totally inconsistent with every principle of humanity. Situated as we are, the principles of Christanity cannot be carried out in the administration of government. My father was a soldier of the Revolution. He taught me when a child, that it was my duty to defend the honor and glory of my country; but, in the war with Mexico, I was never upon a battle-field that my eyes were not suffused with tears; and let me assure you that, as far as my influence extends, it shall be exerted to avert the terrible evil of war, which should never be resorted to but in the last extremity. You allude also to slavery; upon that subject I am a northern man with northern feelings, but I find at the foundation of the government, our fathers recognized this as one of the compromises of the Constitution, and I am bound by my obligations to maintain it. It can only be abolished through the influence of moral power, or of revelation upon the mind. You speak of our great bereavement, and for your kind feelings of sympathy; let me assure you I thank you from my heart."

During the delivery of this address, the President spoke in a firm, clear voice, occasionally evincing feeling and emotion. All present were convinced that he delivered the sincere effusions of his heart. At its conclusion the company rose to depart. He bade each a cordial farewell, when Harriet J. Moore, taking him by the hand, remarked that she had been reminded of King David, who, at the loss of his son, lifted up his voice and wept, and used this language, "I shall go to him, but he cannot come to me." She expressed the desire that, in the midst of all that surrounded him, he might seek seasons of retirement, in which he could commune with his own heart and his Heavenly Father, and thus be enabled to witness a preparation for a re-union. "I have also felt," said she, "a deep sympathy with thy dear wife, and trust this may be your happy experience." To which the President replied, "I assure you, Madam, it is my desire." After a message of love to his wife from the women-Friends we left, and in passing out of the room the President extended a cordial invitation to the company to visit him again, assuring them that they, or any of their friends, should always be welcome at his mansion.

For the fulfillment of the religious visit for which E. Newport had obtained a minute from her Monthly Meeting, she again left home on the 5th of Twelfth month, 1853, with Elizabeth N. Clinger (Cox) and Charles Kirk for companions.

From C. K.'s diary :—

"We passed through Wilmington and East Nottingham. At noon on the 7th, when we stopped to dine, E.'s feelings were soon arrested for the landlord, who had once been a member of our Society. Her remarks evidently reached the witness for Truth in his mind, his feelings being greatly tendered.

When we left we could not prevail upon him to take any compensation for what we had eaten or for the provender given the horses."

The next religious service which is noted, was a visit to a slave-holder. "He received with kindness the close testimony against slavery delivered by E. On the 8th, had a meeting in the afternoon in a baptist meeting-house at Hereford, Md. 10th.—Had a solemn parting with our venerable friend Eli Matthews, of Gunpowder. It appeared as if his work was done, and that he had nothing to do but await cheerfully the summons to a higher life, which E. told him she felt was not distant; and thus it proved.

First-day, 11th.—Had three meetings, one in an Academy at Reisterstown, one at Dover, five miles distant, held in a Methodist house, and another in the evening at Reisterstown, which was large. At all of these meetings the people were very attentive. 12th.—At Westminster, the county town of Carroll Co., Md., we held a meeting in a Methodist house. The people were kind, although the evils of war and slavery were plainly presented to them.

Returned to Finksburgh, and had a meeting in the school-house. Lodged at a Friend's house, for whom and his family E. had pertinent counsel. 14th.—Had an opportunity with another family, and in the evening attended a meeting which had been appointed for us in the Mound Meeting-house. This was a free, open time. 15th.—Waited all day in order to have a meeting at Westminster, which was held in a Methodist house. The grant of another had been given by the Elders, but the Minister objected, because slavery had been alluded to in our previous meeting. At this time E. reminded the people of what John Wesley had said of the system of slavery. He declared it to be "the sum of all villainies." She was favored to speak with so much power, that Truth was victorious. One of the prominent members expressed his satisfaction, and many, by their kind manner, gave evidence of a similar feeling. 16th.—Proceeded to Uniontown, where we had an evening meeting. Thence to Nathan Haines' at Pipe Creek. 17th.—Held an appointed meeting in the Methodist meeting-house at Liberty, ten miles distant, but owing to the inclemency of the weather it was small. 18th.—At the meeting of Pipe Creek, E. had good service. Visited a blind man in the afternoon, who had lost his sight by blasting rocks. 19th.—Rode 30 miles to Frederick City. Had an evening meeting in Coppersmiths' Hall, but E.'s mind was not relieved. 20th.—Were at a funeral at Woodsboro. E.'s testimony was delivered with life and power. We met in the Methodist house in the evening. The religious element was felt to be at a low ebb, and it was a poor time. At Harper's Ferry, and at Charlestown, county town of Jefferson Co., Va., we had no meetings. These were the only two places between Westminster, Md., and Greensborough, through which we passed without having a religious opportunity with the people. We could but compare the state of the country to that of Egyptian darkness—so dark that it could be felt."

Extract from a Letter.

12th mo. 19th, 1853

My last letter was mailed from Westminster. Since then we have been pursuing our daily route, sometimes under deep depression and sore conflict of mind, at others have been favored with a faith so firm and unshaken that the Power which put forth will go before and prepare the way, that there has been an unflinching confidence in seasons of the greatest trials. We found after we left the settlement to which I referred, that we were not clear of that place. This I knew soon after we started, but felt that we were doing right in going on to Westminster, there being some service also required between the two places, and it would be accomplished without much extra riding. This we did; but the Minister being now at home, and hearing that when we were there the doctrine of original sin was treated adversely to his views, he objected to our having the house, although there were others who would like to have made way for us to have a meeting.

I, however, felt released. But another trial awaited us. There was no freedom to go forward, and no sight afforded as where to go. While waiting, another application was made, and full liberty given for a meeting, which was held.

Having been detained two days and one

night, we proceeded to Westminster. We found that the minister of the congregation, who had before granted the use of their meeting-house, had also been absent on that occasion, and he now was not willing we should occupy it. Here was a strait, for greatly did I desire a release, but found none. It appeared, however, that two houses had been offered, both belonging to Methodists, who were in disunity with each other. We felt free to accept the one we had not used previously, and Charles had no further trouble about it, which was a great relief to me, for really his burden is no light one; still he has proved himself to be both willing and adequate to perform every office, both great and small, which has been required. How much I feel for those who are with me.

I have just been querying with C. if he has strength enough left to look forward? He says he cannot look back. We were not at liberty to leave W. till Sixth-day morning, when we had no prospect beyond reaching Pipe Creek. We had gone but a little way, however, before the clouds dispersed and left no doubt as to the direction in which we should go. There is a heavy load upon me. Two meetings to-morrow, and then we go to Berryville. . . . . . .

E. N.

Diary Continued.

23d.—"Arrived at Winchester and put up with our kind friends Henry Sidwell and family. On our way stopped at Berryville, but no way opened for a meeting.

24th.—Went to Hopewell. Attended meeting there on First-day morning, and in the afternoon went to Winchester and had a meeting by appointment in Friends' meeting-house. This was a highly favored season. Our friend was enabled to declare the Truth with life and power.

26th.—Went to Berryville to attend a meeting which had been appointed for us, but it being Christmas time many of the people, both white and colored, were engaged in drinking and frolicing, and had forgotten all about it; and it might have been truly said that "there was no room for the babe in the inn." We returned to Winchester, and on our way visited a family where E. had much close service.

27th.—Made two family visits, and took an affectionate farewell of our friends with rather heavy hearts, expecting to be for weeks if not for months among strangers. Their thoughtful care in providing lunch for the hour of need, when we might not meet with suitable meals in crossing the mountains, was very grateful, and it proved at times of great value to us. With feelings more easily imagined than described, we pursued our course toward the mountains. Lodged at a tavern. We had not gone far next morning before E. informed me we should have to return. We did so, and she had a satisfactory opportunity with the landlord, after which we left peacefully. That evening had a meeting in the Presbyterian meeting-house at Romney, the county town of Hampshire Co. It was tolerably satisfactory.

29th.—It snowed fast part of the day. We travelled 31 miles, and lodged at William Pool's, on the top of the Alleghany mountains.

Letter from E. N.

TOP OF THE ALLEGHANY MOUNTAIN,
12th mo. 29th, 1853

—— ——:—Here we are this wintry evening installed in comfortable quarters, but the elements remind us that the state of things without is indeed comfortless. The wind whistles from every quarter, resounding almost like peals of thunder upon this lofty mountain; yet all within seems tranquil, at least for the time being,—and this should be numbered among our blessings. We are sitting by a tremendous open fire, but are under the necessity of changing our position frequently, to make all parts of the poor tabernacle comfortable.

We are greatly inconvenienced by poor lights. As proposed in my last letter, we went to Hopewell, and attended meeting there on First-day morning, then returned to Winchester and had an afternoon meeting in that place. Joseph Branson and wife accompanied us. On Second-day went to Berryville to attend an appointed meeting, but we found the place in much commotion, it being not only "Court time," but a day for hiring slaves. We saw at least one hundred of these poor creatures standing in the streets, some intoxicated, some running to and fro, but most of them appeared to be in high spirits. To us the scene was one of distress beyond the power of description. It was extremely cold and blustering, but the slaves, so far as we could see, were tolerably well clothed, and were all, no doubt, in their holiday attire. How helpless their condition! Some might make a good exchange in a home, but as it was a long-established practice, that such changes should take place every year, there was nothing permanent in store for them.

The white population were of a class to feel but little interest under this excitement, in getting together for the purpose of a religious meeting, and I could not help rejoicing in the feeling of releasement from further effort.

It is one of the darkest places I have ever known, and this appears to be the general testimony. In consequence of not being instant in season to what I felt required, but from which I desired to be released, we had next morning to return, after having started, but we were not long detained, and reached a town called Romney in time to have a meeting appointed for the evening. What good can all this mortification and suffering of the poor creature do? The people are so superficial and priest-ridden, that there seems to be but little place for the Truth in its simplicity.

The meetings are generally quiet, and often the audiences are remarkably attentive. The responsibility of going farther at this season of the year, and taking my companions into bodily and mental suffering, seems sometimes greater than I can endure. The horses, too, have claimed much thought and pity; but not one ray of light gleams on a backward path, and the impression is that home, if reached, would be but a cheerless abode under the circumstances. Such have been the exercises of my mind, but a comfortable quiet has been attained, and the evidence renewed that if we are attentive to our spiritual Guide, no harm will come to us. We concluded to-day, that could our friends at home know our whereabouts, they would think of us as being in a tried situation, passing as we are through this extremely cold region. We had supposed we might find our way hemmed in by drifted snow over some of the high cliffs, but we have got along with comparative comfort. We arrived at a little town called West Union, about 4 o'clock. It had been a hard drive for the horses, the snow falling and the roads in some places being very heavy in consequence of having been inundated by late freshets. At noon we found a good place to feed our faithful animals, while we took our lunch in the carriage, this being as comfortable a spot as we could find. Evening.—Just returned from attending a protracted meeting composed of different denominations. It was to me as a little brook by the way. No slavery here, and an honest desire to be fed with substantial food evidently prevailed. . .

Diary.

"The weather was extremely cold, and the horses slipped so much, I wanted them rough-shod, but was told the nearest blacksmith was 11 miles distant. Next day before noon it again began to snow, and by night the ground was covered to the depth of six or eight inches; we rode 24 miles and had an evening meeting in a Methodist house, at West Union. The congregation had expected to use the house, but postponed their prayer meeting to accommodate us. We felt that it was a season of divine favor in which the Gospel was preached to attentive listeners.

31st.—Travelled 30 miles through the snow and lodged at a public house. Before leaving, next morning, E. extended salutary counsel to the family.

The 1st of the week and 1st of the year, 1854.—Had two meetings to-day in Pruntytown, County town of Taylor County, Va., one in the Methodist house, at 3 o'clock, P. M., and the other in the Baptist house, at 6½ o'clock, P. M. In this town E. made a visit to a lad of 17 years of age, who had been dangerously injured while wrestling with another boy. He was admonished in the spirit of love. The wife of the landlord had some relatives who had been Friends, which no doubt occasioned her to feel more interest in us, and she was very kind. We had a meeting with the family. When I asked for my bill our host would take no compensation.

Letter from E. N.

PRUNTYTOWN, First mo. 1st, 1854.

My Dear J.:—Another year gone! Where

will this time next year find us? in time, or beyond "the border?" If the latter, I trust it may be in that enclosure where none say, I am sick, nor sorrowful, nor sad! How fervent are my desires at times, that I may no more flag on my journey, but run the race set before me with alacrity and joy of heart, be it long or short. We rode 8 miles this morning to this town, famed for riot and wickedness; and although I was in hopes of getting through without stopping, we have been here since 11 o'clock, and had two meetings. How often I wish some one more able had been put forth. Oh! it is hard work for flesh and blood! There are seasons of abounding, but they are few and far between, and the work is so heavy! It is so difficult to obtain access to the people in such a dark condition, and yet they are willing to listen . . . . . .

C. K.'s Account Resumed.

2d.—Started for Clarksburg, but had not gone more than two miles, when in crossing a gutter, upon the edges of which the ice had accumulated, the front axle broke. There was a house near by where our friends staid until I could return to Pruntytown on a sled and get a new one. 3d. Arrived about noon at Clarksburg and obtained permission to hold a meeting in the Presbyterian house, which proved a season of favor. 4th, had a meeting in the evening at Weston, the County town of Lewis County, in the Methodist house. Elizabeth spoke for some time, but sat down before her mind was relieved. The Minister at once pronounced his benediction, and the people scattered with the feeling that our friend had not been treated with due courtesy. They believed it was because of our testimony against slavery, and their Minister had been told, also, that we were "heretics."

5th.—E., not feeling easy to proceed, we remained in order to have another meeting in the evening. There was a boarder at the hotel where we were staying who had once belonged to our Society, but who had joined the Episcopalians. He was anxious we should have a meeting in the house belonging to that denomination, but the Minister was not willing that a "woman should preach in his church." The congregation who had before accommodated us, were willing that we should again occupy their house, although their Minister did not give his free consent. We accepted their kind offer, and had a good meeting, the power of Truth being felt to prevail over all. We have found a number of persons whose antecedents were in some way connected with Friends. Such are invariably kind and attentive, and many of them express an interest in us, and sympathy with our mission.

7th.—Lodged at a house kept by a widow. Next morning, E. expressed a wish to have a meeting with the people. The landlady offered her house, and at 11 o'clock it was filled to its utmost capacity. Elizabeth addressed them for an hour and a half.

In the afternoon, travelled 16 miles, and put up at a poor tavern, so poor, that we left next morning without breakfast, although we had nine miles to ride before we could get any. Had an evening meeting at Newark, which was satisfactory. E. also had religious service in the family, at whose house we lodged.

10th.—A meeting was held in the Courthouse at Elizabethtown, in which our friend was greatly favored. In the morning when I called for our bill, the landlord said it was paid. I asked, in what way? He said the people of the town had paid it, because they thought it was right.

11th. Rode through rain and mud, and stopped at a house, the occupant of which owned, we were told, 1200 acres of land—yet he and his two daughters lived wretchedly. The teakettle sat before the fire without a lid, the tongs had but one prong, and other things were in a like dilapidated condition. There are not many slaves in this immediate district, but the effects of the system is to be seen and its spirit felt almost everywhere.

12th. Held a meeting in the Court House at Ripley, the county town of Jackson Co., but Elizabeth's mind was not relieved. 13th. E. in bed with a severe cold. The houses are very open, and not unfrequently the windows need the glazier. Last night I counted seven broken panes in one window in the Court House, and the people are not at all particular to shut the doors after them. 14th. E. still very poorly, and does not feel clear of this place.

15th. First day. We had two meetings in the Court House to-day which were tolerably comfortable.

16th. The roads were *very* bad, we just escaped an upset. Immediately ahead of us were three men with a three horse team. The horses had fallen upon the ice and were loosened from the wagon, but the ground was so slippery they could not get up. The only way to relieve them was to roll them over and over to one side and down a bank into the mud. This was a steep hill with sloping sides; the water from the springs had run over the road and frozen, and the late rains had made it as smooth as possible. After the men had removed their wagon out of the way, I asked if we could get up? They answered very decidedly, "No! that nothing living could go up there." Our horses had been rough-shod the day before, and I had a hope that we would have less difficulty on that account, and we did accomplish it in safety, and were truly thankful for it. As it was near night we looked about us for some place of shelter. We had been told of one not far off, where the people sometimes accommodated strangers, but when we applied they thought they could not take us in. I plead with them, for it was raining fast and we knew not where to go, still they declined. I turned away with a heavy heart, but had not gone far when one of them called and said, "you may come, we will do the best we can for you." The house had but one room—in size about 16 by 20 feet. It contained two beds and a weaver's loom, and in it the cooking as well as the eating was done. After we had been there about fifteen minutes, the men we left on the hill came to see if I would take my horses and draw up their wagon, as in it they had venison and other things which they did not like to leave out in the rain all night. Remembering we had left our homes for the good of our fellow-men I could not refuse them. I have described our reception room. The sleeping apartment was some yards off, and to reach it we were obliged to go through rain and mud. It was about the same size as the one we had left, but had no windows. There were three beds, and two women, four rough looking men and myself to occupy them. I think we were as thankful for that night's lodging as for any other. As we were the first who came our horses were sheltered, but four others were hitched to trees, and stood all night half knee deep in mud and water. 17th. Started early, as we had the Pocatalico river to cross. We found, to our great regret, that owing to the rain and the melted snow, it was impossible to ford it. The boat had broken loose and gone down the river, so that nothing remained for us but to wait till the waters abated. We found a house which had windows, but its inmates, in common with many of their neighbors, appeared to lack many of the comforts of life. Many of the people of these counties are ignorant and indolent; one-third of the men, and a still greater proportion of the women, are unable to write their names. The blighting effects of slavery are seen all over the land, which would yield abundantly if properly cultivated. 19th. With the assistance of a person who had formerly lived at the North we drove through the river, the water coming within three or four inches of running into the carriage; but we got through safely, dangerous as was the passage, and we felt grateful for the favor. We then rode sixteen miles over a very bad road to Charlestown. Put up at a Temperance Hotel, which, to our surprise, we found to be a very poor one. The proprietor seemed kind, and soon after breakfast next morning, when he was told we wished to have a meeting he met the proposal with energy; he was an active member of the Methodist Society, and we had a large and satisfactory meeting. On our way from meeting were out in a severe thunder shower.

Letter from E. N.

CHARLESTOWN, 1st mo. 20th, 1854.

My Dear J.:—I have made several unsuccessful attempts to write to the loved ones left behind, who are now far, far distant—separated by mountains high and towering—hills still more difficult of ascent—streams of the Kanawha and Pocatalico, some of which it has seemed as if we had ventured upon at a risk of life, and roads almost impassable, with accommodations sometimes so poor as to be beyond the pen to describe! But now that the cloud is somewhat less dense I hope to succeed in imparting information that may cheer and comfort. Before I proceed further let me say, that although the clouds have been sometimes dark and portentous, yet there has always been a glimmering of light from the "polar star" sufficient to direct us, so that we have received a certain evidence that our course, however difficult, was the one appointed by Him whose promises fail not.

I will not describe the past—*that* I shrink from—but will give a little sketch of what has opened before me. You may have heard of a letter written to W. W. Longstreth, and this will have prepared you to hear of a prospect, which although it had passed again and again before the view of my mind ere I left home, yet it had been treated as a thought not to be entertained. During the first four weeks of my journeyings it frequently presented, but was dismissed as a guest upon which I could bestow no attention. But at last the time came when the presentation was so imperative, that it was not in the power of my mind, with all its holds of defence, to turn it aside, except with the reservation, that after other claims which seemed to have a prior right had been attended to, this should receive the consideration its weight demanded. I cannot depict to you the conflicts which day after day and night after night were produced by the prospect of going to New Orleans. I felt I must either yield, or give back and become a blank in both the visible and invisible creation. It was therefore cause of great thankfulness in this hour of extremity to recur to W. W. L.'s visit and offer. So that when I felt I could no longer withhold a knowledge of the concern, I wrote to him, but have as yet received no answer, nor do I expect one until we reach Maysville. When I wrote to W. I fully believed that E. N. C. would feel herself excused from going farther, but felt no liberty to say a word to her about it. Since then she has written to a friend giving this impression, and I feel now, that if no sister-spirit feels she can sacrifice all that will be required in the prosecution of so arduous an undertaking, and not only so, but can render such aid as a sympathetic spirit can yield, I shall most certainly be at liberty to return with C. and E. I know not upon whom the lot will fall, neither am I anxious, but can say now, and oh! may I not have the bitterness of death again to pass through after expressing it, that I am resigned either to go or return. But these meetings! Oh that some one might be sent to aid in their laborious exercises! I have a heavy cold and have been quite poorly with it, but E. and C. both keep well, which I have esteemed a great favor. In testing the matter I have often felt that I would rather suffer than to see either of them do so. The meetings we have had for some time past have been seasons of such deep wading, as to yield an undoubted evidence that the stream cannot rise higher than the fountain. So where the "seed" is, there must the servant be so far as is necessary to be made acquainted with the nature of the food convenient to hand forth. . . . . . .

Diary Continued.

31st.—"Crossed the Big Kanawha River on a boat propelled by four horses. Our road was along the river, and the streams emptying into it from the surrounding country were much swollen, and there being no bridges, we could not cross them. We stopped to consider what we should do. Then Elizabeth informed us that she had not felt her mind clear of Charlestown, but she had hoped to be able to pass on. She had felt that after crossing the river, if it were not right for us to proceed, the way would be closed. To our humbling admiration we found this to be the case. We returned and put up at the Kanawha Hotel. This caused a great conflict, but we succeeded much better than we expected in the attempt to hold a meeting for the colored population. The Methodists were willing we should have their house, and proposed that the colored people should occupy the floor, and the white people the galleries. This plan was carried out, and the meeting was a favored one. There were many of the first-class present in whom could be witnessed much Christian feeling. It is said some of the slaves are kindly treated and are taught to read and write. E's feelings were particularly enlisted for some old men whose hands bore evidence of hard labor, but whose withered flesh and hoary locks proclaimed their earthly pilgrimage nearly over. The countenances of these, though subdued, yet bore an expression of religious fervor. We were obliged to remain till the 23d on account of the swollen streams. We then started for Barboursville, 40 miles distant. The roads were very rough and the weather very cold.

We lodged on the way at the house of a slaveholder, whose wife talked much of her kindness to her colored people, and appeared to think if they were well clothed and fed, that there was no sin in holding them as property. She spoke of the slave *trader* as being worse than a thief or robber, and when I told her I had never heard an abolitionist use stronger language than she had, she was surprised and did not understand how that could be. Strange indeed that a rational being should conclude that food and clothing could atone for the withholding of the precious boon of liberty! Elizabeth had religious service in this family. 25th.—In the evening had a meeting in the Methodist house, which was satisfactory. 26th.—We were preparing to leave in the morning, when a man called to see us and said they did not want to get rid of us, but he "thought there was a prospect of another break-up of the roads, and at the last thaw the stage stuck fast and it took three yoke of oxen to pull it out of the mud." This was not very encouraging, but we reached the Guyandotte in safety, although it rained all day and was too stormy in the evening to have a meeting.

27th.—Had a meeting in the Methodist house, but E's mind continued under an exercise under which she was as one in bonds, and there was no liberty to proceed."

One of E. N's letters was dated from this place, from which the following extract is taken:

GUYANDOTTE, First mo. 28th, 1854.

. . . In coming here we stopped at Barboursville, where we had to stay two days to obtain a meeting, but it was one of those opportunities that compensated for all through which we had to pass. In consequence of the want of education and the right exercise of their mental powers, the people through this district of country lack enterprise. Although there is often a manifestation of kindness, yet their inertness stands in the way of self-denial even in little things. There are exceptions, it is true, but it is not unusual for Charles to be obliged to harness his horses and do all that is required in getting the carriage ready, and then have a full bill presented as if it had been done for him. I sometimes think that C's example will be a benefit to them in various ways. We came to this place on Fifth-day, when it rained as fast as I ever saw it. We were under the necessity of staying till Sixth day evening in order to have a meeting, and greatly to my disappointment we are still bound here. We are at a comfortable Temperance house, where the presiding minister has his home. When I found I could not leave without an effort for another meeting, Charles talked with him about a suitable place. He told him he was engaged to go from home to preach a funeral sermon, and that opened the way for us to-morrow. I hope we may be able to leave here in the afternoon. The waters are so high that we shall be obliged to take passage on board of a boat on the Ohio, which lies close to us. The running of these boats is very uncertain, so we cannot tell when we shall get off. We have not heard from home for more than five weeks, and you cannot wonder that there are times when the heart becomes faint under some of the privations endured. We are anxious to reach Maysville, where we expect to find letters. This has been a long day, and there has been ample opportunity for reflection. But for an all-absorbing sense, that I know nothing as I ought to know, I should suspect that a state of indifference was closing the avenue of feeling, but I believe, this sense of nothingness, if properly understood, will direct to a source whence a sufficiency will be derived to sustain life. Paul declared that in all states he was content, he knew "how to be abased and how to abound." . . .

Diary Continued.

"As we proceed on our journey the states of the people occasion greater suffering. So heavy is the moral atmosphere, that for some time past we have not been able to take a clear, full breath. Those who have not travelled under such a concern, cannot realize what individuals pass through who are brought into close sympathy with the spiritual condition of their fellow-men, who have chosen to serve mammon rather than a God of justice, of mercy, and of love. Still I have never for a moment doubted the propriety of our coming, nor the authority of the mission. 30th.—Crossed three streams to-day; the banks of them were all dangerous, so that the women preferred walking up, muddy as they were, to riding. The Big Sandy River divides Virginia and Kentucky at this place. Passed through Cattlesburg, Ky., about noon. E. felt a weight upon her spirit, but said nothing about it until we had gone about a mile and a half, and were informed we could proceed no further on account of the height of the streams, over which there were no bridges. We turned about and reached Cattlesburg in safety, notwithstanding the dangerous condition of the roads, and held a meeting in the evening in the Methodist meeting house.

31st.—As we could not proceed further by land, the horses and carriage were placed on board of a steamboat and sent to Maysville, Ky., and we took passage for Greenupsburg, the county town of Greenup. This county is rich in iron ore—there were 12 or 14 furnaces in blast at that time.

2d mo. 1st.—This evening had an appointed meeting, and as usual, were indebted to our Methodist friends for a house. Peace was the reward. Our dear friend's mission has seemed like the ushering in anew of the Gospel dispensation of "Glory to God in the highest, on earth peace, good-will to men." She has quoted largely from the Scriptures, especially from the precepts of the blessed Jesus and his Apostles, showing that if these were practised, they would have the effect to remove all the evils which are abounding in the world. I believe, from the testimonies borne by Elizabeth, she clearly foresaw the desolation that would follow a refusal to liberate the captive by peaceable means. Our worthy Friend, Isaac Parry, remarked, when he heard of E. Newport's concern to visit the South, "I highly approve of it, for I believe it will be one more visitation of mercy to that people, and if they do not bow in mercy, they will have to bow in judgment."

2d.—Arrived at Maysville about 8 o'clock, P. M., where we met our friends Lydia and

William W. Longstreth, who purpose accompanying E. Newport to New Orleans. E. N. Clinger and I feeling released, we proceeded by steamboat to Pittsburg. From that city we travelled homeward on the pike and reached the city of Philadelphia in about eight days."

In conclusion, C. Kirk says: "Had it not been that we had continued evidence of divine care, and that the Good Spirit was ever near to aid us, it would have been impossible for us to have endured either physically or spiritually the trials through which we had to pass."

Neither Wm. W. nor Lydia Longstreth have in their possession a particular account of the religious labors of E. N. while they were with her. From their private letters and a few notes kept by L. L., it appears that, so far as the way opened for the prosecution of E.'s concern, it was faithfully performed. L. L.'s mind was prepared for this service in rather a remarkable manner.

As she was walking in a part of the city distant from her home, she was forcibly impressed, as if she had heard an outward voice, that she would receive a note from her brother, W. W. L., acquainting her with his prospect of going to New Orleans with E. Newport, and asking her to accompany them. She had had no intimation of W.'s intention. In a day or two the note came, and she felt that she could not do other than accede to the proposal.

As has already been stated, W. and L. met with E. N. and her companions on the second of First month, 1854. Those who had been with E. in her arduous labors thus far, turned homeward, and the newly formed trio proceeded on their journey with chastened spirits. L. L., in her note-book says—"My feelings were indescribable when I landed in Kentucky in view of the importance of the mission."

They took passage for New Orleans in the first-class steamer R. J. Ward. In consequence of the boat being heavily laden it was a tedious journey.

They had, as fellow-passengers, Madame Sontag, her husband, Count Rossi and troupe. The former was social and agreeable.

Lydia writes—"Amid all the gaiety with

which we are surrounded, the mind is bowed under a weight of exercise that presses especially upon E.'s spirit, while brother W. and I, as fellow burden bearers, share it. We are anxiously looking forward to the time of our arrival in New Orleans, and desire that we may be preserved in the path of humiliation which lies before us. We are sometimes cheered with a gleam of hope that we shall be enabled to fulfil the work to the relief of our own minds, leaving the results with Him who waters the plants in due season, remembering the declaration, "Cast thy bread upon the waters and it will be found after many days."

We desire the sympathy and help of the spirits of our friends at home. May they intercede at the throne of Grace that strength and ability may be furnished to go when and where the Master shall require.

Second mo. 10—Opposite Arkansas.—The weather is fine; the river is about 20 feet higher than usual. The planters are plowing; the willow trees have budded and the cattle are pasturing upon the grass, which is fresh and green. When the boat stops, a long plank is all that is needed in landing or boarding the boat."

Letter from E. Newport.

Steamboat—200 miles from Louisville,
Second mo. 6, 1854.

Dearly loved ones:—I have taken the pen to pour forth the feelings of a heart filled with a variety of emotions, occasioned by a struggle to appear cheerful among the multitude, which has cost me the strongest effort of which I was capable; but for the present the victory has been obtained, and once more I feel that I can adopt the language, "Thy will be done;" but the work is arduous, the attainment is small, and there is much in my nature opposed to this continual exposure to the gaze of the curious and the scrutiny into the motive for doing thus and so. What can support but a *constant* reliance upon Him who has sustained me through many deep conflicts and trials?

When did C. and E. reach home?

After they left, I went with W. W. and L. Longstreth to their hotel. On First-day morning arrived at Louisville, where we went on board the largest boat I ever saw. Here was a mixture of all grades of people. I was asked by an elderly lady 'if I had anything good for her to read.' I told her nothing that would interest her, as what we had was an exposition of the views of the Society of Friends. She replied, 'Oh that is what I would like.' After reading some of the books, she said she fully accorded with the belief in the influences of the Good Spirit."

Our friends held a meeting one evening in the Ladies' Cabin, which had been announced by a written notice "that Elizabeth Newport, a minister of the Gospel in the Society of Friends, and her companions will hold a meeting for worship this evening, at 8 o'clock, to which all are invited." E. had not been well and kept her room all day, and until the gong was sounded as a signal that the hour for the meeting had arrived. It was a mixed assemblage of about 100 persons—several clergymen being present, also Madame Sontag and her friends. W. explained the manner of Friends meeting together for the purpose of divine worship—that when gathered they endeavored to turn the mind inward. The Scriptures, in which they believed, testified that whatsoever was to be known of God was man-fest in man. The company were very quiet. E. was favored to explain some points of doctrine to the satisfaction of her hearers, but after speaking about twenty minutes her strength failed and she was obliged to sit down. After a short time she again arose, but had not spoken long before she fainted. As soon as practicable, she and Lydia withdrew to the state-room. W. W. L. thanked the people for their respectful attention, and said that owing to our friend E.'s indisposition the meeting would close. In their joint names he bade them farewell, remarking that, although they would soon part, and never in human probability meet again on earth, yet he hoped they might know a re-union in Heaven. After this opportunity there was an increased interest manifested by the passengers, many of whom had previously been kind and attentive; and next day when they learned that E. was better, they appeared much gratified. They wanted to know more about our Society and its principles.

On the morning of the 12th many of the passengers left at Vicksburg. Some of them expressed their good wishes and their interest in the mission of our Friends, and said they were favorably impressed with their views, so far as they had learned them. The differences of opinion relative to religious subjects, had formed no barrier to their social commingling. Elizabeth felt the first step to be taken, after getting to New Orleans, would be to have a public meeting, and after that to visit some of the families who had been afflicted last season by the yellow fever; but the future was much hidden, and W. advised her not to dwell upon it, as what was immediately before her was fully as much as she could bear, and appeared to be at times more than her physical nature could sustain.

On First-day evening, the 13th of Second month, they arrived at New Orleans, the weather being warm and pleasant.

On Second-day morning William called upon S. F. Ashton, who took him to see his wife. She very kindly went with W. and L. to look for a suitable boarding-house, but all were full. On their return to the hotel, they found that during their absence Jacob Barker, who had heard of their arrival, had called, and left with E. N. an invitation for them to make his house their home. In the afternoon he escorted our women Friends thither, greatly to their relief, not only because it was a remarkably pleasant place, but the exchange from a hotel life and from the idle gaze of the curious, was especially grateful, and was a favor they felt could not be over-estimated. In writing to her family, L. L. says: "We have met with some kind friends, which is very grateful to us, but we know right well that our strength and support must come from our Heavenly Father, and to His will we desire to give our undivided attention. This leads us into close baptisms. I can bear but a small part of the weight and exercise that presses upon E.'s spirit, but brother W. helps to bear her up, he being brought under the same feeling. We are desirous that what is done here may be done under Divine guidance—that the seed sown may be left to be watered by the Divine Hand, and that all may be to His glory. I want my dear children to be watchful and careful, that the enemy does not sow tares in my absence, that I may not have to question leaving them in order to discharge an apprehended duty."

"Jacob Barker has the most pleasant house of any that I have seen in this city. His wife is in very delicate health, on account of which they have our sincere sympathy. The kindness we receive could not be exceeded. J. D. Marsh and wife have shown us considerable attention. Through the courtesy of J. D. M. and S. F. Ashton brother W. was introduced to some prominent members of the Methodist Society, who used their influence, and obtained permission for the use of their meeting-house in which to hold an evening meeting. The house was new, and a very large one, but the evening was stormy, and the assembly was rather small. Many of those present were colored persons. W. W. L. writes, "E. gave them a very good discourse, treating principally upon the Christian doctrines peculiar to our Society. After she closed, I expressed our acknowledgements for their quiet attention, and informed them that the minds of my sisters were drawn to visit, in the love of the Gospel, such of the sick and afflicted as might desire to see them. When the meeting closed, persons of respectable standing in the community waited to speak with us, one of whom accompanied us to the lodgings of E. and L., and made arrangements for visiting the House of Refuge for girls. So far as we could observe, all who were present were satisfied with the religious exercises of the meeting, and we can safely say that we have as yet met with nothing but kindness; even our fellow-passengers on the boat from Louisville to this place seemed unwilling to drop our acquaintance, and when we meet in the street stop for a talk."

Of the appointment next day L. L. says: "We were at the House of Refuge for girls under 16 years of age. Our feelings were deeply interested. E. made a suitable address, directing them to that principle within them which reproves for doing wrong and comforts for doing well. I, afterward, arose with the invitation of Jesus, 'Suffer little children to come unto Me and forbid them not,' then added a few sentences, which was a relief to my mind, and which I left with them as a testimony of my love to encourage and strengthen them in well-doing.

Our work is not done here, when it is we shall probably go to Montgomery, Ala. I hope the Good Spirit is at work preparing some one to join us, if it is right that we continue to labor in this South land. If not, I trust we may return with peaceful minds to our beloved homes. At times the heart is full to overflowing, when I feel the responsibility and accountability I am under to my Heavenly Father, who has given me all that I have, with life, breath and being. I know He can take care of me in the midst of dangers. He has given me also to feel this language, 'Whithersoever I send you I will go before and prepare the way for you.'

He has indeed prepared the way for us, showing us our path, and at times strewing it with flowers, the rich perfume of which refreshes and cheers us onward in the fulfilment of manifested duty. Wherever our lot has been cast, we have found kind and sympathizing friends, whose countenances have given us the encouragement of which we have stood so much in need.

It is exceedingly grateful to know, that although far separated from our beloved families and friends, yet there are hearts that beat with warm sympathy for our little band. I do not think we have been sent here because of its being the worst place of all others, and hope our coming may not deter any, but desire that such as are called may be ready, at the Master's bidding, to gird on the armor and enter into the service which He has designed for them. May grace, mercy and peace rest upon each of us."

The daughter of W. W. L., in writing to her father, expressed a fear that he might receive bodily harm, because of E. N.'s views in regard to slavery. He replied, "If Elizabeth keeps to her gift in the Gospel, and so far I am satisfied on that point, she will be preserved from saying or doing anything that will involve us in peril. The whole journey so far has been one of no ordinary trials."

Our friends made a few family visits in the city of New Orleans, greatly to their satisfaction. E's mind was drawn toward one or two planters who resided on the borders of the Mississippi river.

When they acquainted their friend J. B. with this concern, he at once offered to go with them. On board the boat they met with E. Lawrence, a planter, to whom Jacob introduced them.

In conversation with L. Longstreth, it was discovered that one of her daughters had gone to the same school, near Philadelphia, with a sister of his. He was very friendly and invited them to his house. They being thus cared for, J. Barker, after going about ten miles, felt easy to return home. Of this visit E. Newport gives the following account in a letter written on board the boat as they were on their way to Mobile:

LOWER MISSISSIPPI RIVER,
30 miles below New Orleans.

. . . We visited E. Lawrence, a planter, who is also a U. S. Senator. He had just returned from Washington. His wife is a lovely woman, who is as earnestly desirous of fulfilling her duties as any one with whom I ever met. They live about 40 miles above New Orleans.

On First-day morning we had a meeting with E. L. and his family, and in the afternoon one with the slaves, about 160 in number. As the wife was in the practice of gathering their colored people on First-day, P. M., we proposed to her to pursue her usual plan. It was really affecting to see one so young read, kneel and pray, and then sweetly unite her voice with her people in anthems of song and praise to the one eternal Father, who has made of one blood all nations of the earth.*

At the close of our meeting they came and shook hands with us, and assured us that they were acquainted with the "spirit within," to which we had called their attention, as a Guide,—a Comforter in suffering; and which could alone give an assurance of an entrance into that city where small and great meet together, and the servant would be *free.* Poor creatures! how my heart aches for them in their servile degradation! and for their masters too, under *their* sense of suffering and

*In talking with one of the old men, E. N. remarked that it was very grateful to her to find their mistress was in the habit of mingling with them for the purpose of divine worship. He replied, "she always does, and her mother did so before her."

responsibility! But little can be done; the mere sight of us brings before them our testimony against slavery, and arouses a sense of the injustice connected with the inhuman system. They sometimes advance and answer their own arguments while we sit in silence; and although we can see that they endeavor by every effort in their power to sustain their positions, these are so futile that they often wind up in direct contradiction to what they said in the beginning. On our return to New Orleans we were kindly met by our friend, J. Barker, who is now with us on our way to Mobile. I have suffered much under a prospect of further service, but now feel relieved, and if this continues, I shall press on homeward—nothing can keep me but a return of the same binding obligation.

Extracts from L. L——'s Notes.

18th.—' E. Lawrence was met at the landing by his family who gave him a warm greeting, after a temporary absence, and extended to us a cordial welcome. It appeared to me that I could breathe more freely after leaving New Orleans. The oranges were hanging thickly upon the trees which formed a hedge around the house. There were other trees which bore sweet and delightful fruit. The weather was very balmy and pleasant. Our chamber was fragrant with orange blossoms, and by putting the hand out of the window we could almost touch the trees laden with flowers and fruit in varied stages, from the petals just fallen to the ripened orange. Next morning was rainy, and the soil being such as to forbid travelling in wet weather, we were relieved from the unpleasantness of feeling that we were preventing the family from attending, as was their custom, their place of worship, six miles distant.

E. L. was a sugar planter, and gave us much information in relation to the manufacture of that article. I visited the "sugar-house" and found the art was brought to great perfection. We also visited "the nursery," a long building, where the mothers who worked in the fields brought their little children for the day, each having its cradle and sauce-pan of rice. Their food was prepared by "Old Aunty," who fed and took care of them. We looked into the "cook-house" too, where each family received its rations ready for eating—thus saving the weary people the time and trouble of grinding corn and making bread when they should be resting and sleeping."

L. L.'s account of the religious opportunities with the family and with the slaves, is similar to that given by E. N., except that she alludes more fully to E's exercises as having been very appropriate and satisfactory. A brother of E. L.'s wife lived near, and though young and unmarried, had many slaves, which were his by inheritance. L. says "we were told that he was grieved with the practice of holding his fellow-men in bondage, and felt the responsiblity so great, that he rarely left them, but devoted himself to the good of his people, doing what he could to make them comfortable. Information has been received that not long after our visit, this young man not only manumitted his slaves, but provided for them. A call was made upon the sister of our host, who had married a planter, and who sensibly felt the injustice of unrequited labor. In these three families slavery existed in its least offensive aspect.

21st.—Having freely handed forth what was required, there was liberty felt to depart, which we did under deep feeling, and with an earnest expression of gratitude from our friends for the visit. The previous night had been one of watchfulness, lest the boat in which we were to return to New Orleans should pass without our hearing it. The morning was bright and we could tread the deck with the peaceful retrospection that we had faithfully performed our duty. Our progress was slow, and we did not reach the city till about 3 o'clock in the morning. Feeling released from further service in this place, we made some parting calls in company with J. Barker and wife, and after dinner bade adieu to New Orleans, and rode four miles in the cars to the steamboat on Lake Ponchartrain, where we had good accommodations.

A short time previous this boat had collided with another steamboat, in consequence of which our captain was apprehensive that he would be arrested, and therefore, as we neared a particular point, he secreted himself. When dinner was ready the 'waiter' asked brother W. to take the head of the table as the Captain was absent. That W., a Friend, and known to be opposed to slavery, should have been invited to preside at a long table, when there were many other gentlemen from the adjacent States, was more than we should have expected in a country where Friends were looked upon with a jealous eye.

On arriving at Mobile, our friend, J. Barker, who had accompanied us thus far, escorted us to the "Battle House," a large and fashionable hotel. We were detained here till four o'clock next day, and were subject to the gaze of the curious and the remarks of the less polite, so that when the time came we most cheerfully took our departure. The banks of the Alabama river are lined with woods; the water was turbid and unusually high, so that some of the trees were immersed up to their branches. The foliage of the willows was about half-grown, and trees resembling the judas tree were in full bloom; the blossoms of many others were bright, and the live oak and cedars were perfectly green. Occasionally, a high bluff, from 80 to 100 feet, rises from the river, and at Clairborn, a flight of steps with a roof over it, is the means of ascent to the top of the bank.

26th, First-day. — We arrived at Montgomery, distant from Mobile 420 miles. The road to the Exchange Hotel was so rough that we were apprehensive that the omnibus would be overturned. The freshet had rendered the bridge dangerous over a creek, and we were obliged to alight and walk some distance in the mud, but the soil being sandy, it was less objectionable than it might otherwise have been. We proceeded to West Point that night by railroad, and when once seated in the car, we were comparatively comfortable. Upon reaching there next morning at 6½ o'clock, we were told that we should be obliged to await the subsiding of the waters of the Chatahoochie river, which covered the ground to a considerable depth on both sides of the bridge.

2d mo. 28th, 1854.—Being now able to pass over the river in safety, we started at 8 o'clock, A. M., for a six miles ride in the stage, and then to take the cars for Augusta. Several of our fellow-passengers had also been detained by the freshet; among them were Capt. Boylan and his daughter, from Raleigh, N. C. He was an editor, and had a plantation on the Yazoo river, where they had been making a visit. They seemed disposed to join our little company, and we subsequently became much attached to them. A widow lady also manifested her kindly feeling and kept near us. Her home was in the South, but she had spent considerable time in Philadelphia at one period of her life, and had a decided preference for the Northern manner of living. We had much conversation upon the testimonies of Truth, as held by Friends in general, as well as that of slavery. She freely acknowledged her dislike to the peculiar institution of the South, and heartily wished the country was clear of the abomination. At parting, she expressed her unity with us, and her sympathy with the service in which we were engaged. A gentleman who resided near Baltimore, and who had been South on account of the death of his father, offered us the services during the journey, of a colored woman who had been his father's nurse. He was taking her and her little boy to his house, that they might be more comfortable than they would have been in their former home. We of course did not require attention of that kind, but we had many friendly talks with the poor woman, in which E. gave her a great deal of excellent counsel, that, if heeded, will have a tendency to soften the trials incident to her condition. She was earnest that we should *buy* her, but was told that all that we could do for her, was to desire her freedom with that of her people.

The usual way of mending roads in this country, is by "corduroying" them in the worst places. The mud was deep, but we arrived at the station in good time. When the cars came, they brought a number of slaves bound for New Orleans; their overseer was a man of unpleasant exterior. Although the system compels those who hold slaves to be familiar with persons of his caste, yet they profess to abominate them, and are ashamed of such intercourse. Reached La Grange at 12 o'clock, and stopped to dine at a neat looking house by the road-side. The country through which we passed is extremely poor. At 4 o'clock, P. M., arrived at Atlanta, rested for two hours, then proceeded to Stone Mountain, where we had supper, and prepared for spending the night in the cars. It was a clear evening, and we could see the mountain rising abruptly to a great height. It is composed of granite, and on the top was a tower. It is a place of resort in warm weather. Before day-light next morning, we came to Augusta, Ga.

Stopped at Aiken for breakfast. The house stands on a hill, and is a handsome building and well calculated to accommodate many boarders. Weary of waiting among the crowd, whose curiosity seemed insatible, E. N. proposed our taking our seats in the car which was standing near. We had been there but a short time when E., upon looking up, saw the car was on fire; it had caught from the stovepipe, and but for a timely discovery the damage might have been much more serious. When the fog, which had been dense, fell, it turned to frost,—a peculiarity of this hilly region.

At the junction of the Wateree and Congaree rivers, the country was overflowed to the extent of two miles. The waters ran rapidly, and the embankment with the tressel work of the road was carried away for the space of about fifty feet. A boat was provided to transfer the passengers and baggage, but as it would not accommodate more than nine persons at one time, it was slow work. When all were ferried over, we found there was but one passenger car and a baggage car attached to the locomotive; these were to convey quite a retinue to Columbia. Here we decided to spend a day, as it was doubtful whether we could proceed on our journey until the freshet abated. Through this pleasant place I was escorted by C. Boylan, regardless of my friendly garb, which rendered me conspicuous.

Arrangements were made to convey the passengers to Camden, and to avoid the inundations we rode fifty miles. Losing our way, we were obliged to procure a guide, who took us over a road that was not so good as the one we should have taken. One of the horses gave out, and we were compelled to sit in the carriage, in a pouring rain, and see the conductor pass on and leave us. One of the passengers went on horseback to request him to send us another horse, which, when it came, would not pull. In a short time we were agreeably surprised to see a gentleman with three buggies and a baggage-wagon coming toward us. We hailed him, and he lent us a mule, and we proceeded in better spirits. When we arrived at the ferry the evening was fast closing around us, and a fog hung over the river, which I feared would prevent the boatman from seeing the landing, and there were seven vehicles besides several horses to be taken over. The water covered the ground for the distance of half a mile. The ascent from the river was very steep, and the earth being completely saturated, the horses could not draw us up the hill. We alighted, and with the assistance of an extra horse the empty carriage was brought to the top. Had it not been for the little light emitted by the moon and the white sand which helped us to distinguish the way, our ride would have been a dismal one. After going about five miles, and stopping twice to fasten on the "breast-pole," we reached Camden in the rain about 8 o'clock in the evening. Engaged our room and ordered supper, for we had taken no refreshment through the day except a light lunch. It was 9 o'clock before the other passengers arrived, and sleep being more desirable than food, we retired, anticipating a long night in which to rest; but at 5 o'clock in the morning we were called, and told the cars would leave at 6 o'clock. We hurried on our clothes, and found that the omnibus was waiting. Breakfast was out of the question, although we had eaten no supper. We rode to Middletown, and were then four miles from the next train of cars, which was prevented from making a connection with the road at this place in consequence of the tressel work over a marsh or swamp being either carried away or inundated. While waiting for wagons to carry the baggage and mails, a nice vehicle drove up to the door; the owner not having arrived, brother W. engaged the man to take Elizabeth, Catharine and myself over to the railroad. By this means we escaped a heavy rain, being sheltered in a very good house, occupied by a single gentleman, an old colored woman and her grandson, a child of eight years of age. When we applied for breakfast, we were told that they did not keep a house of entertainment, but as we had been fasting they would accommodate us; and we were furnished with a good meal. The car in which we travelled was an exceedingly dirty one, although the conductor had a colored man to "clean it in compliment to the ladies."

At Raleigh, our friends Catharine Boylan and her father left us for their home. We missed them greatly, for they had not only been agreeable companions, but they had relieved us from a good deal of unpleasantness which would have attended our novel appearance in that country, and were instrumental, too, in procuring many little comforts which we would not have had if there had been no one acquainted with the habits of the people to speak for us. In the conversations that occurred on the subject of slavery, these friends frequently expressed their sense of the responsible position in which they were placed, and the daughter, especially, wept bitter tears in speaking of the poor slaves she so longed to liberate. When we came to the river we crossed in a little boat by moonlight, a few at a time. Arrived at Petersburgh in the night. Next morning, when we reached Richmond, we expected to have time to breakfast, but found the cars already in motion, so that we contented ourselves with the remnant of the lunch, which we had been urged to take by a person who had been very kind to us in the difficulties through which we passed on account of the great freshet in Carolina. Took the boat for Washington. Passed Mount Vernon while at dinner. From W. went to Baltimore in the cars, arrived there at 7 o'clock P.M., and reached Philadelphia at midnight."

In the 4th mo., 1854, E. Newport returned the minute granted her for the Southern visit, with the information that, so far as the way had opened for its performance, it had been productive of sweet peace, and she could feelingly adopt the language of the Psalmist, "Return unto thy rest, Oh my soul, for the Lord hath dealt bountifully with thee."

In the 11th month, E. N. applied for a a minute to visit the meetings of Salem Quarter and to appoint meetings as duty might require. The concern was united with and Mary H. Schofield (Childs) and Wm. Griscom joined in the service. This labor of gospel love gave satisfaction to those visited and to the friends who accompanied her. Remarkable instances of a clear perception of individual states were of frequent occurrence, and it was believed that the seed sown would bring forth fruit in due season. E.'s mind was drawn to call on a friend who lived in a small village near a river which it was their purpose to cross in order to attend an appointed meeting in the evening. When they arrived at the house it seemed a most unsuitable time for a visit. The person was particularly engaged, and several of his neighbors were assisting him. He however came forward and they were invited to alight. In a short time dinner was ready and the Friends and neighbors all sat down together, and before they left the table, E. gave expression to her feelings, and it was an interesting opportunity.

In consequence of a strong wind they were unable to get over the river and were obliged to ride 8 or 10 miles farther than they would otherwise have done. This was the more trying as the weather was *very* cold and the roads not good. Passing through a town they called at a store to purchase a buffalo robe to shield the women from the piercing wind. The owner of the store coming out to the carriage to speak to them, Elizabeth's feelings were at once arrested. After he left, she said to W. G., why didst thou bring that man out here? W. replied, he is a very clever man, and—E. checked him, saying, do not tell me anything about him. When they arrived at the place where they designed to lodge, they felt very much discouraged about the evening meeting, as the cold was increasing and the mill dam over which they had to pass, was covered with ice, making the road dangerous. But upon reaching the meeting-house they found it nearly filled, a number having ridden several miles notwithstanding the inclemency of the weather. Elizabeth was greatly favored in testimony; addressed an individual state, describing his life as if she had known him intimately. After meeting W. G. was told that this was the case by a friend who had not fully sympathized with E. N.'s peculiar gift, but as he heard her, his doubts had been removed. He knew she had had no opportunity of knowing anything of the individual in question, except from internal impressions. Next morning the name of the storekeeper, to whom allusion has been made, was incidentally mentioned, when E. requested that nothing should be said about him before her. W. G. was convinced that it would be right to offer this individual a visit. They did so, and were most kindly received. The wife was a member of our Society, but the husband was not. E.'s concern was principally for the latter, whom she encouraged to be faithful to the divine monitor within. After a pleasant salutation for all, they parted under the feeling that they had been rewarded for obedience to this requisition.

In the summer following, E. N. wrote to W. Griscom, inquiring if in a neighborhood she designated, there might be found a class of persons which she described, who were not members, but professors of our Society, and if so, whether he and his wife would bear her company in a few family visits. The answer was in the affirmative, and in a few days they entered upon the service. When E.'s concern was mentioned, to the Friend at whose house they had been cordially received, he named a number of individuals living near by, to all of which E. N. answered *no*. She then asked to have other names of which he might think, *written*. After looking over the list a few minutes, she selected those that impressed her. At one house when the family was gathered, the hired people, as is the custom in some places, were also brought in. E. made some general remarks, and then sat in silence a long time, when she quietly gave W. G. to understand, that she could not proceed while a certain person was present. W. soon judiciously effected his withdrawal, after which E. addressed with power, a visitor who came into the room just before the meeting. She opened his spiritual condition so clearly that he felt no doubt as to the authority of her exercise. Thus they went from house to house, the spiritual eye being anointed to discover, not only the heavenly treasure which was laid up in some minds, but "the hidden things of Esau" were also brought to light and testified against in a wonderful manner. In a family consisting of the parents and grown up children, the gospel stream was poured forth until every vessel was filled and every heart was tendered and contrited under the baptizing power of "the Word." A solemn supplication followed, in which access was granted to the throne of grace, and the influence was such, that when E. arose and took her seat, she exclaimed with fervor, "Glory, glory, glory!! Wm. G. says, "it was a most memorable occasion." One of the families visited, soon afterwards became members of the Society of Friends, as E. N. predicted.

On their way home she inquired if they would go near a certain Friend's house? This visit was a remarkable one. E.'s testimony was sympathetic and encouraging, but she clearly foresaw that ere long the Friend would be released from the cares of life, and in this she was not mistaken. In a comparatively short time he was suddenly removed from "works to rewards."

At the Monthly Meeting held Seventh month 19th, 1855, E. N. informed her friends that her mind was drawn in gospel love to the meetings composing Concord Quarterly Meeting, to some families belonging to Goshen Meeting and others remotely situated; and also to appoint meetings as the way might open. Our friend M. M. Evans accompanied her.

Her religious services throughout this visit were attended with many close baptisms. In the Eleventh month she acquainted her friends with an obligation for further service within the limits of Concord Quarterly Meeting. Unity was expressed with her concern and she was encouraged to do what her hands found to do, under the guidance of the divine Spirit.

In the First month, 1856, accompanied by Joseph Walton and M. M. Evans she attended Birmingham Monthly Meeting. A Committee was appointed to make the necessary arrangements for the family visits and she was encouraged to faithfulness in the discharge of her duty. One of this Committee remarks in relation to E. N.'s service that she was favored to clearly see the state of individuals and to address them pertinently, encouraging all to walk in obedience to the manifestations of Truth as revealed to them. Some families who were not members, but who were in the habit of attending Friend's Meeting were also satisfactorily visited. On one occasion, in a family meeting, they sat in silence a considerable time when the opportunity closed without anything having been said, greatly to the disappointment of both parents and children. E.'s mind was exercised but there was no liberty for expression. Some time after this, she met with the parents of this family, when her feelings were awakened with tenderness and sympathy for the husband. In addressing him, she repeated the text, "Except ye be converted and become as little children, ye shall in no wise enter the kingdom of heaven." She alluded to the work that was going on in his soul, which had enabled him to overcome much, and had brought him near the kingdom, and it was her belief, that if he were continually watchful he would be preserved in this simple child-like faith. She had a clear impression that his days were numbered, and that before many months the call would come to him suddenly, but she believed his lamp would be "trimmed and burning." Six months subsequently, this friend retired in usual health; in the night his wife was awakened and found him speechless. He passed away in a very short time.

In another family, Elizabeth's testimony to a young woman was remarkable. She told her that her heavenly Father had entrusted her with precious gifts, and that if she was not willing to come more fully under the operations of His grace, so that they might be strengthened by exercise, she would experience a spiritual death, and that her path would be one of darkness and gloom. The intellectual gifts with which she had been endowed, would be retarded in their growth, until she would at times feel life almost a burden. But if she would be faithful to the revealings of the Holy Spirit, she would come forth as a bright and shining light in the fulfilment of her Christian mission among the spiritually poor, the lame, the halt, and the blind. This young person freely partook of the bitter fruits of rebellion, as predicted by E. N., but there came a time of overwhelming sorrow, occasioned by the removal of a young and beloved sister, and under this suffering she renewed her covenant and soon after yielded to what she felt required of her, and subsequently became an acknowledged minister of the gospel. At a place where there were several children, E. turned to one of the little boys, after a short period of silence, and said, "So my little friend thou wonders what this Quaker preacher comes here for? Well, we have a dear Heavenly Father, and if we love Him we shall be willing to serve Him, and I feel it required of me to visit Friends' families, which is a great trial; and thou too will find that we cannot always do the thing we would like to do. If I mistake not thou wanted to go out to play and not stay with us during the meeting, and had been persuading thy mother to let thee go." She then described his character and urged him to take heed to what he knew to be right, by which he would be preserved from the temptations that surrounded him, and he would be enabled to give up his own will and yield obedience to his widowed mother. When the friends had gone, the little boy asked his mother, why she told the preacher he wanted to go on the ice and not stay to meeting? When assured that she had not said a word about him, he looked surprised and replied, "Well, mother, God must have told her!" At another time E. addressed an individual whom she believed was standing upon the edge of a precipice. She felt the danger to be imminent and urged him to seek for divine strength to enable him to overcome his enemies, saying if he did not, deep suffering and humiliation awaited him. She alluded to his intellectual endowments, which were calculated to make him eminently useful to his fellow men if they were only brought under the operations of divine grace. It was a touching appeal, and it brought conviction with it. Since the death of E. Newport, this person told one of her friends, that all she said to him at that time was true, and if he had heeded her warning he would have been saved bitter suffering.

An obligation rested upon E. N. to attend the funeral of an entire stranger to her. In allusion to the individual she remarked that "he was not taken away in *judgment* but in mercy from the evil to come." Afterwards it appeared that very different views had been advanced from the pulpit the day before. This person had a vendue, and, as he was bringing a horse out for sale, he fell and died immediately. Some of the people who were there said, "This was a judgment because he had spoken too favorably of the horse." Elizabeth knew nothing of the particulars of the case, and her sermon was thought to be a remarkable one.

Letter from E. Newport.

Tenth mo. 4th, 1855.

My dear M:—It was very pleasant to receive so cheerful a letter, and I trust thou wilt endeavor to abide under the "shadow of the vine." This is a probationary pathway for all, but some appear to be less tried by adversities and reverses than others. It is the end, however, that crowns all, and therefore that which we should most strive after should be to hold out, and this will require the exercise of faith and patience. These are twin sisters and one necessarily brings the other into exercise. . . .

It will never do to place ourselves out of the reach of meetings, so that however delightful on some accounts the proposal made to us may be, I must relinquish the thought of it. I live only a day at a time,—this we know is so literally, but the injunction "take no thought for the morrow" applies especially to the life of the inner man, which is so readily affected by outward circumstances!

Still there is a remedy for this pressure in the exercise of that Christian spirit of which the apostle testified—"The life that I now live is by faith in the Son of God"—this is the faith that I feel the need of possessing, and yet it can never be attained but through grace—I sometimes think there is some increase.

. . . It has been a consolation to find thou hast made an effort to attend meeting in the middle of the week. I have felt the necessity laid upon me to encourage young mothers to attend to the pattern shown them "in the Mount," in relation to clothing their little children; and I ardently desire that thou mayst be willing to attend more strictly to that which will place thee upon a more independent footing, and enable thee to carry out thy own convictions, rather than the customs of the world, or the views of others. Thou knowest I am not an advocate for *mere* uniformity, but for simplicity; *true* simplicity consists not so much in cut and color, as in that which is convenient and that does not require an undue amount of time or labor. The guide is before thee, *follow it.* It will not only redeem, but beautify and adorn, and will impart strength to conform to all the requirements of truth. Trust it—it has never led its votaries astray. . . .

E. N.

Bucks Quarterly Meeting and Makefield Monthly Meeting.

At the Monthly Meeting held Twelfth month 18th, 1856, E. N. was granted a minute of concurrence to attend Bucks Quarterly Meeting, and to visit the families of Makefield Monthly Meeting. From Charles Kirk the following account of this visit has been received :

"E. Newport was accompanied by Margaret Hazleton and myself. Having obtained the approval of Makefield Monthly Meeting, we commenced the service of visiting families on the 18th of First month, 1857, the thermometer indicating a temperature of two degrees below zero, and the roads in some places being almost impassable from snow drifts. Rode seven miles in a sleigh facing a very strong north-east wind, and attended their First-day meeting, which was a low, humble season. In the afternoon, amid a severe snow storm, visited several families, and lodged at our kind friend's Joseph Flowers. On the 19th we were completely blocked in, and were unable to make any visits. 20th.—After shovelling snow and breaking the roads, we succeeded in visiting four families, in which individuals were closely and feelingly addressed. 21st.—The opportunities this morning were memorable occasions. E., in speaking to a young man, was very interesting on the subject of reason, telling him it was not sufficient to guide him safely, but that revelation which *had not ceased*, would bring him into a state of peace and happiness. She reminded another of his early convictions, and warned him to take heed to the secret impressions made upon his mind, or he would be landed in ruin. With a third, she was led into close sympathy, believing, if he had followed the revealings of Truth, he would have been a much brighter light than he then was. When we bade this individual farewell, he fully acknowledged the correctness of E. N.'s views. 22d.—Visited several families, and attended the week-day meeting. Dined and had a religious opportunity with our aged Friend Joseph Briggs and family, and in the afternoon made eight family visits. Next day the same number were visited. 24th.—Six families were called upon to-day. A solemn appeal was made to one individual to induce him to apply more earnestly for heavenly oil, lest his lamp should go out and he be left in darkness. 25th—First-day.—Our dear Friend was favored to declare the Truth with much power. Made a number of visits, the labor continuing arduous. 27th.—Eleven families were visited, in each of which the gospel was preached. Several of the opportunities we had to-day were very interesting. Individual states were feelingly spoken to. 28th.—Visited twelve families, in which there were much labor and sweet counsel. 29th.—The presence of the Good Spirit continued with us, and was sensibly felt as we went from house to house. 30th.—This was a hard day, both spiritually and temporally. Visited thirteen families. 31st.—Rained hard, so that we made but two visits. Second month 1st.—Were at Makefield meeting. It was a favored season. Made also several visits.

2d.—Attended Buckingham Monthly Meeting. The language of olden time in relation to those who "killed the prophets and stoned those who were sent to them," was used as an illustration of the disposition to stifle divine impressions and to "quench the spirit;" it was a searching testimony. 3d.—Were at Soleberry Monthly Meeting, a favored meeting. 4th.—Attended Wrightstown Monthly Meeting, in which the gospel was freely preached. In the afternoon visited several families. 5th.—Makefield Monthly Meeting was held at Newtown, at which we were present. The truth reigned. Made a number of family visits and closed our labors within this district, 126 families and parts of families having been visited. Many and deep were the baptisms through which our beloved friend passed in its accomplishment! There were not only spiritual exercises to be endured, but the weather was severely cold, the thermometer at some places standing at 22° below zero. But E. N. was a perfect example of patience and endurance, never complaining of hardships or privations, however great these might be. She was ever mindful of the comfort of her companions, and entered into their feelings to a remarkable extent. On one occasion a friend who was with her being much fatigued with a hard day's journey through rain and mud, concluded that he would not enter into the spiritual exercise of the family meeting, which was held that evening. At the earliest opportunity, E. asked why he withdrew his shoulder and was not at his post? This friend who travelled a great deal with E. N., and was a true "helper" in the peculiar labor frequently required of her, said, that he never afterward dare shrink from the travail of spirit so important on such occasions.

7th, First-day.—Were at Bristol, notice having been given of our intention to attend that meeting. It was a time of divine favor. By a firm reliance on the everlasting Arm, our friend was enabled to fulfil her mission and return home with a peaceful mind.

Genessee Yearly Meeting.

In the Fourth month, 1857, a minute was granted E. Newport to attend Genessee Yearly Meeting and to visit friends and others within its limits. John H. Andrews was her companion and sympathising burden-bearer throughout this visit. Lydia Longstreth was also a fellow-laborer the greater part of the journey. From brief notes kept by J. H. A. and L. L. the following account is taken:

"Sixth mo. 11th, 1857.—Left home to accompany E. Newport in her religious visit to Genessee. We had the company of several Friends who expected to attend the Yearly Meeting. The road through the mountains was truly picturesque. Two of the bridges across the ravines were 130 feet high, and there were four others varying in height from 40 to 100 feet. While the grandeur of the scenery filled us with awe and admiration, we could but marvel at the wonderful capacity of man that could plan and execute a route so circuitous and difficult. At Canandaigua we were met by our kind friend Edward Herendeen, who took us a distance of seven miles to his house, where we received a cordial welcome from his estimable wife Harriet.

On Seventh day, the 14th, attended a meeting of ministers and elders. It was a time of deep feeling, several lively communications were offered; the one from M. Brown gave proof of greenness in old age.

On First-day the house was filled, many attending who were not members. Affectionate addresses were delivered, among them one from E. Newport, in which there was an impressive warning against intemperance, and encouragement given to an individual to do what he could to aid others in resisting the intoxicating cup, which must sooner or later involve its votaries in ruin. At the close of the meeting, notice was given of one to be held, at the request of E. Newport, at that house in the afternoon.

On Second-day the Yearly Meeting convened. There were present many elderly persons, and also a large number of young people, whose appearance was cheering, giving hope for the future. The exercises of the day were in unison one with another. Much was said on the importance of faithfulness to manifested duty. Early in the meeting on Third-day, E. N. expressed a concern to visit men's meeting, which was united with. She had words of consolation for the aged, who had passed through deep trials, and who would shortly be gathered to their eternal rest. Her feelings then flowed toward those who had wandered from the fold, and she exhorted those who were strong to labor with the weak, that all might be brought into the true sheep-fold. She queried if there had not been a disposition to cut off, rather than to restore, and earnestly plead with Friends to do what they could to bring back those who, through discouragement, had left the Society. The power and solemnity which attended her appeal cannot be described. It was sensibly felt by the meeting, and thought to be, by many, peculiarly appropriate to their condition. Our dear, aged Friend, John Watson, seems closely united to us in spirit. On Fourth day a public meeting for worship was held. E. Newport was prevented from attending by indisposition. 16th.—The meeting was large, and a feeling of love and harmony prevailed. Margaret Brown was engaged in a living testimony for all present, and then offered a sweet and solemn prayer for those who were sent forth with a gospel message for the people. Under a precious covering the meeting closed.

Next morning we had a religious opportunity before parting with our friends, in which individual states were addressed. There was deep feeling in bidding farewell to those of whose hospitality we had so freely taken. E. Herendeen took us in his carriage to Canandaigua. From thence we went to Mendon. The country in the neighborhood of Mendon is beautifully picturesque. There is a hill near Friends' meeting-house in the shape of a hay-stack, from the top of which there is a view forty miles in extent. Within the range are the highlands of Canandaigua Lake, and also several villages that are many miles distant.

On Seventh-day quietly rested. On First-day were at Mendon meeting, which was very large and made up of different sects. E. was much favored in testimony. Several Friends called in the evening, and we had an interesting religious opportunity. Next morning made two visits to the sick and infirm, in both of which words of comfort and salutary counsel were offered. In another visit, encouragement was given to attend to the openings of Divine light upon the mind. 23d.—Proceeded to Rochester.

Letter from E. N.

ROCHESTER 6th mo. 23d, 1857.

—— ——

. . . . When I first left my home I felt as a pilgrim in a strange land in which I did not expect to find a sympathizing spirit, but it has proved far otherwise. There are those who remember my being here fifteen years ago with interest, and have manifested it. S. Hoopes will tell you of our meeting and mingling together, which I believe was a mutual pleasure, but she is allowed to return in peace while I am bound here in spirit with the suffering seed, not knowing what will befall me, save that " bonds and afflictions " await me from city to city, and from place to place, still, under the feeling that the " Holy Spirit witnesseth," and the promise continues, " I will go before thee," I have no reason to doubt or to murmur; for truly I have often known " hard things to be made easy and bitter sweet." We arrived at Wm. Cornell's on Sixth-day, where we were so kindly received and our wants so promptly attended to, that a home feeling was soon begotten. Wm. brought us to the residence of P. Frost, where we expect to remain until to-morrow, when we shall leave for Hamburgh to attend the Quarterly Meeting.

I want much to see you all, but must seek after a spirit that will bring resignation, even during these long and distant separations. May the blessing of Him who "tempers the wind to the shorn lamb" be with you. May He guard and protect you from all that would wound the precious life, and may there be an increase of that love which qualifies to bear each other's burdens, and sympathize with each other's cares, and finally prepare for a commingling in the blessed abodes of rest and peace. . . . . . .

E. N.

Narrative Continued.

24th.—Left Rochester in the cars for Buffalo. Passed through the "Indian Reservation," where E. N. had a meeting in 1842. All the Indians are gone except a few families, who were still living upon the land they had purchased back from the "Ogden Company." How sad that these poor people should have been so shamefully treated by the "pale faces!" Reached Buffalo at 10½ o'clock, and took the stage for Hamburg, distant 11 miles. Here we were met by two kind friends with invitations to their houses. We went with John Webster, whose wife gave us a cordial welcome. Next day attended their Monthly Meeting. Elizabeth spoke of the danger of unfaithfulness, and how, by frequently resisting the convictions of duty, the reason *might* become dethroned. We were told there was a case present similar to that described by her. Seventh-day had a religious opportunity with the family with whom we dined, and attended an appointed meeting in the afternoon at Boston; but the people E. wished particularly to see were not present, it being difficult to get the laboring class together during the week, so it is probable we shall have to return to this place.

On First-day morning made a family visit, and rode seven miles to Collins to attend that meeting. The house was filled with all classes of people, who were very attentive. E. spoke for more than an hour with gospel authority; some present thought it a time that would be long remembered. Dined at N. Sisson's, and had a religious opportunity with the family.

Then rode 20 miles, and lodged at J. Webster's. Received a letter from Margaret Brown, in which she expresses a belief that E.'s trust and confidence would continue to be in the Holy One, looking to no other source for help; and that she doubted not her mission was one that would gather the outcasts of Israel and the dispersed of Judah, and would also awaken the lukewarm and careless professor. She added, "With us the fields are white unto harvest. Come soon and tarry long."

30th.—The Preparative Meeting for ministers and elders was held in the morning, and in the afternoon the Select Quarterly Meeting; this was a favored time. The elders were exhorted to be faithful in doing what their hands found to do, with the belief, that labor rightly performed would strengthen the Society, and be instrumental in bringing forth valiants as in the beginning. The Quarterly Meeting next day was a good meeting, in which E. N. had much service.

On Fifth-day the Youths' Meeting was held, which was large. E. was led to speak on

"Modern Spiritualism." The matter was close and plain, and it was a memorable day.*

Sixth-day we rested. On Seventh-day had a meeting at Abbott's Corners, but it being the time of the celebration of American Independence, the people were otherwise engaged, and the meeting was small but satisfactory.

First-day were again at Boston. The house was much crowded, and E. spoke very interestingly for more than an hour. It was thought to be a season of Divine favor. We dined with a person not in membership with

*Another friend furnishes the following in relation to this circumstance: At the Quarterly Meeting on Fourth-day, E. N. alluded to "Modern Spiritualism" in a peculiar manner, so as to lead to the impression that she was a believer in it, and then abruptly stopped. It was the occasion of much uneasiness among Friends, and many inquiries were made of her companion, J. H. A., what it meant. He answered, "I do not know what it means, but be patient, I think it will come out all right." It was a time of much excitement on the subject in that vicinity, and E.'s remarks, with the uneasiness it had occasioned, were freely discussed; so that next day a large number who had embraced those views were present, when E. took up the subject, and commented clearly upon it to the satisfaction of her friends, and to the disappointment of those who had classed her with the Spiritualists.

Friends. E. had a close testimony to leave with him, and directed his attention to that which had in early life pointed out the path in which he should go. In the afternoon held a satisfactory meeting in the house of the Free Will Baptists, where E. had a meeting fifteen years before. We were at the house of a Friend who had a garden of beautiful flowers, in which it appeared as if almost every kind was included. This enclosure was referred to as teaching a moral lesson of the need of watchfulness and care, so that every disposition and propensity of our nature might be rightly trained and kept in order; very close labor. Returned to J. W.'s arriving there at 11 o'clock P. M., having had two meetings, made three family visits, and travelled 24 miles. Next day made several family visits.

7th mo. 7th.—Had religious opportunities with two families this morning, and then went to Spring Brook, and had an appointed meeting. It was small, the men being too busy to attend; but I thought the women, like the one at Jacob's well, might tell the men of what they had heard.

8th.—Made a call upon a young man, not a member. A remarkable time, in which the high position to which he was called was pointed out, and he was told that unless he turned from his present course he could not fulfil his mission. He and his mother manifested much kind feeling. Had a meeting in a Universalists' meeting-house, which was tolerably well attended and was satisfactory. Had a religious opportunity in a family, wherein a Physician was spoken to, and his state portrayed in a remarkable manner.

On Fifth-day were at the public meeting for worship. Next day made a visit to a Baptist minister, and were kindly received. The power of Truth reigned over all, and the testimony was accepted in the love in which it was given. It was one of those visits that cannot be described." Additional particulars of this visit were furnished by our dear Friend, the late Isabella Webster. She says: "E. N. thought she was at liberty, and had expected to leave next morning, but she went to the door, turned toward J. W., and asked if there were not some Friends living in the direction toward which she pointed. He replied there were three families in that direction, nine or ten miles distant. She remarked, 'I must see them;' and added, 'there is something beside for me to do, but I cannot yet see what it is.' After visiting the families alluded to, she asked the Friend at whose house they were, to name over the ministers of a small village near by. He did so, and when he repeated the name of the Baptist minister she said, 'I must see him.' He willingly granted an interview, in which E. told him he had been under an exercise of mind in relation to taking pay for preaching, and that he had felt that he ought to lay the matter before his congregation, but he was hesitating about it. She bore a close testimony in other particulars, which he acknowledged to the Friend who accompanied them was true, and asked him why he had told E. about him. The Friend said he had not done so, that he was not aware of his scruples. On her return she remarked to J. W., 'I found what I had to do, and am now ready to proceed.'"

Letter to M. E. T.

HAMBURG, 7th mo. 13th, 1857.

My Dear M.—We have not been detained by the outward elements, but the spirit has been so bound from day to day that there was no liberty to go forward. It is nearly three weeks since we came to the house of a dear friend, with whom we are now staying, who was one of the first settlers in this country. We expect to leave to-day after dinner. Thy letter was received, and I was glad to hear from you. I hope thou art better. Exert all the care thou canst, first over the mind, as that is the operator. Be slow to act, and when thou dost move, act wisely; be slow to speak and swift to hear the voice of wisdom, then thou wilt increase in understanding and knowledge. The monitor within will most assuredly point out safe stepping stones, and, as thou art careful to observe these, thy progress will be sure, and thou wilt be established upon a firm foundation. Then the bodily and mental powers will become strengthened, and thy last days will be thy best days—yea, even the noon of thy life shall become vigorous if, my precious child, thou wilt only hearken to, and obey the voice of wisdom. This will lead to an attention to that which will exalt the affections, and prepare thee also to take up the cross, even in *very* little things. I have seen this clearly. Since I last wrote, I have passed through much conflict of feeling in view of going farther. You have all passed before the view of my mind, and I have been enabled to petition our Father in Heaven on your behalf, with fervency of spirit. . . . .

E. N.

Narrative Continued.

Made several interesting visits, and in the evening, called upon a person whose health was fast declining. E. had an impressive testimony to leave with him.

11th.—Attended a very large meeting at Hamburg, notice having been given. The Gospel flowed freely. The states of many were ministered unto, and at the close of the meeting, which was 2½ hours long, the feeling was that the work in this place was finished. Many persons came to say farewell, and to express a desire for our preservation. In the afternoon a number called at J. W.'s, which occasioned E. to have three religious opportunities, in which the states of individuals were pointed out to the admiration of those present. Next day took leave of our kind friends, whose house had been our home for nearly three weeks. In the quiet which preceded our departure, E. gave individual counsel and encouragement. J. W. accompanied us to Buffalo, and next morning we took the Lake Shore railroad for Toledo, distant 292 miles, where we arrived at 8 o'clock, P. M.

7th mo. 14th.—Proceeded by "rail" to Adrian, where we procured a coach and rode 2½ miles to Jonathan Harned's. Fifth-day afternoon had a meeting in a school-house, nine miles distant, and afterward had a favored opportunity in a Friend's family. On Sixth-day visited several families. In the afternoon we were out in a violent storm; the lightning was almost incessant, and it appeared as if the wind would overturn the carriage. On Seventh-day we remained quietly with our friends, feeling the need of rest. First-day morning attended Friends' meeting. The labor was hard, but E. was favored. Friends are few in number. One family, who came four miles in an ox-cart, are among the most diligent in attending meetings. On Second-day J. Harned accompanied us to

Toledo. The wife of the Friend with whom we dined, when she learned that our wish was to have a meeting that evening, drove around and invited all the members and professors to meet at their house at 8 o'clock. It was a small, but a very satisfactory meeting. Some Orthodox Friends were present. All were encouraged to a faithful discharge of individual duty. We find wherever we go that Friends take a deep interest in our concern.

On Fourth-day attended the Preparative Meeting of Adrian, and made two visits. One to a Methodist family, who were in great affliction from the loss of a son, aged 19, who was drowned a few days before. He was the oldest of six sons, and had been, his mother said, a dutiful child all his life. We were much pleased with the children, whose conduct bore evidence of the growth of the good seed which had been sown by their parents, who expressed gratitude for the visit. 23d.—Were met at Battle Creek by Jonathan Hart. The desolating effects of discord are sadly apparent in this country. It is a great trial to E.'s sensitive nature, but she is remarkably upheld. May the labor not be in vain.

Attended meeting on First-day, to which many, not members, came. 28th.—This afternoon the select preparative meeting was held, which was small. The monthly meeting was larger, but one end of the house accommodated all. This visit appears like a feast to the dear Friends, who have given us their company at J. Hart's. In the evening held a meeting for the people generally, and the house was nearly full. Made several social visits.

8th mo. 2d.—First-day attended Battle Creek Meeting, and had a meeting also in the Methodist meeting-house. Called at two places, where the visits were acceptable. We were in this neighborhood ten days, and attended six meetings, beside visiting many families. 3d.—Accompanied by J. Hart, left for Jackson, distant 45 miles, which we reached in a little more than an hour. We proceeded to the State Prison at once, arrangements having been made by which we could see the prisoners at their dinner hour. We found about 360 seated in the dining hall. When they had finished their meal, the warden told them to sit still, and a *gentleman* would address them. The Inspectors from different parts of the State were there, many of whom knew nothing about Friends. When E. commenced speaking, all the officers, both male and female, crowded into the aisles until they were filled. As she appealed in pathetic language to those who had seen the error of their ways, many hearts were softened and the tears flowed freely, and when she advised them to look over the past, and see how they had fulfilled their duties as husbands, fathers and sons, some of them sobbed aloud. She next addressed a more hardened class; the message was solemn and impressive. The doctrine was simple and practical, and easy to be understood. The quiet was perfect, and the spectators looked on with amazement. There was one young man whom we had seen on our way to Battle Creek, when the sheriff was taking him to the prison. His was a life-long sentence for burglary, with an attempt at murder. E. addressed him particularly, and he wept aloud — it was deeply touching! After the meeting we were taken outside the door to see the prisoners pass out. They marched in single file, each with his hand placed on the shoulder of the one in front of him, there being about twenty under the charge of one keeper; thus they went to their different workshops. We then visited the female department, and had a satisfactory time with the women, twelve in number, who were sewing under the care of a matron, who was the wife of the chaplain. As we passed through the prison we saw several doors closed. Upon inquiry found their occupants were sentenced for life to solitary confinement, and were allowed to see no one. Their crime was murder in the first degree. E. said if it *could* be allowed, she would like very much to have a door, to which she pointed, opened. The overseer replied, he was a very desperate fellow, and he had no liberty to do so. The superintendent was then applied to, who said it was against the rule--but, like others, having been wrought upon by E,'s discourse, he added, "I will take the responsibility." There were two doors, the outside of wood, and the inside of grated iron. The prisoner came forward to the grated door, and listened attentively to E.'s address. The scene was affecting beyond description. He was a colored man, who had killed another in revenge. We were told that if we would remain till evening, all should be collected in the chapel, but E. felt her mind relieved, and we left for Detroit, where we arrived at 6 o'clock.

Third-day crossed over to Canada, where J. Hart, who had accompanied us 120 miles, left us. Rode in the cars to Woodstock, a distance of 120 miles, and there procured a carriage to take us to Otterville, but E. being very sick, we were obliged to return to W. for the night. The next day E. N. being better, we again started, and arrived at Pickering that evening.

8th-month 7th.—Engaged in the service of family visiting. Our friends encourage us to fulfill faithfully our prosprect.

9th, First-day.—Had a large meeting in Friends' meeting house in the morning, and afterward made a very satisfactory visit. In the afternoon attended an appointed meeting in the village of Pickering, which was composed mostly of other religious professors; it was large and satisfactory.

On Second-day visited two families, and then proceeded by the Grand Trunk Railroad to Bellville, where we went on board of a steamboat. Here we spent the night, and upon arriving at North Port, hired a conveyance to Jacob Cronk's. Attended the Fourth-day meeting at Green Point, where many women were assembled, but the men being engaged in harvesting, few only were willing to leave their work. Visited a number of families, and had a large and interesting meeting at West Lake, and one at Picton in the afternoon.

17th.—Our friend, T. N. Stinson, took us in his carriage to Brighton. It was rainy and cold. Arrived at N. Brown's at 10½ o'clock, P. M. They had retired for the night, but soon had a good fire to warm us.—Went to Yarmouth, and attended the Half-year meeting. The youth's meeting was very large, and was a memorable occasion.

On 6th day were at Malehide, where we had a laborious meeting, the people having been prejudiced against Friends.. Next day dined at Freeman Clark's, and from there went to J. H. Cornell's.

On First-day were at Norwich, and had a satisfactory meeting. In the afternoon had one appointed in the Town Hall at Otterville, which was large and interesting. The audience was attentive, and was composed of different societies, among whom were several ministers. E. was powerful in testimony. L. Longstreth having received intelligence of the indisposition of her husband, left for her home on Second-day. Upon arriving there, she found, greatly to the relief of her mind, that Elizabeth, wife of Charles Kirk, was willing to accompany E. N. through the remainder of the journey. F. Clark and wife were with our friends in their visits to the families of Norwich Monthly Meeting.

On Fourth-day, after religious opportunities in the families of Samuel and J. H. Cornell, they left for Rochester, and on Sixth day attended that Monthly Meeting. As they were going into meeting, they met E. Kirk, to their inexpressible satisfaction. E. N. opened in the Monthly Meeting her concern to visit the families composing it, but believed it would be right to attend to some service within the precincts of Farmington before entering upon that duty. In accordance therewith, on First-day they attended Farmington

Meeting, and also visited several families in that neighborhood.

On Second-day went to Palmyra. Had a satisfactory opportunity with the family of Pliny Sexton, and proceeded to Williamson, where they had an appointed meeting. Made a number of visits, attended South Farmington Meeting, and returned to Rochester.

On Sixth-day commenced visiting the families of Wheatland, which they accomplished, and attended that Meeting on First-day.

Second-day—Engaged in family visits to the members of Mendon.

On Fifth-day were at that Meeting, and finished their labors in this district on Sixth-day. The day following, entered into the service of visiting families in the vicinity of Rochester Meeting. Seventy-four families were called on, and three meetings were attended.

On Sixth-day they went to Buffalo, and had an appointed meeting in the Unitarian Meeting House, which was large and satisfactory. The doctrine preached was plain and simple. Lodged at A. Griffins, and next day returned to Canada.

On First day were at Pelham, where E. had remarkable service. They were aided in their journey by kind friends, and reached Lobo on the 21st of 9th mo. Next morning, engaged in family visiting, which occupied about three days, and the labor was accomplished to mutual satisfaction.

26th.—They started for Yonge Street to attend "Canada Half-Year Meeting." Were at the meeting of ministers and elders on Seventh-day.

On First-day, the meeting for worship was very large. Second-day the meeting for business was held, and on Third-day, the Youth's Meeting—both of which were interesting opportunities.

Fourth-day.—Had a meeting at White Church, and one at Uxbridge on Fifth-day. In the afternoon returned to N. Brown's.—Next evening held a meeting in the Town Hall at Whitby. N. and M. Brown accompanied our friends to Toronto, where they had a meeting in the afternoon in a Baptist Meeting House and one in the evening in a Methodist Meeting House, which were large and interesting. Throughout their journey in Canada they were most kindly cared for by Friends.

A letter from J. H. A. to his wife containing a particular account of their meeting at Pelham and some other places.

YONGE ST., CANADA WEST, 9th mo. 26th, 1857.

. . . . It was a deeply interesting meeting at Pelham. E. expressed a view that the day is approaching when the principles professed by our Society will outweigh all opposition in Canada, and that there were instruments being raised, who, although but striplings now, will be enabled, *if faithful*, to break down the bulwarks which priestcraft was attempting to erect. I never heard her more prophetic nor more powerful; individual states were opened with much clearness, and many acknowledged the truth of her testimony. All are very kind and anxious to do what they can to assist us, and desire to be visited in their families. The way is marvellously opened in the hearts of the people.

On Second-day we started for Lobo, and, after a ride of 146 miles, arrived at John Marsh's, whose heart and house were open to receive us. In three days we visited all the families, nineteen in number, and, on Fourth-day, attended the meeting at Lobo. It was a remarkably favored season. The Gospel stream flowed freely. The whites and blacks all sat together. In visiting families, the young men came in and sat with us in their working clothes, without delay, which pleased us, and E. frequently addressed their individual states and conditions. J. M. said if she had known them all their lives, she could not have spoken more truly. The communications were so unlike, there was no difficulty in placing them.

We visited two colored families who were fugitive slaves; they own 100 acres of land, and good houses and barns, and had money at interest. First-day attended meeting. N. and M. Brown are here, and gave us a warm greeting. This morning we had a large meeting, the house was crowded with people, and many could not get inside. E.'s discourse was searching and forcible. This afternoon we have a meeting appointed at New Market, two miles distant. I asked a friend (a minister) if he would not go and help Elizabeth. He replied "No, she needs no human help, and does her work well." Second-day, yesterday afternoon, we attended a meeting in what is called the "Christian Church;" it was large, the aisles, windows and doors were all full. E. delivered a powerful discourse. After meeting, a young woman came to her and said: "Thou wast here to-day to give some of us consolation." The opportunity was indeed crowned with blessings. . . . .

On the 6th of 10th month, our friends left Toronto for Lockport, where they arrived at 3 o'clock P. M. They visited three families that afternoon, and four families the next day, which comprised all the Friends of that place. In the afternoon, they went to Rochester, still accompanied by N. and M. Brown. They attended the Quarterly Meeting held at Mendon, which was a time of favor; some friends felt that it was a crowning season. This closed their religious labors in that part of the vineyard, and, in the afternoon, J. J. Cornell took them to Rochester. Next morning, Tenth mo. 10th, after an opportunity with P. F. and family, in which there was much deep feeling, they turned their faces homeward with thankful hearts, in that they had been mercifully favored to travel nearly 4000 miles without incurring an accident. Their gratitude was increased in being permitted to know a re-union with the loved ones at home, whom they found in usual health.

Letter to Phebe Frost from E. N.

PHILADELPHIA, 11th mo. 12th, 1857.

My beloved friend :—It was far from my expectation, when we took our departure from your comfortable and hospitable abode, that so long a time should elapse ere I wrote to you.

Although, apparently, I can offer no sufficient reason, yet there is a cause why I have been disqualified for almost all social and relative intercourse much of the time, since my return.

The obligation again to enter the field of service, after having been so long separated from home and its endearments, has so weighed upon my spirit, and has been attended with so much suffering, (greatly increased, I know, for want of submission) that until a few days past, I have not been able to acquiesce sufficiently to see the *time* of departure. Nevertheless I have thought much of you and your kindness. The word *kindness* conveys but half of that which is in my heart, and lives there in lively remembrance.

We expect now to leave home on next Sixth-day for Scipio. I gratefully remember W. C.'s reply, that he would do what he could to aid us, when I asked him, if we *must* go to Scipio, if he would lend a helping hand. My ignorance of what our movements will be is such that it would not be worth while to write to him. When opportunity offers, please remember me affectionately to him and his wife, with the assurance of a continued interest.

With the expression of endeared affection for thee, thy sister, and nephew, and many other dear friends,

Thy attached and grateful

E. NEWPORT.

For the accomplishment of this unperformed service, our friends again left home on the 27th of the Eleventh month. Arrived at John Searing's at 4 o'clock next day, 29th. First-day, attended meeting at Scipio, in which E. N. was silent. In the afternoon, several friends called to see them. They had expected to commence at once to visit families, but E. having taken a heavy cold was confined to the bed for two days, and on Fifth-day was not able to attend meeting, but in the afternoon visited three families. On Sixth-day rode a number of miles and made two visits. On Seventh-day E. was again unable to go out. First day attended meeting, where she had some vocal service. Next day visited three families, and had a parting opportunity with J. Searing and family. Third day morning, at 6 o'clock, started for Auburn to meet the 10 o'clock train, but on the way the carriage broke down, and they were obliged to hire a lumber wagon. This detention occasioned them to miss the cars, and they were under the necessity of remaining at A. till next morning, when they left for Albany. By taking the night boat from Albany to N. Y., they reached home the day following.

To J. H. A. from E. Newport.

PHILADELPHIA, 12th mo. 17th, 1857.

My dear friend:—It has been upon my mind for some days to communicate to thee something of the state of my feelings since our return from our late toilsome journey, although I have been so much indisposed as not yet to have been out of the house. My mind continues to feel not only a release from the weight under which it rested from the time of our return in the Tenth month, until we entered again the field of service, but the covering is one of peace in which there is no alloy, which I esteem a *great* favor. The capacity to enjoy home, with its duties and responsibilities, was never more fully appreciated than since my return. Thou doubtless hast also thy reward. I am sensible the effort on thy part called for great self-denial in various ways. Energy and perseverance marked thy course, as well as discrimination and judgment! In the enjoyment of the rest and peace into which, I trust, we both have entered, may we not prove ungrateful recipients of the blessings around us; especially thou, my friend, to whom a longer release from such duties may be granted, and who art surrounded with innumerable mercies! Mayst thou be steadfast, having thy feet shod with a preparation of the gospel, so that thou may not be tempted to cast away thy shield. . . .

Farewell in that fellowship of feeling that admits of no dissimulation.

E. NEWPORT.

Several accounts have been received respecting our dear friend E. Newport's services during this visit, all confirming the facts that in many instances she was remarkably led, and that subsequently many of her prophecies were fulfilled. Among those which have been enumerated, was the case of a young man towards whom E. was especially drawn in close sympathy with his spiritual exercises. In a family meeting, she told him she foresaw that, if he were faithful, he would be obliged to tread a peculiar path, and one in which his *faith* would be closely tried. He would have openly to declare truths that had been unfolded to his spiritual vision, which the people were not yet prepared to receive; and said there were individuals present who would have to sustain him in so doing. She then made known to those assembled what these views were, thus strengthening the faith of the young man in her as a prophet. In an opportunity with a young married couple, E.'s exercises flowed toward the husband, while the wife was hungering for words of encouragement from one so highly gifted as she felt E. to be; but she had so little for her that it had the effect to depress her spirits, and to make her feel that she was unworthy and of very little account. Of this she said nothing, except to her husband. In a few days afterwards these friends met E. in another family, the members of which she separately addressed. After a short pause, she said, "Is there anything yet lacking?" and then, in almost the same language that the young woman had used in expressing her disappointment to her husband, E. described her feelings, and gave her such counsel and encouragement as met the witness in her own mind and satisfied her.

To J. H. A. from E. N.

PHILADELPHIA, Ninth mo. 8th, 1858.

"*Esteemed Friend*—The enclosed letter was received this morning. The Friend appears to feel himself much aggrieved, and I am entirely at a loss where to place him, as thou knowest, in many instances, I never heard the names of individuals whom we visited, and in others took no note of them, so that they passed from my recollection. This I have often found was the case, more especially when having been faithful to that which impressed my mind, I have felt the answer of peace. Although that which was delivered may have been close and very trying to express, yet in proportion as the mind was clothed with the spirit of submission and a consciousness of my own insufficiency, the sense of suffering with those to whom I have been drawn in the love of the Gospel, has occasioned a willingness to submit the cause to them, and to the swift witness within them, and never upon any occasion that I can recollect asserting that to a *certainty* things were thus and so. At this moment I seem afresh introduced into the humiliating and suffering baptisms through which my poor mind has passed on such occasions, and could I have believed there was any other means of acceptance with my Heavenly Father, but that of going from house to house, how gladly would I have availed myself of it. I have plead many excuses again and again, such as unfitness, incapacity, and my own short-comings; but the result of so doing has been a sorrowful sense of the withdrawal of Divine protection, and a feeling of deep poverty. Although I have no message to send to this Friend, I would like him to know that my mind never rested more quietly and sweetly than after that service, and I have not for a moment felt that I had any commission to retract, or take back what was expressed."

A Friend, in relation to some of the religious opportunities at which he was present, writes that they were seasons never to be forgotten by those who participated in them. The representations relative to the conditions of those addressed, and the power with which E.'s language was clothed, tended to the conviction that she had a correct view of what she foretold, much of which has since been verified. He says, at one time, a Friend (a minister) about to leave the room, came to E. to bid her farewell; she queried, "Art thou in a hurry?" "No," he replied; she then asked him to sit down awhile. The company soon gathered into silence, when she spoke to this Friend in a remarkable manner; she had close service also for others. Her testitimony for N. and M. Brown was encouraging. At a meeting for worship, she addressed a state with so much clearness, and in so powerful a manner, that many present could not fail to recognize it as applicable to a person present, who had openly espoused atheism, but to whom E. N. was an entire stranger.

When about to leave the neighborhood, she felt she must see this individual in his own house. The opportunity, though a close one, was peculiarly touching. Some things she then said to him have been verified, and there has been a marked change in him in regard to several particulars.

The young man to whom reference has been made, again met E. N. in the year 1859, and had an instructive and deeply interesting interview with her. On that occasion she laid aside her usual reticence, and narrated many events which had occurred in her experience, remarking that it was very unusual for her, but she felt a perfect freedom to do so. Among them was the following incident: At the first meeting of ministers and elders she attended, after she was acknowledged a minister, she was very closely led in describing the condition of an individual present, and her testimony was so peculiar and so pointed, that many thought her mistaken. Among these was an aged mother in the church, who made a remark to the effect, that she "did not know about this kind of prophesying." As E. highly esteemed her, it was a deep trial, and she soon felt that she must go to see her. This was greatly in the cross, but after a time finding her peace consisted in yielding to the impression, she started, but on arriving at the house her courage failed, and she paced up and down before the door several times, feeling that she could not enter, nor could she go home. She finally rang the bell, and the Friend herself came to the door. Upon seeing E. she immediately said, "Come in my dear, be not afraid, the Master has been here before thee." A close union existed between these two Friends ever after. The Elder accompanied E. upon several missions of love, and proved herself "a mother" indeed.

The same individual attended a meeting in 1863, where E. N. was present, in which he felt required to address closely a particular state, and was followed by her with a confirmatory testimony, while at the same time she handed forth such encouraging counsel, that he was made to rejoice even in the deep baptisms through which he had to pass. He accompanied her to her home, and after a pleasant social evening she remarked, that long before she knew that he had entered into a certain religious service, she had seen him engaged in such a work, led by the Divine Master as a little child just learning to walk; she had prayed for his preservation, and wanted him to continue in child-like humility and dependence, which would preserve him in every day of trial. He saw her again in 1868, when her health was very feeble, and on parting with her, he was deeply moved by the thought that it would be a final one. She said, "Farewell; I feel we shall meet once more in mutability." This surprised him, as he had no expectation of being in Philadelphia very soon. In the following year, however, he was at West Chester, Pa., where she was spending a few weeks with her children. She was unable to attend the meeting in which the Friend had much to communicate, but told him she had travelled with him in his exercises on that occasion, and also said that she had a view of trials in store for him, the nature of which she depicted; but she felt assured that he would witness preservation, if his dependence was upon God alone. The Friend says her predictions have been remarkably verified.

Such was the prejudice existing in some minds in relation to E. N.'s peculiar gift, that at one time when she attended a monthly meeting with a minute to visit the families belonging to it, an Elder remarked to a Friend before meeting, that he hoped that he would not be one of the committee appointed to accompany E. Newport. He was, however, named for that service. He concluded he would go with her that afternoon and then leave the charge to others. Being disposed to test E.'s powers of spiritual perception, he proposed they should visit a member, who had not been to meeting for twenty years, and of whom he felt assured she had no knowledge whatever. After sitting a few minutes, E. addressed the Friend, bringing into view many incidents of personal experience, and among others, the reason why there had been a discontinuance of attending meetings, and also mentioned the length of time this discouragement had existed, all of which the committee-man knew to be true. The person visited, in much tenderness of spirit, acknowledged the truthfulness of what had been said, and the Friend needed no greater evidence than he had received, of the right authority of E. N.'s concern, and continued with her throughout most of the visit, encouraging her in the faithful performance of her arduous duties.

They were passing the house one day of a person who had declined receiving a visit, when, without anything having been previously said, E. remarked to the Friend accompanying them, "Thou needst not stop at this place, for here lives the Friend who will not receive me"

At one time, being on a social visit to a relative, her mind was drawn toward a family in the neighborhood, where the husband was sick with consumption. She saw only the wife, and told her that she was impressed with the feeling, that before her husband was taken from her, she would have to bear another heavy affliction. The family, except the husband, was at that time in good health, but very soon a son, a young man, was taken ill, went into a rapid decline, and died before his father.

On a certain occasion, when in company with a Friend, a stranger to her, who at that time was numbered among the gifted ministers in our Society, E. N. was about to leave the room, when, turning around suddenly, she sat down without speaking. After a silence of about five minutes, she thus addressed this individual: "I feel impressed, my brother, to say to thee, 'Mind the Light. Trials of a conflicting nature await thee. There are secret enemies at work to injure thy moral character, and to ruin thy reputation as a minister of the gospel—they are subtle and insidious. There is an under-current of jealousy, and thy footsteps are watched for the purpose of finding some mistake on thy part. Temptations surround thee on every side! What can preserve thee from these powerful enemies? *Nothing,* but keeping thy eye fixed upon the Light within. Not depending upon externals, but alone upon the saving power of Christ within thy own breast. Oh! my brother, I tremble at the sight presented to my mental vision! If thou art not watchful unto prayer, thou canst not resist the torrent of persecution that will assail thee. If thou yields to impulse or allows a spirit of uncharitableness or prejudice to take possession of thy mind, even for a time, thou wilt lose ground, and go faltering on thy way. Thy gift in the ministry will dwindle, and thou wilt be robbed of thy usefulness. But if thou cultivates the spirit of love and forbearance, day by day, and hour by hour, thou wilt be able to stem the current, and come forth purified and prepared for a great work, not only in our Society, but among others, for God has gifted thee. Remember thou must suffer the *Spirit* of Christ to take entire possession, as it will, if thy sole reliance is upon this inward Power. 'Him that overcometh, will I make a pillar in the temple of my God, and he shall go no more out.'" She then spoke to his wife, and told her that she too had a mission to fulfil, which was to aid her husband in standing firm when reproach and censure were heaped upon him, and to encourage him to be patient and kind, so that he could realize that condition which would enable him to say, "Father, forgive them, they know not what they do." But if she were not faithful, she would become a stumbling block in his way and in that of others. She again turned to the husband, and in a most impressive manner said, "I repeat, *eye the Light*, my brother; nothing else can preserve thee in the hour of deep trial that awaits thee." Subsequent events have proved that E. N. had given to her a correct view of the future in relation tothese individuals.

In the summer of 1857 she visited a family wholly unknown to her, even by name. She addressed appropriately each member of it except the wife. After a period of perfect stillness, she then turned to her, and in a remarkable manner recurred to the period when, a few years subsequently, this friend had been in a state of extreme physical prostration for the space of forty hours, during which there was no power to move a muscle or utter a word, and yet the spirit was active. She entered with much feeling into the different experiences through which she then passed, and told her it was designed, she believed, to prepare her for the Lord's work. That she had suffered deeply from the fact of not having been comprehended, but encouraged her to be faithful to the whisperings of the Divine voice, and bade her be of good cheer, that although deep trials awaited her, if she were obedient to what was required, she would in time be enabled to overcome them all. Her prophecy has been wonderfully verified, and although many years have passed, the visit is fresh in the minds of the family, and they hold in tender and grateful remembrance the stranger, who so fully and sympathetically entered into their several states.

From another source the following has been received:—

"Having travelled in company a few weeks with our dear Friend Elizabeth Newport, I feel to relate some particulars relative to the peculiar manner in which she was led during some of the family visits. On one occasion we had dined at a friend's house, and were about to leave, some of the company were already in the carriage, when a message was sent out, requesting them again to come into the house. E. was led to speak to individual states in a powerful and searching manner, by which all hearts present were melted. What was uttered were truths to the writer's personal knowledge. At another time, after the morning meal was concluded, and we were about rising from the table, she addressed all the members of the family, entering into their states in a pointed and peculiar way. In my own family she was equally favored, especially in her communication to me. She was enabled to declare my very thoughts, which had never been previously uttered. In a third instance, we were going from one neighborhood to another, over a road to which E. was a stranger, and came to one that turned off the main road which we were travelling. She suddenly stopped the driver and said, 'please turn into this road.' When we came to a house she requested him to inquire 'if the family were willing to receive a visit.' The request was granted. After sitting some time in solemn silence, E. felt that some one was absent, and inquired of the father. He answered, 'My son.' She said,

'I feel my mission is to him, and we will return when he gets home.' The time was named, and we went again. E. was led to point out, in a powerful manner, the sad, downward course the young man was pursuing. She alluded to his past and present life, and to the fearful results if he did not repent and turn from his evil course. She cited him to that Divine power, which could alone enable him to return to 'the Father's house.' After the interview, his father acknowledged the truth of the plain testimony, and the Divine source whence it came.

I could narrate many more incidents quite as interesting and instructive as the foregoing if time permitted." H.

The following circumstance was relate l by a friend who was accompanying E. Newport to an adjacent Meeting. On their way they stopped at a hotel to refresh their horses. They found a company gathered for the purpose of attending the funeral of the son of the landlord, who had died from intemperance. Persons and circumstances were alike unknown to E., but the latter were unfolded to her spiritual vision, and she was impressed to warn the father of what might befall him, which she did with great solemnity. She told him, if he did not retrace his steps, he would soon follow his son by a premature death. The friend said, her manner was impressive, and her discourse was powerful.

Another person states, "In going to a neighboring Quarterly Meeting, I rode alone, except my driver. I felt depressed, and lonely, and as if there was no one that could enter into my state, no one to sympathize with me. I stopped at a friends' house to dine, but there was no enjoyment for me in social mingling, and soon after dinner I ordered my horse, feeling, that when I withdrew from externals, I could indulge in thought and feeling. Just as I was about to leave, my host said, 'S., thou hadst better not go. Elizabeth Newport will soon be here, and she is a wonderful woman, and can read one through and through.' I replied, 'No. I do not want to be within her reach. I have heard of her remarkable gift.' As I made this remark, a carriage drove up, and E. N. and company entered the house. I stood with my bonnet on, ready to get into my carriage. E. shook hands with the friends, who were all strangers to her, and then with me, and at the same time looked earnestly at me. All sat down and, as with one accord became quiet. In a few moments E. turned toward me and addressed me very close ly. She told me just how I felt--that I wanted to get away and be alone, that I might indulge my morbid feelings. She described the surges of my inner life. Said that a gift in the ministry had been intrusted to me; that I had a peculiar path to travel, and that many would not fully understand nor appreciate me; but my peace and growth depended upon the exercise of this gift. She spoke of the good I might yet do, and what a ministering spirit I might privately become to many who needed the aid of my spirit! She exhorted me to cultivate all my powers, and the sense of *loneliness* would leave me. She described my character, and impressed upon me the necessity of perfect obedience to every opening of Truth to my mind, without copying others. I departed with a heart full of gratitude, that my heavenly Father had commissioned His faithful servant to speak the word of cheer, and freely to enter into my state, and my faith was renewed in divine inspiration."

In the latter part of the year 1858, with the concurrence of her Monthly Meeting, E. N. engaged in a visit to some Friends and others within its limits. The concern was principally confined to those who were not active or prominent members, and her labor of love was acknowledged to have been acceptable and edifying.

At a Monthly Meeting held in the Eleventh month, 1859, E. Newport and Ann Weaver informed Friends of a concern which had weightly impressed their minds, in relation to a meeting for worship being held on First-day mornings, in the northwestern part of the city, for the accommodation of such members of our Societv as are remotely situated from other meetings.

The proposition was favorably entertained, and the Friends were encouraged to attend to their feelings in regard to it.

Information was received at the next Monthly Meeting, that several satisfactory meetings for public worship had been held, and a committee was appointed to meet with these

Friends and to consider the propriety of establishing an Indulged Meeting. Thus originated the meeting which is now held at the corner of Seventeenth St. and Girard Avenue.

The following letter was written by E. N. while on a visit to Westchester, to the Friends of the Indulged Meeting, after her health had become too feeble for her to mingle regularly with them in their meetings for Divine worship.

WEST CHESTER, 2nd mo. 1st, 1869.

Dear Friends of the Indulged Meeting.—Under a renewal of the cementing influence, which I have believed to be a measure and manifestation of the Father's love, my feelings have been drawn towards some of you with whom I have been wont to mingle in social interchange of feeling, and also when gathered with one accord for divine worship at the long established place, as well as at the "little meeting." I have no doubt the few continue to meet, though it may be, at seasons, under discouragement. Dear friends, my desire is that you may "hold fast to the profession of your faith without wavering." My attachment to the meeting of which I have been for so many years a member, rather increases than diminishes. Although I sometimes compare myself to an empty vessel set aside as of little use, there are seasons, when under the distilling influence of that which attracts and cements, as in the bond of true fellowship, my spirit is clothed with an ardent desire for the growth and preservation of those dear friends, who under a feeling of leanness and incapacity are too much disposed to excuse themselves, even when the mind has been awakened to a sense of responsibility connected with a clear manifestation of what is required of them. Here is a cause of suffering not only for the individual, but for the body. Many have been the changes that have taken place by the removal of those whose spirits seem yet to breathe a sweetness which excites a desire, that, so far as they followed Christ, we may pursue the same course! Then there is another class that my spirit has saluted; such as feel the weight and concern for the promotion of the good of the Society. Oh! that these dear Friends may be willing to endure the fire, and be steadfast under suffering, with an eye single to the Light, and with no desire for reputation! That they may be willing to withstand every opposing element! Then will they shine forth with brightness, and their example reflect a light, not only upon the pathway of those immediately within the precincts of our Society, but they will be as a beacon to the wayfarer, whom my spirit has saluted on his journey to and fro, with his hands, as it were, upon his loins and the inquiry upon his lips, "who shall show me, or lead me, into the path where my spirit may be refreshed and strengthened?"

With near love, I am your true friend,

Elizabeth Newport.

At the Monthly Meeting, held in Fifth month, 1861, E. N. obtained a minute to attend New York Yearly Meeting. Our friend Wm. Dorsey, who accompanied her, in writing to M. E. T. in reference to this visit, says:

"I remember it well, sufficiently so to give the impression left upon my mind. Thy dear mother, Ann W. Longstreth and I attended New York Yearly Meeting, and I well remember how close it was necessary for me to keep with her. This was a peculiar trait of her character, that those who accompanied her must be in near sympathy and close spiritual travail with her when she was under particular religious exercise. One evening she gave me permission to take tea with a friend, provided I would meet her at a certain place at an appointed hour. I was punctual, but found her anxiously awaiting my arrival, under great exercise of mind. A large company was present, which soon became silent.

She then commenced speaking, and addressed an entire stranger to her with a most emphatic warning, and, at the same time, in encouraging and consoling language, showing the errors of the past, the penitence and reform of the present, and the importance that he should, by watchfulness unto prayer, retain his integrity for the future. I afterwards learned that there was a young man present, whose condition had been faithfully portrayed by this eminent instrument, under the leadings of her Heavenly Guide. After Yearly Meeting, we visited J. Arnold, a man possessing a noble and gentle nature. We attended his meeting on First-day morning, riding six miles over an extremely hilly road. We sympathized with Friends in the difficulty they had to encounter in holding their meetings during the stormy weather of the winter season.

"The meeting was very interesting, and left a feeling of peaceful rest. The next day J. A took us forty miles into the interior. We reached our destination, and held a meeting in the village. At first I feared we should have a small attendance, but the people flocked in, and we had a large and solemn meeting. The next morning we went to the meeting of our dear aged Friend Katy Hazzard—a log house in the woods. This was also a favored opportunity, but the crowning scene was at the house of a Friend in the afternoon, when we had a family meeting. We wished to reach the steamboat landing, forty miles distant, and time was precious, but when thy mother mentioned to me her concern, I felt at once that all other considerations must yield to that. A sweet solemnity ensued. The love of God abounded. After addressing the family with much feeling, she turned to our friend K. H. with words of sweet encouragement and consolation, which came fresh like the oil and the wine. This dear faithful servant of the Lord burst into tears and wept like a child, but they were tears of joy, not sorrow. She was bidden to go on with her work, and although her Master had placed, as it were, the grubbing hoe and the axe in her hand, He would show her how to use them without fear, and she would receive her reward. After this she turned to J. A., and in a beautiful and touching manner, he was given the penny he had so richly earned. Oh! it was a pleasure to wait and serve with her, she shared so liberally with those around her the good things which were placed at her command, whether these consisted in the firm, but gentle counsels of reproof, or the sweet consolations and encouragement to continue in well-doing. Taking an affectionate leave of our kind friends, we started, with light and happy hearts, and reached the river just in time for the evening boat to New York.

. . . "All who came within the sphere of thy dear mother's influence felt its power for good. Her gift of spiritual sight into the conditions of other minds appeared to be exercised only in obedience to Divine command, and I believe that the feet of many, through her faithful admonitions, have been turned to tread the narrow way that leads unto eternal life. Humility was one of the most, if not *the* most marked trait of her character." . . .

Affectionately thy friend,

WILLIAM DORSEY.

Fishing Creek Half-Year Meeting.

E. N., feeling her mind drawn to attend the Half-Year Meeting of Fishing Creek, and to appoint some meetings within its limits, a minute was granted her for that purpose at the Monthly Meeting held Sixth month 20th, 1861. Mary M. Evans and Charles Kirk were her companions in this Gospel labor. By the latter the following particulars respecting it have been furnished :—

They attended the Monthly Meeting of Fishing Creek, and in the afternoon of the same day the Meeting for Ministers and Elders. Next day the Half-Year Meeting was held, in which E. addressed an individual who she believed had decided to join the army.* It was a clear and forcible testimony. C. K. was informed subsequently, by a "pious methodist woman," that before her son went to that meeting he had decided to enlist, but after hearing E. N.'s powerful discourse he concluded not to go to the war, which "rejoiced her heart."

Dined at J. R.'s, and had an interesting opportunity with the family, which was comforting and consoling to the invalid wife, who had been confined to her bed a number of years. Also had a meeting with the family where they lodged, in which there was close service. Attended the "Youths' Meeting," in which E. was favored in testimony.

In the evening had an appointed meeting at Bloomsburg; the silent solemnity which prevailed over the assembly was remarkable. It was held in a Methodist meeting-house, and one of the members remarked to C. K., that "it would be impossible for *them* to get up such a meeting." Rode six miles, and lodged at R. Wilson's. In a religious opportunity

---

*During the late war.

with the family next morning, much appropriate counsel was given.

Visited two families in the northern part of the county, who reside seven miles from the meeting. One of the Friends said she often walked there and back. Had an appointed meeting in a place not far distant, at which were gathered a large number of rough looking people; but upon this, as on similar occasions, the presence of the Good Spirit was felt, and our dear Friend was admirably sustained in the performance of her duty.

On First-day afternoon an appointed meeting was held in Friends' meeting-house. There are but a few members residing here. They are 16 miles distant from any meeting of Friends. At Catawissa there was formerly a large meeting, but at that time there were but one or two members of our Society living in the town. They had a meeting in Friends' meeting-house. C. K. remarks that "the grave-yard was filled, but the meeting-house was empty!" Two families composed the meeting at Roaring Creek. An appointed meeting was also held in that place. Here they parted with R. W. and wife, who had been with them for several days, and E. John took them to Shamokin.

On the 27th attended the week-day meeting, but the "busy season" having commenced, it was small. Dined with P. and R. John. The few families which constitute this Monthly Meeting are widely separated, and are subjected to many inconveniences in attending their meetings. In the afternoon rode six miles to the town of Shamokin, and held a meeting in the Methodist meeting-house at the request of some of the members of that society, who had expected to have a meeting of their own at the same hour, but gave our Friends the preference. It was a highly favored season, in which the gospel was preached with life and power, and a petition was offered that those present might be so imbued with the Good Spirit, that they would be enabled safely to journey through life, and at its close be permitted an entrance into the realms of light and of eternal peace.

From Shamokin E. N. and company proceeded to Maiden Creek, where they were met by T. Lightfoot.

On First-day morning were at that meeting,

and in the afternoon had a satisfactory meeting at Reading.

Next morning they called upon H. Tyson, who was at that time the Superintendent of Berks County Prison.

E. N. had a desire to have a religious opportunity with the prisoners, for which the way was opened. In the afternoon made several visits to the families of Friends, and returned to Dr. Tyson's. Elizabeth's mind not being relieved, she expressed a wish to see four or five prisoners in their cells. Permission was freely granted, but the query was, how should these be designated? She told the overseer that if he would go with her through the corridor, she felt that she could point out those to whom her mind was drawn. This was done, and resulted satisfactorily.

Having fulfilled their gospel mission, they reached Philadelphia that evening, with "peaceful minds."

In the Ninth mo., 1861, Green St. Monthly Meeting granted E. N. a minute, for the purpose of visiting Bucks Quarterly Meeting, to appoint some meetings within its limits, and to visit families, as way might open. In the performance of this service, she was led into close feeling with individual states, and in some instances, the people were astonished as their secret thoughts and conditions were brought into view, and could but acknowledge that these had been revealed to our friend through a divine source, as they were known to none save themselves. Several months after date, E. returned her minute and informed her friends of the peaceful result.

To attend Baltimore Yearly Meeting, to appoint a few meetings, and to visit some of the prisons in that city, E. Newport was furnished with a minute by the Monthly Meeting, held Tenth mo. 23rd, 1862. Mary M. Evans also obtained a minute as her companion. But few particulars of this journey are at command. The visits to the prisons were memorable occasions, our friend being introduced into near feeling with some who were incarcerated for grave offenses. Her sensitive nature rendered her keenly alive to suffering humanity in its varied forms. During the conflict which has left such a deep stain upon the historical page of our country, she was brought into sympathy for all engaged in it, but especially for the young men, who, under the excitement of the hour, entered what they termed the field of "honor and patriotism," but which, in numerous instances, ended in a premature death, or led into evils which are even more to be deplored than the sacrifice of a comparatively innocent life.

With Abraham Lincoln as chief magistrate of the nation, she deeply sympathized. With her mental vision she saw him pacing his chamber at night, absorbed with the momentous questions, which were shaking the Union to its centre, and threatening its dissolution. She recognized his earnest prayer for right direction, and actuated by the Christian principle, which caused her to regard in no ordinary degree the welfare of her fellow beings, she addressed to him the following letter:

PHILADELPHIA, 3rd mo. 1st, 1861.

Abraham Lincoln—Esteemed Friend:— Many there are in the Society of Friends, with whom I am in membership, whose hearts beat in unison with desires for the preservation of our brother, whose nomination and election to the Presidency of the United States has been hailed with an intensity of interest never before equalled. In explanation of the liberty of thus making a claim upon thy time at such a momentous crisis, when the important subjects now before thee necessarily demand the concentration of all the faculties and powers of the mind, I would advert to thy farewell address, in anticipation of thy departure from a home endeared by many tender associations, and to the earnest and ardent desire for Divine assistance in the prosecution of the responsible and arduous duties upon which thou wast about to enter. This is the Principle that the Society of Friends profess as their guide and teacher, which thou hast thus invoked and trusted in, as the only hope of success—the only armor for which thou hast sought and prayed!

Permit me to say that I believe it is an emanation of Gospel love that constrains me to encourage thee, my brother, "to hold fast the profession of thy faith," that no man rob thee of thy crown. Then thou wilt witness, not only the sustaining influence of thy heavenly Father to be around thee, supporting and preserving thee from the power of thy enemies, but by the descendings of a spirit comparable to that which inspired Daniel, there will be evinced a soundness and discrimination of judgment in the course of thy administration, that will, I believe, cause it to be marked by equity and uprightness. And when thou retires from the field of labor, there will be poured upon thee, not only the rich reward of sweet peace, but the blessings of a nation, who will cherish the memory of one, who, in emergencies, exercised sound judgment and steadfast principle, blended with acts of mercy and charity, so as to claim the love and respect of the people in a preeminent degree! Oh! then, my brother, gird up the loins of thy mind for the arduous duties that are before thee, for this is a crisis in our history. Be strong in faith, and doubt not that thy Father will enable thee, in His mercy and His love, to bear whatever He places upon thee.

Thy friend,

ELIZABETH NEWPORT.

Letter to a Young Friend.

PHILADELPHIA, First mo. 10th, 1862.

My Dear Friend— . . . I feel it to be one

of the blessed privileges of a union and fellowship of spirit, that in the absence of all external evidence or personal intercourse, an interchange of feeling may be witnessed and reciprocated, even "as life answering to life." This thou knowest, and also that it is not confined to age nor circumscribed by outward circumstances. My mind during my late visit, often reverted to thee in connection with others of thy age; some of whom having begun in the spirit, have suffered themselves to be turned aside with discouragement, because of the retrograde steps of some who had witnessed the cleansing operations of the fire of the Word, but have returned to the beggarly elements, or to an external reliance; while others, have suffered the mind to become engrossed with political strifes, and have experienced an alienation from their "first love." It has seemed to me, that if there is not a reaction in some instances, some of our meetings must grow weaker and weaker; and yet on occasions when the feeling of leanness has been so great that I have been almost ready to faint under the evidence of the withering effects thereof, there has been a sudden revulsion, and the language of encouragement has gone forth in such a manner as sometimes to cause the query whether it was not a vagary of my own imagination that has thus influenced me. I have not, however, often been left long without the consolation, that although there was much that was calculated to discourage, yet the day-star of hope betokens a brighter and better state of things, and while the work of reformation may be retarded by superstition and bigotry, the Lord has arisen in His power, and will continue to work in the minds of His children, until there is a separation between the chaff and the wheat, and all that is contrary to His will shall be consumed.

Although it is not likely that I shall live to see that day, yet there are those born who will; and in proportion as thou, my dear brother, keepest close to thy Guide, thou wilt be furnished with that wisdom which is from above, that will enable thee to stand firm and steadfast amid all the tossings and shakings, which will be known ere that day is brought forth,—a day of greater light and intelligence than has ever yet been witnessed by the children of men, wherein the swords shall be beaten into ploughshares, and nation shall no more lift up sword against nation, neither shall they learn war any more. The work is on the wheel, and, though for a time we may as a society be driven as into the wilderness, we shall again come forth. Oh, stand firm! Let no man take from thee that which thou hast obtained by close watching, self-denial, and reduction of spirit. Keep the word of His patience—remember where much is given, much is required; and as thy safety consists in humility and child-like dependence, wear this as a robe; let it be the covering of thy spirit; and should the furnace increase in heat, never heed—in proportion to its intensity, will be thy faith in the power that alone can sustain, and bear up, "above all, over all, and through all."

I want thee to know I am often sensible of poverty and a sense of nothingness, when there seems to be no life in me, so that I am thy fellow-pilgrim in travail of spirit, and thy affectionate friend and sister in the Truth.

E. NEWPORT.

Extracts from E. N.'s Note Book.

Ninth mo. 24th, 1861. What a striking analogy between an unsoiled sheet and an unspotted life! May the remainder of my days yield the evidence of purity stamped upon the pages of this little book. "Thou hast a few names even in Sardis, which have not defiled their garments, and they shall walk with me in white; for they are worthy."—*Rev.* 3c. 4v. By an increase of watchfulness may I know every thought and feeling brought under the reign and government of the Prince of Peace, so that I may be found worthy to be clothed with the raiment of the "pure in heart."

Twelfth mo. 14th. Many and varied have been the exercises of my mind since penning the above. During my late visit to Bucks Quarter, what cause had I for thankfulness! Surely He who promised to go before and open the way, has been graciously pleased to prosper the embassy! And what now shall I render unto Him but the residue of my days! Oh Thou who knowest the desire for an increase of that which alone can insure an acceptance with Thee, be pleased to keep the eye uplifted, that through all a watch may be maintained! And, oh Father! not only create in me a "clean heart" and "renew a right spirit," but give me strength to bear, and fortitude to suffer all that Thou seest meet for me to endure! Let not thine hand spare nor thine eye pity, until judgement is brought forth unto victory, and my measure of suffering is filled."

Fourth mo. 6th, 1862. "Great and marvellous are Thy works, Lord God Almighty, just and true are all Thy ways, Thou King of Saints." Amid depression and poverty I can adopt this language. I read and hear much of many worthies who have passed from this state of being, calculated to interest and stimulate the weary traveller; but up to this date all that I have penned has been of a desultory character; though perhaps no one has had more cause to subscribe to the truth of the text above quoted, than poor unworthy I. When I take a retrospective view, many, many are the evidences that come before me of the infinitude of His wisdom, the marvellousness of His love and mercy, His omnipotence and the justness of His dispensations, adapted as they are to the wants and conditions of His children! Truly, who that has come to bow before them but can say with the poet, "For all I thank Thee, most for the severe!"

My health and strength have so given out that sometimes when there are stirrings within, there appears to be no energy to move the pencil.

Seventh mo. 28th. I have been reading Clarkson of late, a work which has always interested me. I was especially impressed with a quotation from Barclay, "A man's conscience is the seat and throne of God, who is the proper and ineffable Judge, and who, by His power and spirit, can rectify its mistakes." Would that we as a Society were more concerned to remove the beam out of the individual eye, rather than seek occasion against a brother or sister, by which the spirit of discord is introduced and a feeling of distrust engendered, which is inimical to that which the blessed pattern inculcated as the life and spirit of vital religion.

8th mo. 12th.—This has been comparatively a day of rest. There has been a sense of quietude which leads me to commemorate and ascribe thanksgiving to Him who has graciously shown me not only the necessity of endeavoring to cast off some of the weights that have sorely pressed, but to trust all, surrender all unto Him whose "promises are yea and Amen forever."

12th mo. 30th.—A long interval, with many vicissitudes of experience, have passed since my last record in this little folio. I hope there has been some little attainment. Attended Baltimore Yearly Meeting, which was a season of favor. Also paid a visit to a dear relative, whom I found much reduced in strength, but very tender and loving in spirit. Not feeling it required of me to leave him to attend meeting on First-day, we had an opportunity in his chamber, wherein our spirits were nearly united, and ability given to speak of that which flowed in freshness and sweetness from the quickening spirit, the Divine word, a sense of which remained as a sweet savor till I took my departure.

I have, of late, taken a retrospect of the past, when it was my lot to be found, as I apprehended, in the fulfilment of a Divine requisition in the exercise of a gift entrusted to me; and I have regretted the inability I often labored under through the weight of mental exercise and the depression of the physical powers, to preserve an account of some very interesting interviews and opportunities with slaveholders and others, as well as the singular manner in which I was led from house to house in different sections of the country. Also, how the mind was preserved for the greater part, under the most humiliating baptisms I ever experienced, in trust and dependence upon Him, whose promises were, verified, that He would "prepare the way and open the hearts of the people." After reaching a habitation, it was no unusual circumstance to retire for the night, without the least sense of the object of our going into that particular neighborhood, farther than a belief that the obligation was to visit some of the families of slaveholders; but who or where to be found, or where to begin, I knew not. Oh! how often upon such occasions, after laying my head upon my pillow, have I, under a suffering sense of the singular course in which we were led, desired to receive some intimation of the direction for the next morning. But the language of impression was as clear as if audibly spoken, "All thou hast to do is to repose in safety, and trust that Power which has hitherto sustained and furnished thee with light and strength sufficient for the day and its requirements. Thou hast need of a renewal of physical strength; then repose thy trust in Me." Often, upon awaking from an unbroken slumber of many hours, the way or course to be pursued would be so clear as to leave no doubt as to the labor of the day. But language fails to express the humiliating baptisms experienced upon entering the houses of those entirely unacquainted with our principles; and this peculiar manner of going among them even many of our friends did not understand; yet there never was an instance in which we were not almost immediately sensible, upon sitting down in silence, of a solemnity, under which utterance was generally made easy and fear removed, so that the Truth was delivered, always, however, with a guarded care to do it in a way that would least shock the prejudices of education.

Some of these opportunities were signally

crowned with an evidence of tenderness and brokenness of spirit on the part of those immediately addressed, while sometimes the wife would sit, with eyes riveted upon my face, expressive of extreme dissatisfaction.

—. —Oh! for a closer walk and a more perfect devotedness of spirit to the principle of light and life, as revealed even to one so short sighted and disposed to yield to doubts and fears. Certainly no one has more need than I, to seek, and that continually, for a qualification to draw near and to dwell by the well-spring of Life, so that I may be endued with faith and hope, and sustained amid the vicissitudes and trials, many of which, though deeply proving, are known only to Him who sees in secret. My spirit has been refreshed by letters from my dear children, all breathing the spirit of affectionate interest and concern for their mother. Sweet, indeed, is the voice of sympathy from those who are a part of our being, whom in infancy we have cradled in our arms and pillowed upon our bosoms, but who have now grown to the stature of men and women, and have assumed for themselves those responsibilities which cannot be fulfilled in the will of the creature. The longer I live the more sensible I am of our need of Divine aid, and the interest and sympathy felt for the young mother is inexpressible. I feel with her in her varied duties and perplexities, surrounded as she is by those of quick and lively sensibilities, and who are very impressible, either for good or evil.

What need for watchfulness, that the maternal mind may be brought under right discipline, which shall have an influence in moulding the characters of the little ones, and imbuing them with a love for truth and candor and with a cheerful and happy spirit; and, at the same time, induce habits of industry and economy, and lead them *Home* to the principle of life and of love within them, inculcating early the doctrine of dependence of the creature upon the Creator. That we are so constituted that in order to enjoy happiness we must impart it to others—that although it is necessary for us to seek daily and hourly for help from our Father in heaven, yet this we can do while engaged in our duties connected with this life; and He who knows us more perfectly than we know ourselves, will accept the secret desire of the heart, and will bless the earnest appeal to be kept chaste and pure and preserved from the follies of the world, even though there be no sound of utterance.

There is sometimes a diffidence on the part of the mother, arising, it may be, from a sense of her own imperfections. She may have yielded to the spirit of impatience, and been brought thereby into suffering and feel her disqualification for the task of imparting the earnest desires of her heart for the good of her child.

This is a condition of mind painful to endure, but it will work out a renewal of strength and a qualification to enter into sympathy with the child, without which all labor is ineffectual; for this is the touch-stone, and when their little hearts are made sensible of this, it has a tendering influence, and an effect to "prepare the way of the Lord," and to "make His paths straight."

I was sweetly impressed, in our little meeting to-day, with the lines of the poet:

"The only amaranthine flower on earth is virtue—
The only lasting treasure—Truth."

Many Friends were out of town and the meeting was small, but there were some interesting children and young persons there, and it proved to be one of those seasons of refreshment to which the figure of the five barley loaves and few small fishes would apply. The opening was limited and the ability also, but there seemed to be a diffusion that might be compared to the dew of heaven. May it rest long enough on the branches to produce a growth.

Third month, 1863. — "Where no law is, there is no transgression." How just how merciful are these conditions! Did we only live in accordance with the light manifested, need we know anything of the law of sin and death by sorrowful experience? Verily I believe not; therefore, if we transgress the law of life, the responsibility rests solely upon ourselves. How important that parents and guardians should impress the minds of children with the simple and efficient doctrine of obedience as taught by the great Lawgiver; and also the grievous effects of disobedience. Greatly have I sorrowed at times, in view of the pains and labor bestowed to initiate the young and tender mind into doctrines, rituals and ceremonies that, if depended on, will ever lead into formality and a lifeless trust in they know not what.

Sixth mo. 3d.—A variety of unforeseen events have transpired since the above date. Our Yearly Meeting has occurred, which was large and interesting, each session furnishing the evidence to my mind that the great Head of the Church was in our midst. An increase of interest was manifested on the part of the young, and the spirit of condescension prevailed notwithstanding for a little season, conflicting sentiments apppeared to produce a disposition opposed to the peaceable and benign spirit which can alone prepare the mind to offer a sacrifice comparable to the beloved Isaac of our hearts. Never was my mind so clearly impressed with the virtue of such a sacrifice, although it may cost great suffering. Yet if "the unity of the spirit in the bond of peace" cannot be preserved without it, I believe it is called for even on the part of those who are baptised with the true seed, and are able to discern that which is lifeless, though it be clothed with the form of godliness. My faith has been strengthened in the view, that as a tender father pitieth his children, so doth much more abundantly our heavenly Father manifest His love and tenderness toward those whose reliance is wholly placed upon Him.

Sixth mo. 18th—Uncle E. Hilles departed this life in his 80th year. His close was peaceful, though his sufferings had been extreme. His life had been one of usefulness, and I doubt not that admission was granted into that city the inhabitants of which "are no more sick."

Sixth mo. 26th, 1863.—A season not soon to be forgotten. Great alarm has prevailed in consequence of the cruel war and the near approach of the enemy. My mind was clothed with sorrow, but was preserved in quietness and trust, and the promise was soothingly remembered—"I will keep that man in perfect peace whose mind is staid on me, because he trusteth in me."

Third mo. 4th, 1864.—Many months have elapsed since my pen has traced a line within this little folio, and they have been marked by a variety of circumstances. I have felt there was cause for thankfulness that in every hour of months of severe indisposition, the mind had been mostly preserved in patience and resignation, though at times the future was obscured and I was left more fully to feel my dependence as the light which had shown upon my path was withdrawn. I am often admonished to live but one day at a time. "The life which I now live is by the faith of the Son of God," said one who had passed "through heights and through depths, through good report and through evil report," and had obtained "by grace through faith," an establishment upon a sure foundation. Oh, this establishment! this immutable foundation! this ever-present faith under every pressure that all things may work together for the more perfect redemption from all that pertains to self! I feel, of late especially, that it is a duty for those who profess to believe in the guidance of an ever-present loving Father, to preserve a cheerful aspect amid petty annoyances as well as greater trials; and if it be required of them to put on a garment of sackcloth, let them wear it *underneath* in quiet submission.

Eighth mo. 13th.—Have just returned from Atlantic City, where all was bustle and confusion. No enjoyment for me except that found in retirement, either upon the beach or in my own apartment.

—. This has been a day of great exertion for a tabernacle so frail as mine has become. Attended a funeral near Horsham of a young man whose transit was sudden, but who, I believe, found admission within the "pearl gates."

Ninth mo. 1st, 1866.—Although two years have passed since I have made a record upon these pages, and the interim has been marked with debility and infirmities, still I feel there is so *much* cause for thankfulness in the review, that language fails in its expression.

Third mo. 9th, 1867.—"Be ye perfect as your Father in heaven is perfect." What is perfection but a state of entire obedience to the unfoldings of light upon the understanding? This is the state to which we are called, and while it involves great self-sacrifices, yet in proportion to the subjugation of our own wills, will the path be made clear and strength furnished to pursue it in cheerful reliance upon One without whose notice not a sparrow falls to the ground.

Third mo. 13th.—How much we not only suffer but lose for want of an abiding faith and trust in that Power which, if submitted to, would overrule for good the destinies of men! Oh, for a constant abiding upon the watch, that naught but the pure gold may be found within my borders!

Third mo. 20th.—"Be careful for nothing; but in every-thing by prayer and supplication with thanksgiving, let your request be made known unto God." Phil. iv. 6.

Fourth mo. 5th.—Oh! the goodness, mercy, love and condescension of a tender Parent, who permits no more to come upon His dependent children than He strengthens them to bear! Though tossed to and fro for a season, apparently with no Pilot at the helm, yet as there is an endeavor to be still and turn the eye toward the heavenly port, there will be a glimmer or a ray to revive and inspirit the poor drooping mind, which now thoroughly understands its helplessness.

Eighth mo. 15.—The family gone to meeting. I took the Testament, but could not read; closed the book and sat in stillness. The Scriptures *themselves* impart no life, no light, no strength, and it is only as the mind is impressed with the teachings of the spirit that they can be read to edification. "The letter killeth." How true this testimony? When will the children of men come to understand it? When will the professor of Christ learn where to look for the teachings of the Holy Spirit? These are not imprinted upon parchment, for however excellent and pure the truths may be that are thus inscribed, according to the teachings of the blessed Jesus, we must come from the letter to the spirit, if we would receive the true unction. "Search the Scriptures, for in them ye think ye have eternal life; and they are they which testify of me, and ye will not come to me, that ye might have life." John v, 39.

Eighth mo. 18th.—"Day unto day uttereth speech, and night unto night showeth knowledge;" so the return of external darkness after a lovely day, beautifully described by the poet as "the varied God," is no more certain than a state of abstinence and want after a season of fullness, in which the spiritual life has renewed its energies, and the soul has been enabled to rise triumphantly, and lift its voice in adoration to Him who has given the victory.

Then when for a time the light may become obscured, and the tongue which had been loosened in praise "may cleave to the roof of the mouth," how important that we seek quietness and endeavor to commune with our own hearts and be still, so that we may not be found off our guard by the reasoner, and thus this state be prolonged through our own inadvertency.

Eighth mo. 24th.—Why make an effort to express a word in this state of emptiness? There is a struggle for stillness, perfect stillness from all anxiety, from all thought of the future. The invitation has been extended to cast all care upon Him whose tender mercies are over all His works.

Extracts from E. N.'s Letters.

—— —— "Let not thy dependence be placed upon any written creed or faith, or outward observance, as that which is known of the Father is manifested within, by Christ—the Word of life and power. The blessed Jesus testified, "for this end was I born, and for this end came I into the world, to bear witness to the truth." Not that He was born that His Father should put it into the hearts of "wicked men" to crucify Him, so that by the shedding of His blood, redemption should be purchased for the sins of the whole world; but in bearing His testimony to the truth, He laid down His life rather than resist or act contrary to the non-resisting principle, "If a man smite thee on the one cheek turn the other also." As His disciples are faithful in bearing their testimony to the truth, and prove their allegiance by taking up the daily cross, they will follow Him so closely that, by the renunciation of their will, they will come into the experience of the death of the cross. And as they continue steadfastly to carry out the doctrine of self-denial, which the Son and sent of the Father, so clearly defined throughout His mission, they will not only know an ascending and a descending upon the ladder which Jacob saw in his dream reached to heaven, which to my mind represents the ascending of the prayers of the pure in heart, and the descending of the heavenly virtues, love, joy, and peace, but they will also be brought to witness that described by the apostle, as having immediately succeeded the crucifixion of Jesus—" the veil of the temple was rent in twain from the top to the bottom, and the earth did quake, and the rocks were rent, and the graves opened, and many bodies of the saints which slept arose and came out of the graves after their resurrection, and went into the holy city and appeared unto many." Thus it will ever be, as the will is surrendered and a crucifixion of all that stands in opposition to the Divine will, is known. That which obscured the vision, the veil of superstition, of prejudice, of creeds and systems of faith, which have their origin in the wisdom of man, is rent in twain, and we are enabled to discern the simplicity of the teachings of the Holy Spirit, so that the earthly nature shall be shaken, and the rocks rent. Those benign dispositions of mercy, love, and charity, that were asleep as in the grave, will arise and come forth with beauty, so that they shall be seen and recognized by those who dwell in the holy city, which can be entered only by such as are crucified unto the world and the world unto them."

. . . . Art thou not sensible, my dear child, of a continual flow of sympathy for thee? Do not be discouraged. I believe this school of suffering will be useful in proportion to an acquiescence on thy part, in child-like simplicity to thy allotment. Thy heavenly Father loves thee and knows with what thou hast been gifted. These gifts need the refiner's fire, and the process may cost thee much suffering; but bear up, better days are in store for thee.

As thou submits to the deep baptism, which may be needful, thou wilt find thy talents, like gold, separated from impurities, and from all that would mar its beauty, ready for the service of the Divine Master. As thou progresses, thou may find need for further refinement: for renewed baptisms, and having submitted thy will, thou wilt be strengthened to come forth with increased power to perform the labor of thy day. Shape thy model, my dear, after the pattern shown thee in the mount. Thus will simplicity become thy clothing, and thou wilt have a standard of thy own, and will not need a borrowed light. As this is adhered to thy most conspicuous adorning will be that of a meek and quiet spirit."

. . . . It seems to me a great attainment to set a guard upon the lips, even in social intercourse. The longer I live the more value I see and feel in silence, that kind of silence which cannot be attained other than by some mortification of self. It is as needful for thee as thy daily food, as in that state only art thou furnished with that discrimination that can enable thee to divide thy words aright even in social intercourse. I have sometimes found solace in the feeling that silence was more expressive, and at times is more eloquent than words. I feel that this is an important era with thee. "I am the true vine, and My Father is the husbandman. Every branch in Me that beareth not fruit He taketh away; and every branch that beareth fruit He purgeth it, that it may bring forth more fruit." John, xv. 1. 2. Here we see that even the fruit-bearing branches need the operation of that comparable to the knife.

Thy benevolence is large, thy sympathy, thy candor, thy humility, are all heavenly principles; yet they need the direction of the Spirit of truth, which will lead thee to discriminate, so that thou mayst diffuse the most healthful influences wherever thou art found.

This pruning or purifying operation cannot be effected without suffering, and if, my dear, thou allows this dispensation to pass without a regenerating influence upon thy mind, I *fear* the design of a wise and gracious Father will be frustrated. In humble submission to the heavenly Teacher, thy weary soul can find peace. Seek not human aid, but look to God alone for a release, and He will come in His own time, and by His power will set the captive soul free. Watch only through this dark and painful hour, and the bright morning will yet dawn upon thee.

. . . . I have been much impressed with the language of Jesus, "A new commandment I give unto you, that ye love one another." As love and reverence are due to the good and gracious Being who formed us, and whom we desire to know more intimately when done with time, how is it that any of us, old or young, are acting at variance with the knowledge we have received of the Divine law, and of the commandment of loving one another, even as we love ourselves!

I believe it to be consistent with the doctrine taught by Jesus, that in all who resolutely refuse to listen to the voice of the internal Monitor, the light will become obscured, and in this state the soul will be separated from harmony, love and peace.". . . . .

——1865.

To S. Andrews and Family.

. . . . . I am sensible that there are occasions when, to the surcharged heart, words are powerless; even the tones of sympathy meet with no response, although they issue from kindred and congenial feelings.

This is a state of suffering known to those bereft of a beloved one, who has been as a prop and staff, and around whom the purest affections have clustered and entwined their tendrils from earliest recollections. Still, I feel an Omnipotent Arm has been underneath to bear up and sustain. Trust it—rely upon it! Truly can I say, I mourn with you in your bereavement of a loved parent, husband and counsellor.

Perhaps no one beyond his immediate family had a more full opportunity of an acquaintance with him than myself. Under all circumstances I ever found him true to his trust. As an Elder, he was quick and discerning, and frank in the expression of his feelings. As a companion and fellow-laborer, "in season and out of season," there was a fitness and adaptation that, I think, few possess. Never, in one instance, have I known him to shrink from service, however humiliating the requisition may have been. He maintained his post in singleness of purpose; yet, when loosened from the harness, in cheerfulness he often found the recreation his nature required. His urbanity and warmth of feeling rendered him a pleasant and useful companion to the young as well as to the old.

With his readiness to discern times and seasons, he was quickly impressed when an exercise called for silence, and entered freely into the labor, so that I may say, throughout the weeks and months that we were engaged together in gospel love in visiting the different parts of the vineyard, the unity of the spirit in the bond of peace was maintained unbroken. . . . . .

E. N.

Second mo. 8th, 1865.

. . . . I know I have much to be thankful for. A few mornings since, as I was pondering upon these things, the query presented, whether I was sufficiently thankful for the numberless blessings and favors which had been bestowed upon me? I was carried back to my early childhood, when I could not have been more than five or six years old. My mind was then awakened to a sense of the goodness and mercy of my heavenly Father, and I thought "I had rather die *now* than live to offend so gracious a Being." And, although I felt deeply sensible of many omissions and commissions since that period, yet my mental eye seemed attracted to a little rill, which, in its meanderings, watered and refreshed every lone and barren spot within its reach; and the impression was received, to cultivate the virtue—gratitude—that this would bless and prepare me to meet the trials of life with calmness and equanimity; that then I need not fear that the eventide of life would be overshadowed, or that a sterile and barren soil would encrust the heart and render it cold and insensible. May the impressions then made upon the mind be realized. . . . .

To a young Friend under deep Trials.

Twelfth mo. 22d, 1866.

"Truly my beloved —— can I say I have been with thee in suffering and in sorrow, and have borne thee, as it were, upon my heart to our heavenly Father. The spirit of supplication has been poured forth on thy behalf, with the entreaty that He would be pleased to give me an understanding of what I should do, or how I should counsel thee, in these seasons of close baptisms. On one occasion, especially, I was as clearly impressed with the feeling as I could have been, had the language been audible to my external ear, to tell thee "to throw down every crown at the footstool of mercy, and there offer up self and all that pertains thereto—that this is what is called for." "I will purify thee in the furnace of affliction." Circumstances are such, that no efforts of thine or mine can reverse them. The only alternative is submission, and in order that this may be complete, it must be accompanied with resignation, even such as will enable thee to say, "Thy will be done."

Flee thou to this Tower—it is thy only safety,—and the alone preparation for strength.

to fortify thoo for the duties that must devolve upon thee. This will enable thee to restrain unprofitable suggestions of thought and feeling, and overcome the impulsiveness and waywardness of thy nature, and then a close watch will be set upon thy lips and upon each act, and thy wants will be supplied from the Fountain whence alone they can availingly come."

Third mo. 22d, 1867.

—— —— There are moments when the surcharged heart can only breathe forth its inner life. It has no power nor language of its own, and no definite recognition. What then can it do, but to wait and watch for the coming of that spirit which can dispel the tones of sadness, distrust and sorrow, and attune to melody. Have we not found that these seasons of weakness and frailty, are but the precursors, if patiently endured, of a nearer access to our Father, whom to know is life eternal, whom to obey is peace and rest? Hast thou not known this? Then cease from anxieties that harrass and weaken both body and mind. Thou needs to husband all thy strength for the work that lies before thee. Bear up above the fluctuations that sometimes sweep around thee, so that the dear lambs committed to thy care may be nurtured in innocency and sweetness; and thy own mind be so preserved under the influence of divine love, that thou wilt be able to make straight steps to thy feet. In order for this, thou must be willing to move upon independent ground, or rather the ground marked out by Him who knows how most effectually to reduce the will of the creature, so as to make it subservient to His divine and holy appointments. . . . .

I hope thou art not looking back, but art pressing onward, with the eye upturned to the only source of good and of strength. . . . . I miss thy society. It is not often that I *feel* alone, but in L.'s absence, the remembrance of dear M. is continually before me. She used to stimulate me to go out, but now what pleasure is there in going alone! I know her sweet spirit is at rest. I know she cannot come to us, and that but a little while will elapse before I also shall take my departure to the spirit-world, but we are so constituted that we cannot help feeling deeply these severings. Jesus wept—may we not? Surely there can be no sin in this, if we seek submission and struggle for resignation.

Eighth mo. 22d, 1867.

—— —— . . . There is a work upon the wheel, and it requires care that the design of the great Architect be not frustrated. There are so many ways whereby this can be done, that it requires continual vigilance on thy part. It is said that the blessed Jesus learned obedience through suffering. If so, how shall we arrive at the state to which we are directed—"Be ye perfect even as your Father in heaven is perfect,"—except through tribulation and suffering? Much may, no doubt, be avoided through watchfulness. Perfect obedience is that to which we are called, and I crave for thee, my beloved—this state of child-like dependence. Keep thy eye single to the Light; it will lead to an establishment upon the sure foundation, so that although the elements be boisterous, thy building shall firmly stand. . . . . . .

How fleet are the footsteps of time! and

where will some who are now upon the stage of being, soon be landed? Not in a land of dreams and shadows, where the rays of light are divided and broken, as they appear through the web of life, but where the beams of the sun of righteousness will surround the obedient and self-sacrificing without change, save as they increase in radiance and beauty. Far, very far superior to that which is seen by mortal eye, even when the western horizon is made gorgeous by the setting sun, will be that which awaits those who have known an overcoming of all that which would obscure the glory which emanates from the throne of mercy and of love, as it shines forth from our Father in heaven.

Tenth mo. 27th, 1867.

—— —— . . . I know it is easier to plan than to carry out that which we desire. I suffer with thee in all thy trials, but do not let them press too heavily upon thee. Try to live above them. The apostle said, "By grace are ye saved through faith;" exercise it; it will preserve thee; it will sweeten the bitter; it will smoothe the rough places in thy pathway. It will make the sterile ground yield a plentiful supply for all the wants and cravings of thy nature. "I will refine thee, but not with silver." I see blessings in store for thee if thou wilt submit in child-like obedience and dependence. Every tender and sensitive feeling of my nature is moved for thee.

As to my dear friend, T. B. L., I have felt deep regret in not being able to see him. I suffered much until I was favored with a consoling evidence of the blissful and glorified state into which he had found admission, even through much tribulation. . . .

Eleventh mo. 7th, 1867.

My Dear Friend—Thou hast often been the companion of my mind, and according to my measure, I have sympathized with thee in the privation and loneliness, that has doubtless at seasons surrounded and pervaded thy beautiful home. casting a shadow over all its enjoyments. But it is meet that we should look beyond the shadow to the *reality*; even to that which is invisible to the mortal eye. Thy precious mother's countenance, in all its sweetness, appears still at seasons to beam upon me as I saw it during the time I sat by her with my lips sealed, though my heart was filled with the desire that my last hours might bear the evidence that marked her every look, that she was in a state of preparation to enter the kingdom of rest and of peace. Truly, of her it may be said—she "being dead, yet speaketh." Wert thou not often sensible, my dear, of the yearnings of her spirit toward thee? Did it not follow thee in thy goings to and fro? did she not plead with thee, not so much by word, perhaps, as by the look of her beautiful and expressive eyes, to be faithful to thy heavenly Father's will? And is it too late? Ah, no! then gird up the loins of thy mind and press forward. Thy mother's God will aid thee; will sustain thee. Be thou faithful to the revealings of Christ in the secret of thy soul. "To him that overcometh will I give a white stone, and in that stone a new name written, which no man knoweth save him who hath received it."

Very affectionately, thy friend,

E. Newport.

Twelfth mo. 25th, 1867.

My Dear ——— . . . . The query arises, how is it that thou so lately comparatively a stranger, should be induced thus to care for one who feels that she has no claim upon thee? Well, my precious young friend, may thy reward be equal to the feeling that crowned the gift in the heart of one who feels that a kindred affection has been ignited, that will diffuse its warmth throughout the few remaining days of my pilgrimage. . . . . To-day my mind was impressed with a feeling that infused not only a *calm*, but a sweetness that was animating and strengthening; under which thy mother's countenance beamed upon me as when I last saw her, so expressive of that heavenly state that enshrined it. And the language that was intelligible to my spiritual ear was on this wise—"Say to my daughter that I want her not to forget to appreciate the blessings that flow in upon her—blessings from beneath and blessings from above—unsparingly poured forth from the hands of the bountiful Giver of every good and perfect gift. The gift of intelligence, of the graces of the spirit, joined to those of inspiration; that which has dawned upon the understanding, and enabled her to know the nature of her obligations to her heavenly Father." This, as near as I can express it, is the substance of what sweetly impressed my mind. Not that I heard, or *believe* I heard, an external sound, or that I am a "*spiritualist*" in the modern acceptation of the term; but I *do* believe our gracious Father is sometimes pleased to permit an intercourse between embodied and disembodied spirits; and on this occasion my feelings were deeply affected with the recollection of the state of my mind, at the interview to which I have alluded. And now, my dear, let me tell thee how my spirit *yearned* toward thee while I sat by the bedside of thy precious mother, poor and stricken as I felt myself to be. I essayed to speak, but had no power to utter a word of what was upon my lips; and when at last I turned to leave her, it appeared as if I was taking with me the blessing that had been given me to impart, and I was ready to believe it was because of my poverty and leanness; and yet the longing was so great to have thee with us, that I lingered in the hope of hearing thy footstep, till at last I felt I could stay no longer, and departed under great depression of spirit, but in love and tenderness, and in admiration of the sweetness and meekness of thy dear mother's patient spirit. Wilt thou excuse the awakening of remembrances of a painful nature? I had no such expectation when I began to write.

In dear love and sympathy, thy friend,

E. NEWPORT.

1st mo. 13th, 1868.

My Dear ———.—How fast the days are passing—almost the middle of the first month of the New Year! How little we know of the vicissitudes the coming one may bring! The great matter is to live up to our convictions. I was interested in an article under the head of "Mind the Light" in last week's *Intelligencer*, and I felt were I a ready scribe, I would like to carry the subject a little further. Didst thou read the appeal to mothers? It will bear several readings. . . . . We, as a Society, need more of the teachings of that in which we profess to believe,—even the guidance of the Holy Spirit in the support of our testimonies. There is great beauty and strength in conciseness. May this be desired by all, rather than enlargement of speech or extended communications. . . .

I retired to the sitting-room to fathom, if possible, the cause of the oppression which has for the past two hours weighed upon my spirit, but as it is undiscoverable I must leave it. It may possibly be a trouble of my own begetting. There are causes enough to weigh down any sensitive mind. The suffering of hundreds and thousands of our fellow-creatures; the prospect before and behind us of darkness and desolation. In the Divine economy man is so constituted that he may, by a perversion of his noble powers, for a time, wield his sceptre after his own evil design, yet in accordance with Infinite Wisdom, the indulgence of every wrong brings its penalty, and will sooner or later work its own destruction. How important, then, that we endeavor so to live that our confidence in a divine Protector may increase. Faith is the Christian's shield, and remains to be "the substance of things hoped for and the evidence of things not seen." . . . . .

I often, especially of late, feel as if I was just beginning to live, now that I have passed the period assigned to learning, and find I "know nothing as I ought to know." How I wish on such occasions that the minds of my children could be inspired with the feeling that is thus enkindled. Thought reaches forth into the infinitude of space, and in its transient flight would enter into the wisdom and economy of Nature's great Architect, that it might bring thence some idea of the magnitude of His power and the beauty and order which there reign supreme; but that only "which is revealed, belongs to us and our children."

2d mo. 12th, 1868.

—— ———. . . .—My heart flows out in love and sympathy toward thee, my dear ——, and I feel to encourage thee to do whatever thy hands find to do, leaving the result to Him who sees in secret, and who abundantly rewards every act of dedication, however small it may seem to be, with that peace which the world can neither give nor take away. . .

At no time since our acquaintance have my

feelings been more enlisted for thee, blessed as thou art with health and every external boon that is calculated to render thy pathway free from the little annoyances that many, to a painful degree, have to contend with. How fervently have I desired that thou mayst be found steadfastly pursuing the course which has been pointed out by the Light within, as the right one for thee to pursue. On one occasion, when my feelings were drawn forth on thy behalf, I believed that this is an important period with thee, and thou wilt excuse me if I dwell a little more earnestly upon the necessity of being "instant in season," lest, while consulting about this or that, its very insignificance may discourage thee so as to put to flight the energy and strength that were at hand, and which would have carried thee safely over the bridge that was firm enough to have supported thee, although the waters may have looked boisterous and threatening. My desire is ardent for thy progress in the path of obedience and self-denial. . . .

To E. N. from a young Friend.

. . . . I felt the sweetness of thy spirit,

there was no condemnation in *that*, and the discrepancy between what I heard and what I thought belonged to me, occasioned deep perplexity but no resentment. Had I been deceived myself, or couldst thou be deceived? I could not help fearing that thou hadst judged from outward observation; that if, with a heart no better disposed, I had dressed *plainly*, a different sermon might have been preached to me. In this state of mind I attended meeting, feeling as if my hands were bound and I a prisoner to thee. "Who shall show us any good?" was all I could utter; and these were the very words with which thou arose, and enjoined upon little children to dwell with their exercises. I felt released from that prison-like state. Clearer views of truth arose in my mind, and deeper convictions of sinfulness.

This I have thought due to thee, beloved friend, in explanation of what I said. If I did not feel thy sermon as applicable to my state when it was uttered, I can appreciate the spirit in which it was spoken, and can confess, too, that I *now* feel the need of rebuke. My practice, as I *now* perceive, has been *very* deficient. All that relates to theory I find must be left, and my efforts directed to performing in humility and love what I know to be right. . . . .

From another.

9th mo. 1st, 1868.

"I did not expect to address thee so soon again, my beloved friend, but as I have been sitting here in my dear mother's hallowed chamber on this the anniversary of the last hours she passed in it, the scenes which then transpired come vividly before me, and with them thou art so intimately connected that my heart turns to thee with renewed feelings of gratitude for the last words of consolation she received on earth. They were precious to her, and the heavenly expression of her countenance seems still to beam upon me, as when she turned to me and said, "How I have been wishing for this!" They were to her an evidence of acceptance that she had been longing for, and I have often wondered why one so pure, so heavenly-minded, who never since I can remember did aught but good, should have needed any evidence of acceptance at the close of such a well-spent life; and it causes me ofttimes to exclaim, How can such an one as I, whose whole life has been spent in the pursuit of earthly pleasures, ever hope to gain admittance within the same Heavenly mănsion!

She, whose last petition was, that her erring child might seek for more enduring treasures, will be heard no more on earth; but I trust it will never be forgotten. Oh! I feel her absence more to-day than when she was taken from us. I thought then more of the blessed change she had experienced, than the loss I had sustained; but as time has passed away I have keenly felt the privation of her Christian example and tender counsel. Thou must excuse me for thus relieving my full heart, but thou hast felt so near and dear to me this day, I could not help it.

I believe I cannot close without expressing at this late date, a deep feeling of gratitude that abides with me for thy instrumentality in awakening me to a sense of my manifold transgressions, and endeavoring to check my course in sin and folly; for although I have not alluded to it in thy presence, I have no doubt thou remembers thy close exercise in thy visit of love to our family. Many years have passed, and little progress has been made toward anything better, yet it has never been obliterated from my mind, nor have I ceased to be thankful for it, and trust it may even yet accomplish that which was intended." . .

E. N.'s answer to the preceding Letter.

9th mo. 11th, 1868.

My Dear Friend:—Thy precious letter came to hand seasonably. I was not aware that at any period of my life I had been instrumental in awakening thy mind to a sense of thy responsibilities. I have no recollection whatever of my visit to your family. This may seem singular to thee, and in order to explain what has often seemed inexplicable to myself, I will relate a view I once had while wading under deep feeling in the prospect before me. Our children were young, and there were many discouragements, and besides, I felt the magnitude of the work and my own unworthiness and unfitness to engage therein. While reasoning with flesh and blood, there was presented to my mental vision a beautiful clean mat; and the impression was, such as this thou wilt find at the door of every house; examine thy feet at the entrance, for unless thou art careful to leave all that is imparted to thee at each house thou enters, the mat at the door will be soiled, and the work will be marred.

Under the responsibility that I continually felt, there lived with me such an absorbing desire to fulfil my mission with peace, that in many, and I might say, in almost all cases, I never recurred further back than to discover whether I had faithfully followed my Guide; and that I should have been instrumental in imparting consolation to thy precious mother I cannot understand.

Never did I feel my own insufficiency more deeply than during the little time I sat by her bedside.

12th.—Weariness so overcame me yesterday that my pen was laid aside.

15th.—Still unfinished, and were I to follow my inclination this letter would not meet thy eyes; but, my dear friend, my heart is yearning with emotions that are prompted by near affection, which I believe to be as enduring as the source whence it has its origin.

In regard to the future, the film is not yet removed from my eyes. This living day by day is a test, and sometimes a close one, of Faith and Trust; but I find there is no other way for me, and my continual watchword is found in the poetic language,

"Be still, nor anxious thoughts employ—
Distrust embitters present joy;
Thou canst not want when God 's thy Friend."

This often brings to me the spirit of repose and resignation. Ungrateful, indeed, it would be were I to express an idea that would cast a shade upon the holy and benign influence which results from a dependence and trust in the guidance of a loving Father. Ah, no! full well I have known the peace and rest which have been spread as a canopy over an unquiet, restless, panting heart in days past, when in a land of darkness and exile. I knew my children needed a mother's care, for amid all there came to me tidings of their sickness, and there was no evidence that our labors were of any possible service, still the sound vibrated upon the spiritual ear, that I was in my right allotment. Then was my weapon of warfare thrown down, for there were seasons when I was torn as between earth and heaven, and my peace returned unto me, and I was made renewedly sensible of the healing virtue of that Power which revives and prepares for fresh sacrifices." . . . .

Third mo. 21st, 1869.

. . . . "It is not worth while for me to attempt to express my sense of thy kindness and thoughtful attention to thy friend. It is as a green spot in my heart, and often when debility seems to have clogged all the courses of nature, and there is no ability to give expression to the bubblings up of the spontaneous feelings of the spirit, yet in the depths of humility the fervent desire has arisen to the Father of Spirits, that He would be pleased to preserve, purify and prepare thee for a vessel in His house—even a "*beaten*" vessel! that so the truth might be sustained and circulated by and through thee. This appears to me to be a day in which every man had need to find an independent standing, even that standing which the truth only can confer." . . . . .

Third mo. 24th, 1870.

My dear ——, I commenced writing to thee on Second-day, but my strength gave out for the time, and I put it aside as not worth sending. I often feel impoverished, and yet I have cause for thankfulness, there are so many seasons of union and communion with divine and heavenly intelligences. Wilt thou be alarmed, my dear friend, when I say, I am confirmed in the belief that a kind and beneficent Father has constituted His intelligent creature man, so as to enable him to hold communion, "large and high," with Himself, and at seasons to exalt His name, His power and glory? When He reveals Himself through the spirits of the just made perfect in such a way as to satisfy the mind of the presence of a dear departed one hovering near, how soul-sustaining and precious are these emanations, or angel-visits, though "few and far between" they may seem to be. These soothing influences have a tendency to solace and sometimes to confirm our trust in seasons of great weakness and distrust, for however we may have been favored with access to, and support from, the Great I Am, times of weakness are inseparable from humanity. . .

. . I find of late I ought to have dotted down some scraps of pure, unsullied thoughts that have gone forth to some dear ones to whom I have felt bound by ties stronger and closer than those of consanguinity; for are not those of affinity heaven-born? Is not their origin from the *Fountain* of love?

Sometimes when quietness and repose are spread as a canopy over the face of nature, my spirit has saluted some of these dear ones in their pilgrimage Zionward, in near fellowship—sometimes in suffering and sometimes in rejoicing, with thankfulness of heart for the inestimable blessing thus furnished, of an intermingling of spirit with spirit during our sojourn here. Language fails at this time to convey a full sense of the heart-felt desire for the growth and advancement of those who having known of the goodness of a loving Father, yet are falling short of the mark of the high calling in Christ. While in deep humility I have had a view of my own short comings, yet I have adored His name, in that I could see as the book of remembrance was opened that all my life long He had extended

His loving kindness to so frail a creature and unprofitable a servant. But I must close.

In near affection,

E. N.

Second mo. 9th, 1871.

——— ——— . . . . "I am often led to wonder that one of thy temperament should have been attracted toward an individual with so little of sufficient interest to create an attachment in another so richly endowed with the blessings and enjoyments of life. As I have dwelt upon the subject, my spirit has been lifted, my precious friend, on thy behalf, to Him who scans our thoughts and knows the secret workings of the heart,—that He would be pleased to continue to bless thee and aid thee in overcoming thy spiritual enemies—that thy Light may shine with increased lustre, and brighten the paths of those around thee, that they may be induced more earnestly to seek after an acquaintance with the secret source and spring of feeling, from which thou art deriving thy spiritual sustenance." . . . .

Affectionately, thy friend,

E. NEWPORT.

In the winter of 1865 our dear friend, E. N., took a heavy cold which resulted in bronchitis. From this time she was frequently unable to attend meetings, and was prevented from entering into active duties, but her interest for the Society of which she was a member was unabated, and her desires for its growth and advancement always continued. Her friends ever received a cordial welcome, even when from the increase of disease, she was unable to converse much with them. Words were not required to convince those who mingled with her that she was supported by that faith "which overcomes the world," and which had been her armor and shield through the vicissitudes that had attended her life. There were times, when comparatively free from oppression, that she entered freely into conversation, and expressed her views and feelings upon both religious and secular subjects. The free institutions of our country were of great interest to her, and she regarded with apprehension and disapproval everything which threatened their overthrow. The possibility of combining Church and State was to her a matter of grave importance, and she felt that Friends had need to guard with jealous eye, any invasion upon a testimony to a free Gospel ministry. She considered this one of the strongest bulwarks of the Society, and that it needed only to be fully comprehended to be more generally accepted by the honest inquirer.

In a letter written in 1866, she thus alludes to her belief in the intermingling of spirits, even while the soul is an inhabitant of the earthly tabernacle. "Iron sharpeneth iron; so a man sharpeneth the countenance of his friends." Prov. xxvii, 17. Truly this testimony is verified when we are brought face to face with those of kindred minds, and also when being absent in body, spirits mingle and commingle. I believe it is the will of our heavenly Father that this privilege should be at times enjoyed; and I consider it one of the strongest evidences of our spiritual nature, that we are not only permitted to mingle with absent embodied spirits, but also with the disembodied. Do I go too far in assuming this ground? Far be it from me to do so *speculatively*; it is only as my own mind has been awakened to the certainty of it, that I speak.

I feel, however, whenever I approach the subject, it involves that which is sacred in its nature and character."

A few days before her death, she said to a dear friend, that she had as much faith in the growth of the soul in the next life, as she had in her own existence, and also in the recognition of spirits; and added—that it was no speculation with her, but reality—that she had nothing to do with "modern spiritualism," but such were her views long before that subject was agitated. It came to her as inspiration when attending a funeral. A clear sense of progression in the next life was presented, and she felt commanded to give expression to it, which she did, greatly to the comfort of the widow.

In the Fifth month, 1867, she met with a close trial in the death of a beloved and promising daughter. Although generally resigned, yet there were times when this sorrow was overwhelming. In speaking of her bereavement she said—"This lovely flower has been transplanted in a more congenial clime. While it was sudden to me and to us all, yet the work of preparation had been silently going on under the pruning hand of her heavenly Father, so that when the call came, she was ready, and gave evidence to the last of her acceptance, and that the way was clear before her. Her language was, 'The dear Father will receive my spirit; mourn not for me, I am ready to go.' "

In the years 1870–71 E. N.'s physical sufferings greatly increased, but she was always cheerful and patient, and as far as was in her power, administered to the mental and spiritual wants of those around her.

At the time of the Yearly Meeting in 1871, on the afternoon of Seventh-day, she made a visit to the meeting of Ministers and Elders, and delivered a gospel message suited to some conditions present. Her physical weakness was great, but her manner was very impressive. The call appeared almost as from one whose life had been resuscitated, and it was sensibly felt by many. Not being able to remain, she left before the close of the meeting, and as she retired a feeling of sadness covered many minds, in that it was not at all probable that her voice would again be heard in the assemblies of the people.

She told her daughter one day, that she clearly saw that she would be with them about three weeks. She felt that the time of her departure had before been hidden in divine wisdom. She knew that her family felt her necessary to them, and she had passed through intense suffering on that account; but now her light was clear and bright, and she could give them all up and leave them in the hands of their heavenly Father, and trust them all with Him. Her work was almost done, and she felt calm and peaceful.

About two weeks before her death, she remarked to one of her children, that this passage of Scripture had come freshly before her as applicable to our religious Society—"O Jerusalem! Jerusalem! how often would I have gathered thy children together, even as a hen gathereth her chickens under her wings and ye would not." "Oh! I feel that there are so many who will not be gathered into the true fold. There is a sifting time coming, and I pray for these that their faith fail not, but that they may abide the turnings and overturnings of the Hand that would effectually separate the wheat from the chaff. If these keep humble and are obedient to the teachings of the pure inshinings of the Light, it will be as a lamp to their feet; and although they may often have to tread the wine press alone and sometimes have to wade through deep waters, yet if they are faithful and keep simple in doctrine, they will be instrumental in gathering many from the by-ways and the hedges, to seek a more intimate acquaintance with the principle of divine revelation. I see another class, who have slidden off and fallen into that dangerous stream, the love of popularity. This will not only rob them of the beautiful robe of simplicity, but they will be landed in the abyss of darkness and suffering."

On the 14th of the First month, she was so ill that the family were called in the night, but she rallied and soon engaged in a touching and fervent supplication adapted to each state.

A few nights afterwards, upon reviving from another sinking turn, she repeated the following lines:

"Sweet is the scene when virtue dies
When sinks the righteous soul to rest;

A holy quiet reigns around—
A calm which nothing can disturb,—
Naught can molest the peace profound
Which their unfettered souls enjoy,—
So fades the summer cloud away,
So dies the wave along the shore,
Triumphant smiles the victor's brow
Fanned by some angel's purple wing—
O grave! where is thy victory now?
O death! where is thy sting?"

On the morning of the 20th her son, who lived in Chicago, arrived. When informed that he was in the house, she clasped her hands and exclaimed—" dear Father, I thank thee." A tribute of thanksgiving was audibly expressed for the favor, and much affectionate counsel was administered to him. On First-day, the 21st, she requested the family to gather around her, when she addressed them separately, with great sweetness and tenderness. She alluded to the approaching separation, said she knew that they would feel a great void, but when the time came she wanted them to loose their hold and let her go; the chain would not be broken, only extended, for love is immortal. Upon being queried with if she had a journal, she replied,

"No; when I have thought of writing, inspiration would leave me, and the text would present, "The life is more than meat, and the body than raiment." During her illness she frequently talked of her earlier life, and related many instances which occurred before her children were of an age to remember them. These, as well as those of later experience, were narrated in a manner, that led to the belief that she thought it not improbable that they would be gathered together in a manner similar to that in which they are now presented to the reader. On the evening of the 22nd, she said—"I do not seem to have been learning anything of late except the lessons of patience and faith—I feel so much like a little child."

"Joy and happiness, dear mother," said a daughter, "awaits thee in thy spirit home." She replied, "I do not aspire to any great things. I crave blessed rest, and to enjoy the love, the sweetness, the mercy and tenderness of the Father."

She several times said, "The time is not long, I am only waiting and watching." Her sufferings and debility gradually increased, but the sweetness of her spirit continued, and was sensibly felt by all who were privileged to be with her. On the morning of the 27th, about the time which she had predicted, she departed without a struggle.

She had requested that her funeral might take place from the meeting-house, at the corner of Fourth and Green Streets, and on the 30th of First month, 1872, many Friends and others were gathered on that occasion. The interment took place at Fair Hill.

A Memorial of the Monthly Meeting of Friends,

Held at Green Street, Philadelphia,

Concerning our friend, Elizabeth Newport, deceased.

The memory of our beloved friend, Elizabeth Newport, wife of Jesse W. Newport, and daughter of James and Margaret Ellison, is precious to many within the limits of this Monthly Meeting, of which, the most of her life, she was a member, and for about forty years a valued minister.

In 1841, she with her family removed to Abington, Pa., but in a few years they returned to this city, and again became members of this Monthly Meeting.

It is not intended in this memorial to enter into the details of our friend's private life, which was in a remarkable degree consistent with her profession as a disciple of Christ; but our object is to give forth a testimony to her faithful adherence, not only by precept, but through example, to the principles and testimonies of truth, as held by Friends.

Her simple childlike faith was beautiful, and under its influence she was made a minister of the Word, which she was often enabled to divide in a manner that brought conviction to the minds of her hearers. Of the goodness and long-suffering kindness of our heavenly Father, she bore abundant testimony. Her earnest appeals, when engaged in public service, to those present, to trust more perfectly and confide more fully in His mercy and willingness to save *all* who come unto Him, are remembered with the desire that her labors of love may not be lost; but prove as bread cast upon the waters, found after many days.

She was endued with the gift of prophecy, and possessed in an unusual degree the spirit of discernment, by which she was frequently brought into a feeling of the condition of her fellows, to whom she was "a flame of fire" or a minister of consolation.

These qualifications were especially noticeable in family visits—a service to which she was frequently called. On some such occasions, so clear were her spiritual perceptions, that she not only pointed out the direction in which she should go, but the particular place where she should stop, although the country and the people were alike to her unknown.

Many instances of remarkable individual visitations through the instrumentality of our dear friend, might be enumerated, wherein she was given clearly to depict the state of mind of those visited, and the consequences which would attend faithfulness or disobedience; but our limited space is adapted only to an allusion to this feature of her ministerial gift.

She visited many parts of the heritage under a religious obligation; and when thus engaged the unity of her friends at home was very grateful to her sensitive mind, particularly in seasons when, by her peculiar gift, she was led into close conflicts and deep baptisms of spirit; for notwithstanding her willingness to be as "clay in the hands of the potter," she was sensible that her treasure was held in an earthen vessel.

In the year 1853—4, she made an extended religious journey into several of the Southern States, while the institution of human slavery existed in that part of our country. When laboring in promiscuous assemblages in the *far* South, she felt herself excused from making special mention of that institution, but in the religious opportunities not unfrequently had in the *families* of slaveholders, a full testimony against the iniquitous system was fearlessly borne. We who knew her so long and well, and remember her gentle and persuasive advocacy of the right, and her fearless rebuke of the wrong, and especially the wrong of slavery, cannot doubt that in this instance she was influenced and directed aright. We recognize in it the controlling agency of heavenly love, which released her from encountering the prejudices of the slaveholder, thereby enabling her to touch their hearts and consciences, and bring them under the powerful influence of her ministrations. Friends who accompanied her speak of the effect produced by her appeals to the slave masters and mistresses, on behalf of their slaves, as well as upon the poor suffering slaves themselves. Large numbers assembled to hear her, and many were touched and softened, and some even moved to tears. Wherever her lot was cast as a gospel messenger, she called the people to that principle, which would lead out of all wrong doing, and enable them to do justly, love mercy and walk humbly with their God.

Through the several years in which she was prevented by ill health from attending meetings for Divine worship, or mingling with her friends, except to a limited extent, she preserved a living interest in all that concerned the welfare of not only her own religious Society, which was very dear to her, but also in that of the world at large. She was not bound to party or sect. Her love for her fellow-men proved its origin by its universality.

The last time her voice was heard in public, was at one of the sittings of the Yearly Meetings of Ministers and Elders in 1871, to which she came in great physical weakness, with a message of gospel love and incitement to greater individual faithfulness. She expressed a deep concern that the members of that body should be watchful and careful of their steppings, and that each should follow the revelations of Truth, as they were received through the medium of that Light which makes manifest the will of our Father in heaven. By many her impressive manner will long be remembered.

Although her sufferings for many months were great, yet her mind continued clear, and her spirit retained its cheerfulness. To those about her she administered counsel adapted to their various states and conditions. Her prayers were earnest for her family, and she desired them, when the summons came, to gently loosen their hold and let her go; for with the eye of faith she beheld the beauty of the Father's house, and she believed there was prepared for her a mansion therein.

In her early youth she had dedicated herself to the cause of Truth, and remained steadfast in the faith, that pure vital religion consists in obedience to the Divine will and love to our fellow-men.

With the feeling that she had "*left nothing undone*" that had been required of her, she passed away on the 27th of the First month, 1872, in the 76th year of her age. It may be truly said in connection with her:

"Blessed are the dead which die in the Lord from henceforth. Yea, saith the Spirit, that they may rest from their labors; and their works do follow them."—(Rev. xiv. 13.)

By direction of the Monthly Meeting,

JACOB M. ELLIS,
LYDIA L. ROWLETT, } *Clerks.*

Read and approved in Philadelphia Quarterly Meeting of Friends, held Fifth mo. 6th, 1873, and signed by direction and on behalf thereof, by

CALEB CLOTHIER,
SUSAN CARRALL, } *Clerks.*

www.ingramcontent.com/pod-product-compliance
Lightning Source LLC
LaVergne TN
LVHW021148110826
845150LV00005B/1158

* 9 7 8 1 4 2 5 5 4 7 1 4 1 *